Why Didn't I Learn This in Hebrew School?

Why Didn't I Learn This in Hebrew School?

Excursions through the
Jewish Past and Present

Eliezer Segal

JASON ARONSON INC.
Northvale, New Jersey
Jerusalem

This book was set in 11 pt. Fairfield Light by Alpha Graphics of Pittsfield, NH and printed and bound by Book-mart Press, Inc. of North Bergen, NJ.

10   9   8   7   6   5   4   3   2   1

Library of Congress Cataloging-in-Publication Data
Segal, Eliezer.
    Why Didn't I Learn This in Hebrew School?: Excursions through
    the Jewish Past and Present / Eliezer Segal.
        p.   cm.
    Includes bibliographical references and index.
    ISBN 0-7657-6076-2
    1. Judaism—Miscellanea.   I. Title.
BM51.S43 1999
296—dc21   98-51384
                                                              CIP

Printed in the United States of America on acid-free paper. For information and catalog write to Jason Aronson Inc., 230 Livingston Street, Northvale, NJ 07647-1726, or visit our website: www.aronson.com

For my mother,
Rhoda Halpern Segal,
for instilling in me the joy of learning

Contents

Jewish Weddings   95

In the Community   121

Introduction

This review, published in celebration of my fiftieth article for the *Jewish Free Press*, summarizes the approaches and motivations that underlie most of the items in this collection.*

As most of my long-suffering readers have probably noticed, an important landmark was recently reached in the history of Jewish journalism with the publication of my fiftieth article for the *Jewish Free Press*. For those of you who might not have been keeping count, my first contribution appeared on November 15, 1990, in the *JFP*'s premier issue, while the Hanukkah feature in the November 30, 1994 issue was my fiftieth.

While I await the lavish surprise party that my editor is no doubt preparing for her most popular columnist, I have been devoting some thought to the purposes of my journalistic endeavors and how they have been received by my Esteemed Readers.

_____

*"50 Down and Many More to Go." *Jewish Free Press*, Calgary, January 19, 1995, pp. 8–9.

One of the greatest pleasures of newspaper writing is the challenge of adapting myself to the restrictions of the medium, especially the need to produce for deadlines ("We're going to press in two hours. Make sure you have something ready") and to compress my wisdom into finite chunks that can be squeezed between the advertisements.

On deeper reflection, I realize that there are some more substantial reasons that attract an academic scholar to the journalistic venue. Chief among my motives is my determination to infect people with my own fascination with Jewish history and culture.

One of the most gratifying responses that I often hear from readers is that they had not realized that learning about Judaism could be so entertaining. Initially, I found such reactions to be odd, but I have come to realize just how widespread this perception is. It is symptomatic of some immense gaps in what passes for Jewish education.

Indeed, I do take pride in the fact that most of the details and trivia that I assemble in my articles are not readily found in popular surveys or textbooks and often have to be pieced together from works that are considered esoteric and scholarly; whereas the prevailing impression that emerges from so much popular writing on Jewish history is that Judaism is an arid and deadly serious system of laws and doctrines, which must be treated with such heavy doses of reverence that it becomes unapproachable for ordinary people.

This impoverishment of our cultural literacy flows naturally from the ideologies to which we have entrusted most Judaic teaching in recent generations, namely the Zionist movement and religious Orthodoxy. For all that these worldviews might diverge over other fundamental issues, they are as one in their determination to erase any meaningful Jewish experience between Bar Kokhba and Herzl, implying that throughout this period Jews did little more than pray, study Talmud, and endure persecution. This misrepresentation does a great disservice to the richness and vibrancy of our history.

In keeping with my own agendas, I tend to emphasize a recurring set of themes. For example, many of my articles are devoted to finding parallels between recent events and topics that are described in Jewish sources from earlier eras. My underlying assumption is, of course, that our ancestors were very much like ourselves and dealt with issues very much like the ones that confront us today.

Another idea that often finds expression in my articles is that Judaism has never been static or monolithic. The tradition has made room for legalists, philosophers, mystics, and others, each of whom has interpreted the heritage in their own distinctive manner.

As is inevitable amid such variety, our ancestors produced varying proportions of wisdom, virtue, eccentricity, and folly. Though my attitude to the Jewish past might not always be a reverent one, it is usually affectionate. At any rate, it is our family and cannot be denied or disowned.

This attitude of amused distance, fueled by my academic dabbling in religious studies, also affects my treatment of other religious traditions. Rather than indulge in polemical diatribes on issues that defy reasoned verification, I enjoy tracing the manifold patterns of similarity, contrast, and interaction that have characterized Judaism's relations with both Christianity and Islam over the centuries. This exercise can lead to a clearer understanding of what is distinctive and what is universal in ourselves.

There were times when I entertained doubts about my ability to continue coming up with original ideas for articles for each impending deadline. After all, won't I eventually run out of novel things to say about each year's festivals?

Experience has taught me that this is not likely to present a real obstacle. The Jewish religious and cultural legacy contains sufficient resources to keep me occupied for the next fifty articles at least.

PART

I

❧

Jewish Trivia
and Exotica

1

✍

How Many Levels Are There in Heaven?*

*I*n a recent session of CBC radio's popular morning "Eye-Opener" program,¹ a caller asked a "good question" about the origins of the English expression "seventh heaven."

The answer that was given referred the listener to the popular Muslim conception of paradise, which is divided into several celestial levels, awarded according to the degree of righteousness achieved during one's mortal lifetime.

---

*"In Seventh Heaven." (*The Jewish Star*, Calgary/Edmonton, Nov. 3--16, 1989, pp. 4-50.

1. The "Calgary Eye-Opener" is an early-morning radio talk show aired on the local station of the Canadian Broadcasting Corporation. One of the most popular segments of this program, and one which has since been imitated in other cities, is the "Good Question," in which listeners pose a factual question to which the research team must find an answer by the following morning.

That may very well be the channel through which the expression reached English. It should, however, be noted that the concept preceded by many centuries the rise of Islam, and has deep roots in Jewish tradition.

THE SEVEN HEAVENS

Some of the rabbis of the Talmud had very precise ideas about the structure of the upper regions. They were presumably influenced by the fact that the Hebrew word for heavens or sky appears only in a plural form: *shamayim*, implying a multiplicity of heavens. Given the special role of the number seven in the Bible, it was natural that this number should also determine the arrangement of the heavens.

The Jewish sages had no trouble finding distinct functions for each of the seven levels. The heavens, mysterious as they are, affect us in many aspects of our daily life, as well as having important religious associations.

Thus, according to one quaint itemization, one heaven is required simply to screen off the light at nighttime, another to store the rain and snow, and still another to house the planets. Others have more religious uses, accommodating the souls of the righteous and the unborn, as well as various levels of angels, the Heavenly Jerusalem, and the throne of God.

According to one legend, the Israelites who assembled at Mount Sinai to receive the Torah were treated to a glimpse of all seven heavens opened up above them.

The Jewish mystical tradition, as it is revealed to us in texts dating from just after the Talmudic period, turned the concept of seven heavenly levels into a key focus of its speculations. According to their imagery, these heavens are actually palaces—*heikhalot*—and the task of the mystic is to ascend as high as he can until he reaches the highest level, where he will be vouchsafed a peek at the throne of God.

In this conception of multilayered palaces, the Jewish mystics were influenced by the verse in the Song of Songs (1:4); "The King [i.e. God] has brought me into his chambers," a verse which had already been interpreted allegorically by Rabbi Akiva, the most renowned talmudic mystic.

THE MYSTICAL ASCENT

The rules of the mystical ascent into the *heikhalot* are quite complex and (as I have had confirmed by my family's 11-year-old expert on the subject) remarkably similar to those of a video arcade game. Throughout his ascent, the mystic is being opposed by hostile angels who stand guard at every gate on the way. The opposition becomes more powerful as the levels get higher.

If the mystic knows the names of the angelic guards he will be granted magical powers over them. Most important, he must collect "seals" inscribed with secret names of God, which will earn him permission to proceed still farther. He is constantly being put to tests, and a terrible fate awaits the one who fails such a test. If he does succeed in his mission, he will be allowed to address questions or inquiries to the Almighty himself.

This type of mysticism also passed into Christianity. The late Gershom Scholem, the leading historian of Jewish mysticism, calls our attention to the testimony of Paul, who describes (2 Corinthians 12:2–4) how he himself had experienced a similar mystical ascent: "Whether in the body or out of it, I do not know— God knows." Paul was caught up as far as the third heaven, where he "heard words so secret that human lips may not repeat them."

Scholem argues that such climbs through the different levels of heaven were probably common among Jews of the time.

The third heaven seems to have been a common stopping-point in the journey and is mentioned in some Jewish works of the period. The Talmud relates how a group of rabbis discoursed so impressively about Ezekiel's mysterious vision of the heavenly chariot that a heavenly voice was prompted to announce: "A place is prepared to you, and a table is set for you—you and your students are admitted to the third level."

CLASH WITH SCIENCE

As Jewish thinkers became more familiar with science and astronomy, the enumeration of seven heavens became problematic.

According to the medieval theory there were at least ten heavens—concentric spheres, each one containing a heavenly body (the seven known planets, the sun and moon, as well as the outer sphere that houses the stars). These heavenly bodies were believed to be "separate intelligences," incorporeal beings of pure thought, who were identified with the angels of the traditional religions.

Maimonides, in his *Guide to the Perplexed* (composed around 1190), tried to reconcile the apparent discrepancy between the Talmudic description and the science of his day. While asserting that the number seven could, if necessary, be justified on scientific grounds (since some levels are grouped together), Maimonides argues that the rabbinic tradition should not be taken literally, but as an allegory about God's guidance of the universe.

Though in a manner very different from the mystics, Maimonides also believed that human beings should strive to experience the higher spiritual levels of the various heavens. To the extent that an individual is capable of contemplating pure, eternal, abstract truth, he can plug in to the lowest of the separate intelligences. For the philosopher, such knowledge becomes the ultimate purpose of religious life.

The determination to ascend through the seven heavens has remained alive in more recent times.

The founder of the Hasidic movement, Rabbi Israel Ba'al Shem-Tov, describes in a letter to his brother-in-law how, between 1746 and 1749, he engaged in a number of mystical ascents, including one where he rose higher than ever before to confront the Messiah himself, who answered various questions for him and provided him with secret charms to facilitate future celestial visits.

Like Jewish mystics from earliest times, the Ba'al Shem-Tov used his heavenly ascent as an opportunity to ask for Heavenly intercession to ward off impending disasters that were threatening the Jews.

The expression "being in seventh heaven" is thus an extremely ancient one in Judaism. Its rich associations make it difficult for me to use the phrase glibly, according to its current vernacular usage, as a mere superlative for extreme happiness.

SUGGESTIONS FOR FURTHER READING

Dan, Joseph (1987). "The Religious Experience of the Merkavah." In *Jewish Spirituality: From the Bible through the Middle Ages.* ed. Arthur Green. Vol. 1, pp. 289–307. New York: Crossroads.

Jacobs, Louis, ed. (1976). *Jewish Mystical Testimonies.* New York: Schocken.

Scholem, Gershom. (1965). *Jewish Gnosticism, Merkabah Mysticism, and Talmudic Tradition* 2nd ed., New York: Jewish Theological Seminary of America.

——— (1965). *Jewish Gnosticism, Merkabah Mysticism, and Talmudic Tradition.* 2nd. ed. New York: Jewish Theological Seminary of America.

2

❧

Why Do Jews Sway When They Pray?*

$\mathcal{T}$he picture of a Jew swaying to and fro in prayer or religious study is one that I have long been inclined to explain on practical grounds. During lengthy periods of standing, it saves wear and tear on the feet. It also enhances one's concentration. As you focus upon the book before your eyes, it is the rest of your surroundings that appear to be swaying in a vague blur, and hence you are less likely to be distracted by the temptations of the environment.

I am not aware of a fully appropriate English word to designate the action. Nor, for that matter, can I think of a Hebrew word that adequately captures the swaying motion of Jewish prayer.

It is to Yiddish that we must turn to get the precise verb, to *shokel*. This fact would seem to indicate that the practice has a particular

---

*"The Meaning of Shokeling." *The Jewish Star*, Calgary/Edmonton, Dec. 1–21, 1989, pp. 4, 15.

association with the Eastern European milieu, and conjures up images of the hasidic *shtiebelach* of Poland and Russia.

In truth, however, the picture of the Jew swaying in prayer is one that has a long history throughout the Jewish world and has often been noted by outsiders as a peculiarity of Jewish worship.

Most talmudic sources actually seem to recommend standing straight and still while praying. These sources emphasize that one's concentration during prayer should be absolute. From Ezekiel's description of the angels of the divine chariot standing "with legs straight" (Ezekiel 1:7), the talmudic rabbis learned that one should hold one's feet rigidly together during prayer.

Jewish law tended to discourage excesses of bowing and prostration and took care to define those points in the service when bowing is allowed.

It is related, nonetheless, that Rabbi Akiva, when praying privately, would be left in one corner and be found later in another because of his constant bowing and prostrations.

THE KUZARI

By the beginning of the Middle Ages, the Jews of Arabia were already notorious for their *shokeling*—to the extent that an old Arabic poem uses it as an image to describe the swaying of a camel.

By the eleventh century, the practice of *shokeling* had come to be regarded as an identifying mark among the Jews of Muslim Spain.

Thus, we find a reference to it in one of the theological classics of the time, Rabbi Judah Halevi's *Kuzari*. This famous work took the form of a philosophical dialogue between a rabbi and the king of the Khazars, a Mongol kingdom in Russia whose leaders had adopted Judaism in the eighth century.

The *Kuzari*, presenting a fictionalized account of the arguments which ultimately persuaded the king to accept Judaism, focuses on a variety of sober topics in the areas of philosophy, science,

Torah, Hebrew language, and Jewish history. Amidst all this serious theology, the Khazar king cannot resist asking his Jewish teacher why Jews move to and fro when reading the Bible.

The Rabbi begins by offering a conventionally held view: "It is said that it is done in order to arouse natural heat."

He then proceeds to suggest his own theory: Originally, there were not enough books to go around, and ten or more individuals would have to share a single text. Each would have to bend down towards the book in order to have his turn at reading, then stand back to let others have a peek. "This resulted in a continual bending and sitting up . . . Then it became a habit through constant seeing, observing and imitating, which is in man's nature."

A similar theory, current in contemporary Israeli folklore, explains that Yemenite Jews are often able to read books from unusual angles as a result of the dearth of books in the old country. Several students would have to sit around a single rare volume, each one observing it from a different direction. The story does indeed have a ring of plausibility.

IGNITING THE SOUL

The phenomenon of *shokeling* during religious study was conspicuous enough to be addressed by the *Zohar*, the classic of Jewish mysticism composed in thirteenth-century Spain. The hero of the book, Rabbi Simeon ben Yohai, is asked by his students why it is only the Jews who move back and forth when learning Torah.

Rabbi Simeon begins his beautiful reply by observing that the soul of a Jew derives mystically from the Celestial Torah. Thus, through hearing a word of Torah, the soul is immediately ignited like the wick of a lamp, as it is joined with its supernal source.

By swaying during Torah study, the Jew's body is actually quivering to the flame-like rhythm of his soul. No other people, says

Rabbi Simeon, possess such a mystical connection to the divine Torah.

Christian observers were also aware of the Jewish proclivity towards *shokeling*. An interesting testimony to this fact can be found in the margins of a thirteenth-century Latin manuscript of the *Histories of Peter Comestor*, a popular medieval retelling of biblical history.

The marginal glosses in question were composed by one Abbas (Abbot) Johannes de Brach, a figure who demonstrates an impressive expertise in Jewish as well as Christian and Greek scholarship, including a measure of familiarity with the Hebrew language.

When he reaches the description of the revelation at Mount Sinai, and to the verse (Exodus 19:18), "And the *whole mount quaked terribly,*" Abbot Johannes makes the following observation, "Thence it is that the Jews still quake at their prayer, representing the quaking at the mount."

The remark sounds uncannily like a typical Jewish midrash, though I am not aware of any Jewish source that presents such an explanation.

A very similar interpretation however is found in an almost contemporary Spanish-Jewish commentary, that of Rabbi Jacob ben Asher, known as the *Ba'al Ha-Turim*. Rabbi Jacob links the custom to a verse a few lines earlier in Exodus (19:16) "And all the people that were in the camp trembled."

It is obvious, in any case, that the Jews in thirteenth-century Europe were known for their *shokeling* during prayer.

CALL FOR DECORUM

By the time we get to the nineteenth century, the emancipated and religiously enlightened Jews of Germany have little sympathy for the traditional swaying during religious services. Shokeling is grouped with other traditional practices which are regarded as violations of the solemnity and decorum appropriate to a place of worship.

A very articulate call for religious reform, composed by Eliezer Liebermann in Dessau, 1818, contrasts the typical Jewish service with that of the non-Jew: "Why should we not draw a lesson from the people among whom we live? Look at the Gentiles and see how they stand in awe and reverence and with good manners in their house of prayer. No one utters a word, *no one moves a limb* . . . "

It is perhaps significant that, according to an uncorroborated report by the historian Heinrich Graetz, Liebermann eventually converted to Catholicism.

This insistence on standing still during the service was justified by the reformers on grounds of promoting respect and orderliness in a house of worship. Over the last two centuries, it came to be linked with a number of related changes in the structure of the synagogue service.

Thus, for example, we now find a widespread use of professional cantors, rather than lay prayer leaders. The *bimah* is moved from the middle of the sanctuary to a stage-like structure at its front. The cantors begin to turn towards the congregants, instead of leading them by facing in the same direction.

CONGREGATION AS AUDIENCE

All these changes, which became particularly widespread in North American Judaism, have legitimate historical precedents or aesthetic justifications. Taken together, however, they produced a common outcome: to place the congregation in the role of an audience, passively observing as someone else conducts the service for them.

Sociologists and historians of modern Judaism have generally understood this phenomenon as a recognition of the fact that significant proportions of the American communities are no longer knowledgeable enough to participate actively in the services. This fact serves at once to reflect and promote alienation from the community.

In fact, one recent sociological study of American synagogue life found that careful observation of different patterns of *shokeling* reveals some remarkable differences between different groups within the Jewish community. One can note distinct variations between the swayings of men and women, modern and traditional Orthodox, and even between parents and their yeshivah-educated children.

Perhaps the humble, much maligned act of *shokeling*, wherein individual Jews move their bodies to private rhythms as they commune with their Creator, is the ultimate act of protest against being relegated to religious passivity. As recognized by Jew and Gentile alike over the ages, it represents something that is integral and unique to traditional Jewish religious life.

SUGGESTIONS FOR FURTHER READING

Heilman, Samuel C. (1976). *Synagogue Life.* Chicago: University of Chicago Press.

Mendes-Flohr, Paul and Jehuda Reinharz, ed. (1955) *The Jew in the Modern World: A Documentary History* 2nd ed. New York and Oxford: Oxford University Press.

Smalley, Beryl. (1983). *The Study of the Bible in the Middle Ages.* Oxford: Blackwell.

3

᠕

Are Smoking and Drinking Religious Acts?*

*I*n reading these days about how Ottawa is adding ever more stringent restrictions to the marketing of cigarettes in Canada, my mind tends to stray to the good old days of twenty or thirty years ago when people could enjoy their simple physical pleasures, before we were educated to the fact that just about everything is injurious to our health.

Traces of these changes can be discerned in traditional Jewish lifestyles as well. Judaism has generally encouraged people to enjoy the pleasures of God's world, and it comes as no surprise that from the first discovery of tobacco, questions begin to blossom forth from the halakhic codes and responsa regarding such matters as its possible use in the *havdalah* ceremony at the conclusion of the sabbath, where a blessing is customarily recited over a fragrant herb or spice.

---

*"A Cigarette and a Cup of Coffee." *The Jewish Star*, Calgary/Edmonton, Feb. 9–22, 1990, p. 4.

Those of us who have prayed in old-style Ashkenazic shuls will certainly have memories of the passing around of a snuff-box during the Shabbat services. Somewhat more disturbing is the widespread custom, still in vogue in hasidic circles in Israel, of encouraging young children to smoke cigarettes on Purim.

HOLY SPARKS OF TOBACCO

The hasidic movement has always cultivated a special attachment to the pleasures of nicotine. This is, of course, entirely consistent with their general philosophy of accentuating the simple joys of life, especially those that appealed to the lower classes of society. As with many other such folk practices, however, smoking came to be looked upon by Hasidism as a religious ritual in its own right, and a mystical one at that!

This point is emphasized in a recent study by the distinguished English Judaica scholar Louis Jacobs.

In his article, Jacobs traces the mystical theme of the "uplifting of the sparks" as developed in the literature of the Kabbalah.

According to this conception, our world consists of a mixture of holy sparks scattered among profane "shells." The goal of Jewish religious life then becomes one of elevating the hidden sparks by performing everyday activities and religious rituals in awareness of their mystical importance.

This idea was given special prominence in the doctrines of Rabbi Isaac Luria (known as the Ari) and the mystics of sixteenth-century Safed and was inherited by the Hasidic movement in eighteenth-century Russia and Poland.

Jacobs notes how the early *hasidim* applied this mystical doctrine to the act of smoking. The Hasidic fondness for cigarettes was well-known and became the target of criticism from their opponents, the *misnagdim*. The *hasidim* justified their habit on theological grounds. Smoking was, after all, a way of elevating the holy sparks.

Some Hasidic masters were conscious that a special privilege had been granted to their own generations: Tobacco had been unknown to the great Ari himself, "because the time had not yet come for the very subtle sparks in tobacco to be released by smoking." But now that almost all the coarser sparks had received their restoration, God sent us tobacco so that the Hasidic masters should elevate these new and subtle sparks!

It was told of Rabbi Israel Ba'al Shem-Tov, the founder of the Hasidic movement, that he once waxed enthusiastic about a student who interrupted his prayers by stooping to retrieve his fallen pipe. The Baal Shem-Tov justified this apparent breach of decorum by explaining that there are subtle souls who can only achieve their perfection through this most ethereal of substances.

The Ba'al Shem-Tov went on to compare cigarette smoke to the "sweet savour unto the Lord" exuded by the sacrifices and to the incense that was burned in the Temple.

As Rabbi Jacobs understands this story, it alludes to the Kabbalistic belief in reincarnation. Some righteous souls cannot bear to return to earth unless they are allowed to reside in tobacco.

One wonders how many such souls continue to hover over the Calgary bingo halls.[1]

MIDNIGHT VIGILS

Another recent study attempts to trace a connection between the Jewish mystical tradition and yet another injurious habit, the drinking of coffee. The current issue of the *Association for Jewish Studies*

---

1. This reference is a familiar one to most Calgarian Jews. The government-sponsored bingo parlors which serve as an important source of income for community institutions (and which are mentioned elsewhere in this collection) are notorious for the quantities of cigarette smoke which they exude.

Review contains a fascinating article on this theme by historian Eliott Horowitz of Beersheba.

The very origins of coffee-drinking, Horowitz notes, are rooted in mystical practices. The beverage was evidently introduced by fifteenth-century Muslim mystics (Sufis) in Yemen as a means for producing the wakefulness necessary for their nightly devotional exercises. In Jewish mystical circles caffeine performed a similar function.

The practice of midnight vigils in mourning for the destruction of the Temple, and in prayer for its rebuilding (known as *Tikkun Hatzot*), was popularized by Rabbi Isaac Luria's circle of mystics in the second half of the sixteenth century. Such rituals had been known before, but only now did they achieve widespread acceptance.

Horowitz suggests that this fact should be understood in connection with another piece of information, mentioned in a responsum of Rabbi Moses di-Trani: Coffee was at this time being introduced to that part of the world, and at least one coffeehouse is documented as existing in Safed by 1580, whose clients were known for staying there well into the night (though not for prayer or mystical devotion).

THE CAFFEINE CONNECTION

This raises the question: Are we justified in suggesting a correlation between the two phenomena? Does the sudden increase in the popularity of the midnight vigil, a custom which had been introduced with little success centuries before, have any connection with the recent availability of coffee in Safed?

Horowitz tests this hypothesis by trying it out on another historical setting, that of seventeenth- and eighteenth-century Italy. Here, as distinct from Safed, there existed a strong local pietistic tradition of *Shomerim la-Boker*, or rising before dawn for penitential prayer.

As the currents of Lurianic Kabbalah began to reach Italy from the Holy Land, devotees made efforts to introduce the *Tikkun Hatzot* into communities like Venice and Mantua—with no immediate success.

It was not until the mid-seventeenth century that the Lurianic midnight vigils began to achieve widespread acceptance, at the expense of the *Shomerim la-Boker* societies. Over a relatively short period of time, the Mantua *Shomerim la-Boker* club, a venerable and once-populous organization, quietly disappeared from history for want of members. Similar patterns characterize other communities.

The reason for this change? Of course there are many considerations to be taken into account, but the introduction and spread of coffee-drinking seems to make an appearance here at the crucial time: the first coffeehouse was established in Venice in 1640, but the drink remained a rare luxury there until the turn of the century. Consumption of coffee became common during the first half of the eighteenth century (and Jews were prominent in its commerce). Now they were able more easily than before to stay awake at night. This is precisely the time when the *Tikkun Hatzot* achieved dominance and the *Shomerim la-Boker* faded into oblivion.

No, we are not suggesting that either tobacco or coffee are habits to be encouraged by Judaism now that we are aware of their dangers to health. What we can however appreciate from the above examples is that a religion does not develop without interacting with the surrounding environment, and that Judaism has always had a special talent for discerning the religious significance of even the most profane activities.

4

ॐ

What's in a Name?*

$\mathcal{A}$ friend recently asked me to verify a theory he had heard, to the effect that the name of the Spanish town Toledo had originally been derived from the Hebrew *Toledot*, which denotes generations or history. While the idea immediately struck me as a historical impossibility, I felt that it nonetheless was deserving of further investigation.

A quick glance at the *Encyclopedia Judaica* did not uncover any support for that explanation of the name, but it did mention that a similar tradition was recorded by one of Spanish Jewry's luminaries, the noted statesman and exegete Don Isaac Abravanel. Abravanel reports that the city of Toledo had been named by Jewish exiles following the destruction of the first Temple. The name by which it is usually referred to in medieval Hebrew writings is

---

*"What's in a Name?" *The Jewish Free Press*, Calgary, Dec. 18, 1990, p. 12.

Tulitela, which Abravanel derived from the Hebrew root *tiltul,* which denotes wandering or exile.

The explanation is reminiscent of many similar traditions, all of which reflect the Jews' firm conviction that their communities dated back to hoary antiquity. Accordingly there could be no doubt that Jews had been responsible for first assigning the names of the respective places. A similar theory derives the name *Polin* (Poland) from the two Hebrew words *po lin,* "Rest here for the night!" reportedly uttered by early Jewish immigrants from Central Europe upon first reaching that land.

Though none of these supposed etymologies is likely to be historically authentic, it is true that some locales in Spain do bear Hebrew-sounding names. For example, the name of Cadiz is generally believed to be derived from the same root as the Hebrew *kadosh,* or holy. The connection however is not a Jewish one, but goes back to the ancient Phoenicians, the great maritime empire centered in what today is Lebanon. The Phoenicians spoke a language akin to Hebrew and built colonies throughout the Mediterranean basin as far west as Spain.

Another important Phoenician port was Carthage, or as it was called in its original Semitic form *Keret Hadashah,* New Town, a popular name for ancient cities, equivalent to the Greek *Neapolis,* which in Italian became Naples and in Arabic, Nablus (Shechem).

Carthage, of course, posed a serious threat to the imperial aspirations of Rome and came close to overcoming Rome altogether. In light of later Jewish suffering at the hands of "the wicked empire," the defeat of Carthage should be viewed as something of a historical tragedy for Jews.

An old history teacher of mine liked to point out a further dimension of the campaign: Had Hannibal succeeded in overrunning Rome, then chances are that the entire western world would today be speaking a language that is substantially identical to Hebrew!

The talmudic Rabbis enjoyed suggesting Hebrew explanations for the names of the cities in which they lived, even if the names were obviously of Greek or Latin origin. For example, the name Tiberias, the Galilean town built by Herod to honour the emperor Tiberius, is explained in the Talmud as referring either to its beautiful view (*tovah ra'ayatah*), or to the fact that it sits at the navel (*tibor*) of the Land of Israel.

The process could work in both directions, and was indulged in by non-Jews as well. The first Greek-speaking travellers to Jerusalem were so impressed by the religious character of that city, dominated as it was by the Temple and the priests, that they never doubted that the name *Yerushalayim* came from the Greek *hiero*, meaning holy.

Or to take a more recent example, a movement in nineteenth-century England wished to trace the origins of the ancient Britons back to the ten lost tribes of Israel. For these followers of the British Hebrew movement there was no question that the very name British was of Hebrew origin, a combination of the words *brit* (covenant) and *ish* (man)!

The quest for Hebrew etymologies did not cease with the migration of Jews to America, though these were often voiced with tongue firmly in cheek. The name America appears in some parodies of American Jewish life as *Amma Reqa*, "the empty people." I personally have always been impressed at the appropriateness of the name of a popular Jewish seaside resort: *Me-ami*, "waters of my people."

Closer to home, the Jewish agricultural settlement at Edenbridge, Saskatchewan was intended by its founders to be read as Yidden-bridge, the closest that the Canadian government would allow to an explicit reference to its ethnic make-up.

And who knows if, when the first Jewish exiles arrived at the junction of the Bow and Elbow rivers, they were not subjected to a volley of hostile arrows, causing them to name the place *Kol Girei*, (later: Calgary), Aramaic for "all the arrows"?

Presumably, their brethren to the north had a more fortunate experience, inspiring them to dub their new home "the land that He has given"—in Hebrew: *Adama natan* (which later became Edmonton).

SUGGESTIONS FOR FURTHER READING

Horowitz, E. (1989). "Coffee, Coffeehouses and the Nocturnal Rituals of Early Modern Jewry." *AJS Reivew* 14: 17–46.

Jacobs, Louis. (1987). "The Uplifting of Sparks in Later Jewish Mysticism" In *Jewish Spirituality: From the Sixteenth Century to the Present*, ed. Arthur Green. Vol. 2, pp. 99–126. New York: Crossroads.

5

_⅋_

Who Stole the
Priestly Breastplate?*

$\mathcal{S}$everal months ago an unscrupulous and underpaid columnist
(myself) published in the pages of this newspaper an article pur-
porting to describe the discovery of the breastplate of the ancient
Hebrew high priest. Having discredited my veracity on the topic,
I must assure my readers that the information contained in _this_
article is actually reliable and true.

As anyone who has ever seen an Indiana Jones film knows, the
question of the fate of the lost Temple treasures is one that has
long fascinated writers of fiction. Among the most distinguished
of such speculators was none other than Sir Arthur Conan Doyle,
the creator of Sherlock Holmes. Conan Doyle composed a story
entitled "The Jew's Breastplate," which deals with the fictitious
theft of that artifact from the British Museum. The story was first

---

*"The Return of the Priestly Breastplate." _The Jewish Free Press_,
Calgary, August 23, 1991, p. 10.

printed in a magazine in 1899, and was subsequently included in a collection entitled *Round the Fire*, published in 1908. The story is admittedly not one of Conan Doyle's better-known works and has rarely been reprinted.

In 1913, there appeared in Piotrkow, Poland, a book entitled *Sefer Hoshen ha-Mishpat shel ha-Kohen ha-Gadol—The Book of the High Priest's Breastplate*. The Hebrew volume told a story that was virtually identical to Conan Doyle's, with one significant difference: the hero was the sixteenth century Bohemian Rabbi Judah Loew of Prague, better known by his acronym, the *Maharal*. In the story, the Maharal journeys to London in order to solve the mysterious theft of the breastplate from the "Belmore Street" Museum.

The author of this story was one of the most popular Hebrew writers of the early twentieth century, Rabbi Yudel Rosenberg. Combining traditional rabbinical education and a broad erudition in general literature, Rosenberg authored over twenty works while serving as rabbi in various Polish communities. He was best known for his collections of wondrous tales about famous rabbis, especially hasidic masters. Most of these stories were works of out-and-out fiction, though usually not presented as such.

The Maharal was one of Rosenberg's favorite protagonists and appears in several of his books. In fact, Rosenberg (who apparently believed himself to be a descendant of the Maharal) is responsible for inventing the one detail about the Maharal with which most people are familiar; the famous *Golem*, the humanoid monster allegedly created by the rabbi to save the Jews of Prague from anti-Semitic plots. So popular did this superhero become that we find it difficult to believe the story had no basis in either fact or legend before Rosenberg introduced it in a book published in Warsaw in 1909!

It appears that several of Rosenberg's stories, whether about the Maharal or Rabbi Elijah Guttmacher, the *Greiditzer Rebbe*, or others, were really Judaized versions of popular whodunits and adventure stories.

The tale of the priestly breastplate was, in any case, destined to be one of Rosenberg's last stories. In 1913, he left Poland for Canada, where he took up rabbinical positions—first in Toronto, and later settling in Montreal—turning his attentions to more respectable rabbinic activities. From this point onwards, his production of stories ceases.

Rosenberg had presumably learned the important lesson that in Canada one cannot get away with publishing fictitious accounts of the high priest's breastplate.

SUGGESTIONS FOR FURTHER READING

Dan, Joseph. (1975). *The Hasidic Story—Its History and Development.* Keter Library: Jewish People and Culture, ed. S. Halkin. Jerusalem: Keter.

Halpern, Solomon Alter. (1981). *The Prisoner and Other Tales of Faith.* Jerusalem and New York: Feldheim.

Robinson, Ira. (1990). "A Letter from the Sabbath Queen: Rabbi Yudel Rosenberg Addresses Montreal Jewry." In *An Everyday Miracle: Yiddish Culture in Montreal*, ed. P. Anctil and M. Butovsky, pp. 101–114. Montreal: Véhicule Press.

6

ॐ

What Does Judaism Say about Birthdays?*

The *Free Press* recently celebrated its first birthday. While anticipating the magnificent staff party, I have taken to wondering what Jewish sources have to tell us about birthdays and their celebration.

One of the first Hebrew expressions any modern Jewish child learns is the word for birthday, *yom huledet*. This phrase goes back to the Bible, to the story of how Pharaoh held a feast on the occasion of his own birthday, at which he restored his chief butler and hanged his baker, in conformity with Joseph's predictions (Genesis 40:20).

In the midrash and in some of the ancient Aramaic translations, the word used to render birthday in that passage is *genosa*, which

---

*"Happy Birthday, JFP." *The Jewish Free Press*, Calgary, Nov. 15, 1991, p. 9.

is the Greek word for birthday. The *genosa* is listed in the Mishnah among the idolatrous religious celebrations on which Jews are directed to avoid dealings with their pagan neighbours. The Mishnah lists both the Greek and Hebrew terms for birthday, a fact which the Palestinian Talmud explains as intended to include both royal and individual birthdays; the former were considered public observances, whereas the latter were observed as idolatrous rites by individuals. It is the Greek term that appears most frequently in the talmudic sources, suggesting that birthdays were considered a foreign practice, not a Jewish one.

In actuality, most of the birthdays mentioned in the Talmud were of the royal variety. We have already mentioned Pharaoh's, and some midrashic traditions claim that Ahasuerus' big party at the beginning of the Book of Esther was also a birthday celebration. This is in keeping with the norm in the Roman Empire, where the Emperor's birth would be commemorated in an obligatory religious ceremony, since the Emperors claimed to be gods. The association with Emperor-worship probably resulted in the birthdays' being held in grave disfavor by the ancient rabbis.

There are, nevertheless, some more favorable references to birthdays, as in the following midrash, which comments on God's declaration that, following the Exodus from Egypt, Nisan (the month in which Passover falls) should henceforward be counted as the first month.

> This is analogous to the case of a king to whom a son was born. He ordained that date to be a holiday. Subsequently the son was abducted, and he remained in captivity for a long period. Some time later, the son was ransomed, and the king began to celebrate that date as if it were a birthday. Similarly, before going down to Egypt the Israelites used to celebrate a past event [namely, the creation of the world]. Subsequently they went down to Egypt and experienced slavery, and God performed miracles for them and they were redeemed. They now began to count the months from that date.

The point of the parable seems to be that, though one's birth is a fine thing to celebrate (even as we mark the birth of the world on

Rosh Hashanah), the anniversary of a subsequent achievement (like the Exodus) can take its place as more fitting occasion for festivity.

It is, therefore, entirely appropriate to wish the folks at the *Free Press* a hearty *mazal tov* on this anniversary of their accomplishment.

SUGGESTIONS FOR FURTHER READING

Lieberman, Saul. (1962). *Hellenism in Jewish Palestine: Studies in the Literary Transmission, Beliefs and Manners of Palestine in the 1st Century* B.C.E.–*4th Century* C.E. New York: The Jewish Theological Seminary of America.

7

ॐ

What Do Jews Believe about the Afterlife?*

$\mathcal{A}$ colleague of mine in the University of Calgary Religious Studies Department approached me a while back in a state of considerable agitation. He (a non-Jew) had been teaching an introductory class on Judaism and, when he began speaking about the Jewish belief in resurrection of the dead, had been stubbornly attacked by a Jewish student who insisted that "Jews don't believe in that sort of thing." The experience repeated itself not long afterwards in conversation with a Jewish friend who mentioned how some of the media reports of Robert Maxwell's burial on Jerusalem's Mount of Olives had noted that Jews traditionally believed that those who were buried in that spot were guaranteed to be first in line when the dead were revived in the Messi-

---

*"When the Dead Rise." *The Jewish Press*, Calgary, December 15, 1991, p. 9.

anic era. "Is that really true?" my friend asked me. "I thought Jews didn't go in for that sort of thing."

I am certain that both these incidents reflect a similar phenomenon among contemporary spokespeople for Judaism, many of whom have no qualms about expounding their personal opinions as those of Judaism. Unfortunately, the state of Jewish literacy in our communities does not allow many of us to distinguish between facts and opinions.

With respect to the subject at hand, let me assure you that the belief in resurrection—that is, the belief that at some point in the future the dead will be restored to their physical bodies—has been a tenaciously held belief among Jews since at least the second century B.C.E. The Books of Daniel and Maccabees, both composed against the background of the Maccabean revolt, refer to this idea explicitly, in the latter as a means of motivating people to acts of martyrdom. Josephus Flavius singles out this belief as one of the distinguishing ideas of the Pharisees, as against other Jewish movements which came to be regarded as heretical. The Mishnah, in an untypical foray into the realm of dogmatics, lists resurrection among the beliefs whose denial will cause you to forfeit your place in the world to come. From then on, there is scarcely a Jewish thinker who does not adhere to this idea, which is reaffirmed thrice daily in the liturgy. The belief also gets inherited by the Christians and the Muslims.

I suspect that the self-proclaimed authorities on Judaism who have denied the existence of this idea were troubled because they had been brought up on the maxim that Judaism, unlike Christianity, is not obsessed with the afterlife, but prefers to focus on this world. I believe that that statement is generally true, but that there remains quite a bit of room between a belief and an obsession.

In fact, I think that it is useful to look at the belief in resurrection, as with any eschatological or metaphysical idea, not so much for what it says about the dead (though our sources are full of whimsical speculations on what we will be wearing then, how we will be transported to the Land of Israel, and what will happen to remarried widows when they find themselves with multiple husbands), as for what it teaches us about the Jewish perceptions of life itself.

I have often wondered how Jews arrived at such an unlikely afterlife idea. Would it not be simpler to believe that we survive death in pure spiritual, disembodied forms? That, after all, was the ideal that was promoted by the ancient Greeks, one that is more befitting a spiritual religion.

Perhaps it is precisely this point that prompted our Pharisaic ancestors to promote belief in physical resurrection. The Greeks, as we are aware, had a decidedly negative attitude towards their bodies and anything physical. The philosophical tradition, much of which has been inherited by Western cultural values, tended to look upon the body as an impediment to true spiritual or intellectual perfection. In their opinion, one's physical and material substance are unfortunate facts of life that we should do our best to minimize or undo through self-denial and withdrawal from the world.

We should note that Jews were not entirely immune from such thinking. A philosophical mind like Maimonides, though including the belief in resurrection among his "thirteen principles of faith," was understood by his contemporaries to be lukewarm in his commitment to the idea. As a rationalist, it is clear that he would have been better disposed to an intellectual, rather than a physical, survival. In the end, he describes the resurrection as a temporary affair, following which people will die again and (if they make the grade) survive as abstract souls.

These negative evaluations of material existence, as promoted by the Greek philosophical tradition and its Jewish sympathizers, were precisely the kinds of ideas that talmudic Judaism was denying in its assertion that our physical being is not a tragedy but part of God's ideal plan for the world. What greater proof of this can there be than the fact that even in the next world we will have bodies?

There is much more that could be said about the values and ideas that are contained in this "dogma." Whether or not one chooses personally to believe in physical resurrection, we should recognize honestly how central the belief has been as an expression of Jewish attitudes to life.

SUGGESTIONS FOR FURTHER READING

Katz, Steven. (1977). *Jewish Ideas and Concepts*. New York: Schocken.

Segal, Eliezer. (1997). "Judaism." In *Life after Death in World Religions*, ed. Harold Coward, pp. 11–30. Maryknoll: Orbis.

Raphael, Simcha Paull. (1994). *Jewish Views of the Afterlife*. Northvale, NJ: Jason Aronson.

8

ॐ

How Much Is a Bird in the Hand Worth?*

*I*n the course of my readings of ancient rabbinic texts, I was recently surprised to encounter a familiar-sounding proverb which translates roughly as "A bird in the hand is better than a hundred in flight." This quotation, so similar to a common English one, was employed by the midrashic author to illustrate a quintessentially Jewish idea, inspired by a passage from the biblical Book of Ecclesiastes (4:6): "Better is a handful of quietness than both the hands full of labour and striving after wind."

Typically, the rabbis of the midrash applied this sentiment to the world of Torah study, observing that "a person who has studied a small amount of *halakhot*, but has mastered them, is preferable to one who has studied large quantities of *halakhot* and midrash, but has not truly mastered them."

---

*"A Bird in the Hand is Better than a Hundred in Flight." *The Jewish Free Press*, Calgary, July 2, 1992, p. 11.

Intrigued by the parallels between the midrashic proverb and its English equivalent, I turned to Bartlett's *Familiar Quotations*. Here I was able to unearth a number of variations on the saying. As expected, there was no mention of either the midrash or the Book of Ecclesiastes.

Some of Bartlett's references were to sixteenth-century English authors, who used the proverb in manners that were very unlike the Jewish sources. Not surprisingly, the lesson was applied most commonly to affairs of the heart. Thus, in Thomas Lodge's *Rosalynde*, the lovestruck Rosader is advised to turn his romantic attentions to the shepherdess Aliena, who is already favorably disposed towards him, rather than to the fairer Rosalynde, who does not know he is alive. "One bird in the hand is worth two in the wood," he is counselled; "better possess the love of Aliena than catch furiously at the shadow of Rosalynde."

Another author of the time, Thomas Lodge, adds sardonically that such advice is "better for the birders, but for birds not so good."

The same proverb reappears not long afterwards in Cervantes' *Don Quixote*. Here, too, it is proffered as a piece of romantic advice, only this time it comes from the hero's loyal companion Sancho Panza, as he urges Don Quixote not to delay in declaring his love for his cherished Dulcinea.

It should be noted parenthetically that Cervantes may have had some Jewish connections. An entry under his name appears in the *Encyclopedia Judaica* which reviews a number of theories to the effect that the Spanish novelist stemmed from New Christian (that is, converted Jewish) stock. Such claims should not be taken too seriously, however, since they tend to be made about almost every important figure in modern Spanish history. Even if one were to concede that Don Quixote's creator was of Jewish ancestry, it is inconceivable that he would have been familiar with obscure midrashic texts.

The conviction that "a bride in the hand" should be snatched up, rather than waiting indefinitely for a better candidate, does appear in talmudic sources. A succinct formulation of the idea is ascribed to the Babylonian sage Samuel, who expresses it in characteristically halakhic terms: "A man should betroth a woman even on the Ninth of Av, lest another suitor beat him to her."

None of this really helps explain how a maxim from a fourth-century Jewish text resurfaced in sixteenth-century England or Spain. Such uncharted wanderings are however quite common in the history of proverbs and sayings, which are usually transmitted by mouth rather than by written word, and express fundamental human truths that are common to all nations and cultures.

9

ॐ

What Is the Origin of the Expression *Oy Vey!*?*

$\mathcal{W}$e can learn a lot about people from how they give expression to feelings of shock or sorrow. Different cultures have formulated a variety of quasi-verbal ways of instinctively reacting to distressing situations. In some cases it will be through an obscenity or blasphemy. Among Jews, however, there are two expressions which are most familiar to us. Ashkenazic Jews will cry "*Oy vey!*" whereas Sepharadim will blurt out the very similar–sounding "*Way, way!*"

The *vey* component of *oy vey* exists in German as well (*weh*), and might have entered Yiddish from there—though, as we shall observe below, this is not necessarily so. The *oy* however does not seem traceable to any outside source. This seems to hold true as well of the *Way* of North African Jews, which does not (insofar as my inquiries have revealed so far) show up in the vernacular

---

*"Oy Vey!" *The Jewish Free Press*, Calgary, March 2, 1992, p. 8.

languages of their Muslim neighbours. These facts invite further investigation.

Oy is actually an old and authentic Hebrew word. It appears with some frequency in the Bible, where it is usually rendered in English as "woe!" It is not always spoken by Jews, and hence we find such scenes as that in 1 Samuel 4:7–8, in which the Philistines are depicted as crying "*Oy!*" in confused anticipation of an Israelite attack.

In the Book of Ecclesiastes, we find a variant of this interjection, pronounced *Ee!* as in: "*Ee* to him that is alone when he falls" (4:10). This form seems to have become the prevalent one by the time we get to the era which produced the Mishnah (first to third centuries C. E.), and appears in such phrases as "*Ee* to me, whether I speak or remain silent!" and "*Ee* to the wicked and to his neighbor!" (By the way, you won't find this form in the normal printed editions of the Mishnah, which replaced the strange-sounding *ee* with the more familiar *oy*. The quotations listed above are from reliable manuscripts).

It is when we reach the period of the Talmud and Midrash (third to sixth centuries) that Jews begin using a new expression in order to give vent to their pain and tribulation: the familiar *vay* or *way!* This word appears in dozens of passages in rabbinic literature, as the equivalent of its older cousins *oy* and *ee*. *Vay* (or *way*) was apparently not considered a distinctively Jewish expression at the time, since the same word was in use in both Greek (*ouai*) and Latin (*vae*), carrying precisely the same meanings as their Hebrew counterparts.

Thus for example, the midrash relates the following charming anecdote about Rabban Gamaliel, who blessed his daughter on the birth of her first child with the rather upsetting prayer "May the word *vay* never budge from your lips." When his daughter voiced her dismay at receiving such a blessing, the doting *zeydeh* explained his real intention: His wish was that she might have many occasions to lament about such domestic troubles as "*Vay*, my baby won't eat! *Vay*, my baby doesn't want to go to school!"

Rabban Gamaliel astutely perceived that there are certain types of parental torments that we learn to prefer over the alternatives.

And just so that you should not be mistaken into supposing that Jews only knew how to suffer, we should make it clear that talmudic literature knows also of an appropriate interjection for joyous occasions: *Wah!* The similarity between the sounds of *way* and *wah* often furnished occasions for elaborate wordplays, which hinted subtly at just how fragile the borderline between sorrow and joy often is.

SUGGESTIONS FOR FURTHER READING

Kutscher, Y. (1963). "Leshon Haza'l." In *Sefer Hanokh Yalon*, ed. S. Lieberman, S. Abramson, Y. Kutscher, and S. Esh, pp. 246–80. Jerusalem: Kiryat Sepher.

Segal, Eliezer. (1994). *The Babylonian Esther Midrash: A Critical Commentary*. Brown Judaic Studies, ed. Ernest Frerichs, Shaye J. D. Cohen, and Calvin Goldscheider. Atlanta: Scholars Press.

10

✤

Who Put the Genie in the Lamp?*

$\mathcal{F}$ollowing in the footsteps of other beloved creations of legend and folklore, the Islamic genie has by now been irrevocably co-opted by the Disney cartoonists. Future generations of children will undoubtedly envisage the genies of the *Arabian Nights* as amorphous blue creatures with the appearance and manic personality of Robin Williams.

The original genie, or *jinn*, was of course a being of a different color. Stemming from the hazy past of ancient Arabian paganism, Muslim tradition enriched the *jinn*'s profile by adding to it features derived from the demons who inhabited Jewish and Christian lore, as well as the more exotic South Asian and African civilizations into which Islam subsequently penetrated.

---

*"The Biblical Roots of Aladdin's Genie." *The Jewish Free Press*, Calgary, June 2, 1994, pp. 6, 9.

The *Qur'an*, Islam's sacred scripture, mentions the *jinn* on several occasions. Some of the passages will evoke familiar associations for readers versed in talmudic legend.

For example, the *Qur'an* relates that King Sulaiman's (Solomon's) mastery of the languages of all creatures allowed him to regiment the hosts of humans, birds, and *jinns* under his command. This echoes the talmudic legends of how the wise monarch exercised dominion over the beasts of the field, the birds of the air, and assorted demons and supernatural spirits.

Solomon's sovereignty over the animal kingdom can be derived in a reasonably straightforward manner from biblical verses such as 1 Kings 5:13 ("He spoke also of beasts and of fowl and of creeping things and of fishes"), but the tradition about Solomon's control over the supernatural realms was derived from imaginative midrashic exegesis of verses like 1 Chronicles 29:23 ("Solomon sat on the throne of the Lord") and Ecclesiastes 2:8 where Solomon recalls how he accumulated *shiddah veshiddot*, an obscure expression that might refer to anything from concubines to cabinets, but which rabbinic midrash identified with the Hebrew word for demon, *shed*.

The *Qur'an* also records stories about how Solomon harnessed the power of the demons (or *jinns*) for his ambitious and demanding construction projects: "They made for him what he pleased of fortresses and images, and bowls large as watering-troughs and cooking-pots that will not move from their place."

According to the *Qur'an*, Solomon died while leaning upon his staff, but his demise did not become known until a worm started to gnaw through the wood of the staff. Had the enslaved *jinns* known this fact, they would not have continued to labor for the king.

Several of the themes in this story can be traced to talmudic writings. Rabbinic legend tells us that Solomon was punished for his overbearing pride when he was impersonated by the demon king Ashmedai and removed from the throne. In this early prototype of *The Prince and the Pauper* motif, the real king was forced to wander the world as a beggar until, as the midrash states it, nothing remained of his former magnificence except the staff in his hand. One version of the tradition states that Solomon never regained his throne and died in abject poverty, a theory that is supported by a very literal reading of Ecclesiastes 2:10: "and *this* [only what I am now holding in my hand] was my portion of all my labor."

The worm in the Muslim story also recalls one of the more marvelous inhabitants of the talmudic bestiary, the *shamir*, a miraculous worm-like creature that Solomon (with the unwilling assistance of Ashmedai) captured and utilized to cut the stones for the construction of the Temple.

The story of Solomon and Ashmedai resurfaces again in the legends of the *Thousand and One Nights*. All of us are familiar with the propensity of genies to get stuck inside lamps and jars. In at least one instance, the genie claims to have been placed there by none other than King Solomon who "sent his minister . . . to seize me, and his vizier had me bound and brought against my will to stand before the prophet [Solomon] as a suppliant." When the *jinn* stubbornly refused to proclaim his faith in God, Solomon had him imprisoned in the jar, which was sealed with lead, stamped with the royal ring inscribed with God's name, and cast into the ocean.

This Arabic folktale shares many elements in common with the talmudic story in which Solomon sends his chief minister, Benaiah ben Jehoiada, to capture Ashmedai. Solomon continued to hold the demon in chains with the help of a magic ring. It was by tricking Solomon into lending him the magic ring that Ashmedai was able to depose the king, and only after taking back that ring was Solomon (according to one version of the story) able to return to power.

When all is said and done, an unmistakable thread of continuity, twisted and complicated though it may be, leads from the pages of the Bible and the Talmud to the cartoon genie of Disney's *Aladdin* films.

SUGGESTIONS FOR FURTHER READING

Fredrick, Dan. (1994). "The Jinn in Islamic Theology and Folklore." B. A. Honors, University of Calgary.

11

⤳

What Did You Know
before You Were Born?*

*A*n intriguing legend from the Talmud and midrash describes how a child, while still in its mother's womb, is taught the entire Torah to the glow of a supernatural lamp that allows it to see to the ends of the earth. It is only at the moment of birth that an angel appears and imposes upon it an oath to live a righteous life, and then slaps the youngster on the mouth or the nose, causing it to forget all that it has learned.

According to this tale, the process of learning in later life does not involve the mastering of new information, but only a review of teachings that were once known, but have subsequently been forgotten.

As several scholars have been quick to point out, this depiction of learning as recollection bears an uncanny resemblance to

---

*"The Angel's Slap." *The Jewish Free Press*, Calgary, October 27, 1994, 8.

a myth that was recounted several centuries earlier, in the concluding pages of Plato's *Republic*. In Plato's well-known myth, the
souls stand ready to enter their new lives with the accumulated
experiences of prior existences, but are ordered to drink from
waters that induce forgetfulness.

Unlike the rabbinic legend, the Greek story posits a doctrine
of transmigration of souls, so that the unborn child's wisdom is
acquired in the course of its prior lives, not by being instructed
in the teachings of the Torah. It is also significant that the Jewish
soul is commanded to make a moral choice, whereas the fatalis-
tic Platonic soul can only *choose* to continue a destiny whose
course was determined by its previous incarnations.

The angel's smack in the Talmudic legend produces total am-
nesia for all, but in the Greek theory of *anamnesis*, the souls quaff
varying quantities of the oblivion-inducing potion. The clever souls
drink no more than they have to, which makes for an easier job of
learning and recalling during their coming lives. Only the foolish
and shortsighted souls make the mistake of rashly and greedily
gulping down excessive doses, dooming them to lives of ignorance
and dull-wittedness.

The theme of the angel's slap was a favorite in Eastern European Jewish folklore. In most versions, the slap becomes a tweak-
ing (*shnel*) of the nose, which is responsible for creating the furrow
beneath the nostrils. The story provides a satisfying explanation of
the sublime and innocent wisdom that adorns the countenances
of newly born infants; they are, according to this theory, still enjoying the residual effects of their prenatal schooling.

Furthermore, the Jewish world had its share of child prodigies
and geniuses who mastered the Talmud at a tender age (such a
person is known in Hebrew as an *Illui*). This phenomenon could
be ascribed to the soul's evading the angel's slap, whether by ac-
cident or design.

The popular Yiddish writer Itzik Manger composed a delight-
ful novella, *The Book of Paradise*, based on the premise that a
mischievous young spirit named Shmuel Abba succeeded in side-

stepping the *shnel*, and then, after he was born, regaled his audiences with a hilarious series of reminiscences about the doings of the righteous in paradise.

My most unlikely encounter with the legend occurred a few years ago while watching a television late-show movie. The film was the 1948 production *Key Largo*, which starred Humphrey Bogart as a disillusioned and battle-weary cynic who found himself among a group of hostages in the power of a desperate gangster. In an otherwise forgettable piece of banal philosophizing, whose connection to the plot now escapes me (unfortunately, my memories of postnatal experiences tend to be very hazy), Bogie began to expound the story of the angel's slap. The legend was related there in its midrashic version, though its Jewish origins were not identified.

Plato, the Talmud, and Humphrey Bogart . . . Hmm? With three such diverse and unimpeachable witnesses attesting to its veracity, the story just might be true. In fact I seem to recall something similar happening to me when I was very young. . . .

SUGGESTIONS FOR FURTHER READING

Manger, Itzik. (1983). *Di vunderlekhe lebnsbashraybung fun Shemu'el Aba Abervo: (dos bukh fun Gan-Eydn)*. Tel-Aviv: Peretz.

Urbach, E. (1987). *The Sages: Their Concepts and Beliefs*. Translated by I. Abrahams. Cambridge, MA. and London, England: Harvard University Press.

12

~

What is the Origin of the Expression *Yasher Koach?**

*E*nthusiastic handshakes, accompanied by the Hebrew greeting "*Yasher Koach*," are the standard expression of congratulations for those who have had the merit of participating in the public worship of the synagogue, especially the reading of the Torah.

The words *Yasher koach* translate literally as "May your strength be firm." A benediction of this sort is always timely, but it is a curious one to be introducing on these particular occasions. Are we really concerned that an individual's powers will have been significantly drained after having mounted the lectern and mouthed some blessings?

The origins of this practice are linked to those of a similar blessing that is recited on rarer occasions; the congregational declaration "*Hazak hazak venit-hazek*" that follows the conclusion of each of the five books of the Pentateuch. The meaning of that Hebrew

---

*"Yasher Koach: May You Have Strength!" *The Jewish Free Press*, Calgary, June 15, 1995, p. 8.

phrase is analogous to that of *Yasher koach*: "Strong, strong, and let us be strengthened!"

From various descriptions of synagogue customs from the medieval period, we learn that the original practice was to wish each participant in the Torah reading *Hazak hazak* upon the conclusion of his *'aliyah*. The reason for this, it appears, was a practical one. According to the ancient procedure, the Torah had to be read while it was standing upright and its text visible to the congregation. The reader therefore had to physically support it by taking hold of its posts. Sepharadic Torah scrolls are normally housed in a special box that can stand safely on the reading table, but to keep an Ashkenazic-style *sefer Torah* straight and not allow it to fall demanded some serious exertion.

It is therefore understandable that bystanders would do their best to encourage the reader to maintain the requisite vigor.

As often occurs in the evolution of religious customs, certain routines stubbornly persist even after their original reasons have ceased to be applicable. Though the Torah is now allowed to lie horizontally on the lectern, we still insist that the reader "support" it by symbolically grasping its wooden posts, and the people next to him continue to pray that the reader's strength will suffice for the task.

Thus, we have found ways to preserve the remnants of two different customs: The saying of *Hazak* has been relegated to the ceremonious conclusions of entire books, possibly owing to a misunderstanding of an old instruction that it be recited "when one finishes reading the Torah." *Yasher koach*, on the other hand, has been adopted as the informal congratulatory formula for the normal *'aliyah*.

The customs we are describing date back to talmudic times, and are attributed there to the heroes of the Bible. When God exhorted Joshua to take over Moses' mantle of leadership, he instructed him that "*this* book of the Torah shall not depart out of thy mouth . . . be strong and of a good courage." Rabbi Simeon ben Yohai deduced that the wording "*this* book" implies that

Joshua was actually holding a Torah scroll at the time. The rabbis discerned in this episode a precedent for saying *Hazak* to anyone who is grasping a Torah.

Similarly, when Moses declared "Cursed be the one who does not uphold all the words of this Torah," the talmudic rabbis understood this as alluding to the obligation to offer verbal support to the person who is holding up a Torah scroll.

Indeed the fear of inadvertently dropping a sacred scroll was not the only fear that troubled participants in the synagogue services. Midrashic tradition speaks of the grave perils that were felt to threaten a person—whether from a hostile Satan or from the person's own carelessness—when he accepted the momentous responsibility of praying on behalf of the congregation.

An interesting twist on this theme is contained in a midrashic interpretation quoted by Rashi in his very last comment to the end of the Book of Deuteronomy. When God (in Deuteronomy 10:2) spoke to Moses about "the first tablets *which* [Hebrew: *asher*] you broke," the rabbis read this as if God were saying to Moses "*Yasher koach* for breaking the tablets," in reaction to the people's worship of the golden calf.

This midrash takes on a powerful poignancy when we bear in mind that the normal meaning of *Yasher koach* is "May you have strength not to cause the Torah to fall." In this midrashic exposition, the usage is ironically reversed, as God reassures Moses saying: You have done the right thing in showing the strength and courage to hurl the Torah before a people that has proven itself unworthy of it.

At any rate, we hope for the strength to uphold both the scroll and its contents.

SUGGESTIONS FOR FURTHER READING

Ta-Shema. (1987). "The Vocative 'hazaq' in the Liturgy." *Tarbiz* 57: 115–8.

13

࿇

What Does Archeology Teach Us about Balaam?*

ℬased on the information supplied by the Bible, it is not immediately apparent why Jewish tradition has been so hostile to poor old Balaam.

Admittedly, at his worst moments, he comes across as a pathetic, almost comical creature, a weak-willed man who is subjected to a humiliating argument with a talking ass.

Yet the same individual is acknowledged to be an authentic prophet who obeys the directives of the God of Israel, in whose name he blesses Israel with some of the Bible's most inspired poetic outpourings.

In light of the above considerations, it is hard to comprehend why the Bible considered him such a formidable antagonist that he had to be executed by the Israelite army.

---

*"Balaam the Prophet." *The Jewish Free Press*, Calgary, July 5, 1995, p. 10.

Our understanding of this non-Hebrew prophet has been enriched in recent years by a remarkable inscription that was unearthed in 1967 in archeological excavations at the Deir 'Alla site in Jordan, not far from the scene of Balaam's activities in the Book of Numbers. The text in question, which was probably composed around 700 B.C.E., was written in Aramaic (or Ammonite) on plaster slabs that might have formed part of a sanctuary or cultic monument. From it we learn of the existence, some six hundred years after Balaam's lifetime, of a religious movement that continued to revere Balaam as its great prophet and spiritual mentor.

Several features in this memorial reveal uncanny resemblances to the familiar Biblical story of Balaam, whose role is depicted in terms that are reminiscent of the Hebrew prophets.

Thus, *Balaam bar Be'or* is said, in the inscription, to be a "seer of the gods" and is the one to whom those gods reveal their intentions in "visions of the night."

The names of the gods who speak to the pagan prophet are also familiar to us from the Bible, including *El* and a council of deities called *Shaddayin* (mighty ones). Balaam is informed in a dream that the people are about to be punished by darkness, drought, and other natural disasters, and he must urge the people to placate the angry divinities.

It is clear, however, that these surface similarities to Jewish religious concepts only serve to enhance the fundamental contrast between the pagan seer and the Prophets of Israel.

We must not lose sight of the fact that Balaam's gods are referred to in the plural, signifying a world governed by disharmony and conflict. In fact, some scholars have suggested that the Bible, in order to prevent any confusion between the divine epithet *Shaddai* and its profaned use among the pagans, deliberately altered its pronunciation, turning it into *shed*[*im*], the common word for demons.

The most glaring differences between the perceptions of prophecy in the Torah and in Balaam's cult become apparent when we read in the inscription how the heathen leader responded to the warnings of doom.

Now, we are all familiar with the typical Jewish responses to impending catastrophes: The people are urged to examine their spiritual states and to take special care to improve their standards of morality and social justice, and to attend to the welfare of the poor.

Not so Balaam. Although the concluding lines of the inscription have been poorly preserved, and several different conjectural reconstructions have been proposed for the Aramaic text, one very persuasive interpretation reads that Balaam exhorted his people to placate their gods by deepening their commitment to the promiscuous activities that were carried out, with the assistance of sacred prostitutes, in the name of the local fertility cult. According to this theory, it is likely that the structure that once housed the inscription had been just such a cultic brothel.

If this hypothesis is correct, then it also sheds light upon the biblical account of how, immediately following the Balaam episode, the Israelites were enticed into committing harlotry with Moabite and Midianite women. That transgression, which brought divine punishment upon the people, is ascribed by Jewish tradition to Balaam.

From the Deir 'Alla inscription we learn that, from Balaam's perspective, such behavior might not have been intended as a deliberate affront to God, so much as it was a pious pagan *mitzvah*.

All these details might help explain why Balaam, ostensibly speaking in the name of the same god, but representing a religious worldview diametrically opposed to Jewish moral values, came to be regarded as such a serious threat to the biblical ideals of spirituality.

SUGGESTIONS FOR FURTHER READING

Hackett, Jo Ann. (1986). "Observations on the Balaam Inscription at Deir 'Allah." *Biblical Archeological Review* 5: 218–22.
Rofé, Alexander. (1979). *The Book of Balaam.* Jerusalem: Magnes.

14

✢

Where Is the Garden of Eden?*

$\mathcal{W}$here is Paradise?

I expect that many of my readers, if confronted by this question, would reply simply: Between Saskatchewan and the Rockies. Alternatively, they might begin to describe some sort of heavenly abode inhabited by harp-strumming angels.

For Jews, the matter involves some further complications. The Hebrew equivalent of Paradise is *Gan Eden*, the Garden of Eden, which is where the souls of the righteous are privileged to enjoy Eternity—at least until the time of the Resurrection.

Now where is this wonderful garden? The Torah provides us with specific geographical coordinates, identifying it as the source of four important rivers. Although we have not yet succeeded in identifying the location, the story in Genesis presumes that it lies

*"The Cherub's Sword and the Wrath of Zeus." *The Jewish Free Press*, Calgary, October 19, 1995, p. 6.

somewhere in our terrestrial world—for otherwise it would be difficult to account for the stationing of a cherubic guard at its entrance to fend off intruders.

Although Jewish legend has dwelled lovingly on the wonders of an otherworldly Garden of Eden, some of our sages have insisted that it is still to be found in its earthly location. A powerful case for this position was made by the medieval Talmudist, exegete, and mystic, Rabbi Moses ben Nahman (Nahmanides). In his treatise on the afterlife, he claimed support not only from the plain sense of Genesis, but also from the testimonies of non-Jewish travellers who claimed to have seen the Garden somewhere below the Equator.

One of the tales that he cites involves a team of medical researchers led by an ancient Macedonian scholar named Aesculapius, who entered *Gan Eden* while touring the Orient in search of medicinal plants. Unfortunately, their discovery of the Tree of Life tripped off an alarm—an angelic flaming sword that ignited the entire delegation.

Nahmanides cited this story from the sixth-century medical treatise, *Asaph the Physician*, where it can indeed be found. In Asaph's story, the tale is adduced in order to resolve a difficulty in medieval medical historiography: How was it that the legendary wise men of primordial times, especially the Egyptians, were in possession of remarkable healing treatments, but their successors in the classical age were forced to resort to experimental research? The solution lies in the tragedy that befell the overambitious party of Aesculapius and his companions, whose sudden deaths brought about an immediate interruption in the transmission of ancient medical lore, compelling later doctors to resort to the less efficient methods of clinical experimentation.

But the story's origins predate even *Asaph the Physician*. Readers familiar with classical literature will recognize its roots in Greek and Roman mythology. Aesculapius (or Asclepius), son of Apollo, was the Greek god of healing. In the Greek version of the story, Asclepius discovered the secret of reviving the dead. (Warning:

Don't try this at home. It requires quantities of Medusa's blood). When he used his skill too liberally, Zeus himself struck Ascelepius down with a thunderbolt.

When Jews retold the story, they demoted Asclepius from a deity to a human physician and replaced Zeus' thunderbolt with the biblical sabre. It followed naturally that the most suitable setting for this event was the unapproachable Garden of Eden.

Thus, Nahmanides inadvertently used a pagan myth to prove the existence of the earthly *Gan Eden*.

Subsequent authors expanded the significance of the story, making it serve as an explanation of how the original wisdom of the ancient Greeks—which the medievals believed to have been derived from Hebrew sources—had come to a sudden end, to be replaced by the misguided rationalism that typified later philosophical thinking.

The thirteenth-century mystical classic, the *Zohar*, gave a different twist to the tradition, claiming that the victims of the fiery sword were the disciples of Plato and Aristotle in the time of Alexander the Great. This was the reason why later Greek philosophy was inferior to the thought of earlier generations (which were closer to their Jewish origins).

Yet another variation on the legend located the entrance to Paradise in the Machpelah cave in Hebron, the tomb of the patriarchs. Since the burial cave itself houses the gateway to *Gan Eden*, it is believed that all those who attempt to enter it will be smitten by the Cherub's sword—even as Aesculapius fell victim to the lightning of Zeus' wrath.

SUGGESTIONS FOR FURTHER READING

Idel, Moshe. (1982). "The Journey to Paradise: The Jewish Transformation of a Greek Mythological Motif." *Jerusalem Studies in Jewish Folklore* 2: 7–16.

15

جسم

Why Is Garlic
Good for You?*

$\mathcal{F}$or several months now a braid of garlic bulbs has been proudly hanging on our kitchen wall. As it happens, this is not simply a matter of personal taste, but it links us to a venerable Jewish tradition.

The Mishnah, in discussing a point of religious law, states that the expression "garlic eaters," when it appears in the wording of a vow, is to be understood as a designation for Jews and Samaritans.

Indeed rabbinic literature is full of praises for this common herb. "It satisfies hunger, it warms the body, it illuminates one's face, it increases seed and it destroys intestinal parasites."

These benefits have been supplemented by contemporary enthusiasts of the herb, who claim that it can cure skin diseases,

---

*"A Garlic Eater and Proud of It." *The Jewish Free Press*, Calgary, January 25, 1996, pp. 4–5.

lower cholesterol counts and blood pressure, reduce hypertension and the risk of heart attack, and may even be able to overcome some forms of cancer and AIDS-related illnesses.

The talmudic commentators offer a different explanation for the Jewish identification as garlic-eaters: An ordinance ascribed to Ezra, back in the early days of the Second Commonwealth, requires Jews to eat garlic on Friday nights. The reason for this, as understood by the Talmud, is because garlic serves as an effective aid to ardor and fertility, enhancing the marital lovemaking that is an essential component of Jewish Sabbath observance.

The inclusion of the Samaritans alongside the Jews as garlic eaters raises some intriguing questions.

The Samaritans, who inhabited the west bank of the Jordan (especially around Shechem and their sanctuary on Mount Gerizim) claim to be the remnants of the original Israelite tribes of Manasseh and Ephraim who escaped the exile of the northern kingdom, though biblical tradition regards them as the descendants of foreign colonists who were transported to Samaria by the Assyrian conquerors.

The Samaritans possess the Torah, in a version slightly different from the accepted Jewish text. Though they observe its precepts meticulously, they do not accept the traditions of the Jewish Oral Torah. This leads to many significant differences between their religious laws and ours.

One such divergence is in the matter of conjugal relations on the Sabbath: Though encouraged by Jews, it is prohibited by the Samaritans. Under the circumstances, how are we to explain their reported enthusiasm for garlic?

One possibility that suggests itself is that the Samaritans had a very different objective in mind when partaking of garlic. Perhaps they felt that the scent of garlic on the breath would actually *cool* romantic urges.

As to the Jewish practice, we would expect that conservative Latin satirists like Juvenal and Martial, who were always so quick to ridicule the exotic and uncouth mannerisms of lower-class

Roman Jews, would have seized upon this point somewhere in their works. So far, however, no such allusions have been found. At best, Martial does have some nasty things to say about effects of fasting upon the breath of Jews (like many Romans, he thought Shabbat was a fast day).

When you think about it, Italians are the least likely people to be upset by the smell of garlic.

Some scholars have sought to discern a reference to this phenomenon in a quote attributed to the emperor and stoic philosopher Marcus Aurelius, who allegedly made an insulting reference to the breath of the Jews.

If the allusion were indeed to the garlic that enhanced the breath of contemporary Jews, then the anecdote could have some interesting implications.

Several historians have argued that Marcus Aurelius was the enigmatic Antoninus, the Roman leader who often appears in rabbinic literature in amicable conversation with Rabbi Judah the Prince on all manner of questions of faith, science, and politics.

It is tempting, though hardly justified, to tie all these speculations together and conclude that the Roman emperor's insulting comment reflected his personal encounters with his Jewish comrade.

The picture becomes more intriguing when we note that Rabbi Judah himself is reported to have expelled a scholar from his academy on the grounds that his breath smelled of garlic. If we link this story to the previous one, then it might be seen as a response to the criticisms of Antoninus.

Not all Jewish authorities were convinced of the medical benefits of garlic. Maimonides omitted from his code all favourable references to garlic eating, whether in connection with the Sabbath or vows. This policy seems to reflect his medical opinion. Speaking as a physician, he advises against anything more than minimal and infrequent consumption of garlic, and never during the summer months.

With all due respect to Maimonides' medical expertise, I prefer to include myself in a long and honorable tradition of garlic eaters.

SUGGESTIONS FOR FURTHER READING

Feliks, Jehuda. (1968). *Plant World of the Bible*. Ramat-Gan: Massada.
Preuss, J. (1978). *Julius Preuss' Biblical and Talmudic Medicine*. 2nd ed., Translated by Fred Rosner. New York: Hebrew Publishing Company.

16

◦♋◦

What Do *Orthodox* and *Cowboys* Have in Common?*

Recently I received an irate letter from a correspondent who had been accessing my articles via the Internet. This individual, who claimed to be descended from Spanish-Jewish converts to Christianity, was taking issue with an article in which I had made reference to the religious practices of the Marranos of Spain and Portugal. The term *Marrano*, he argued correctly, was an abusive and demeaning old Spanish word meaning *swine*—expressing the distaste felt by many veteran Christian Iberians, even for Jews who had adopted the official faith.

I felt the occasion called for apology rather than self-justification. I explained that I had hesitated before choosing the offen-

---

*"'Orthodox,' 'Cowboys' and Other Insults." *The Jewish Free Press*, Calgary, March 7, 1996, p. 8.

sive epithet over the more respectable *conversos* or New Christians, but had ultimately decided that such terms would be unfamiliar to my average reader.

As an aside, I remarked that Jews have a long history of accepting names that were originally intended as derogatory. Perhaps this practice can be traced back to the Patriarch Abraham, whose designation,—*Ivri*, or Hebrew, is understood by some commentators to mean "one who comes from the other side [*'ever*]," possibly reflecting the perspective of the Canaanites who patronizingly viewed him as an alien.

In later generations, Jews consistently referred to themselves as *Israel*. The term *Yehudi* (Jew) is found very rarely in talmudic literature, and in those rare instances where it does appear, it is usually in quotations attributed to non-Jews.

This is consistent with the evidence of Greek texts, where *Ioudaioi* is the name that is normally used to designate our people.

This demonstrates a crucial difference in perspective: Gentiles acknowledged only the truncated province of Judea, as it existed under Persian, Greek and Roman rule, whereas the Jews were always conscious of their links to the glorious days when David and Solomon reigned over the united Israelite monarchy.

Rabbinic Judaism evolved out of the Second Temple Jewish faction known as the Pharisees. The word Pharisee translates as *separatist* and alludes to the fact that the group imposed upon itself extra stringencies in the areas of purity and dietary laws, which set limits to their social interaction with people outside their own group.

The Hebrew word for separatist is normally a term of opprobrium. Ancient texts of the "*Sh'moneh Esreh*" prayer included a condemnation of those who do not make their proper contribution to the welfare of the community.

When talmudic documents mention the word Pharisee (*P'rushi*) as the name of a religious movement, the word is usually being used by their opponents, the supporters of the priestly Sadducee party. When referring to their own origins, the rabbis employed the term *Haverim* (comrades). Eventually, however, the name Pharisee came to be accepted by Jews as a neutral or even an honorable title—in spite of the fact that Christian innuendo has turned it into a synonym for hypocrite in many European languages.

In more recent times, we may note the rise of the *Misnagdim*, who championed the primacy of talmudic scholarship against the nascent hasidic movement and its ideology of charismatic mysticism.

The term *Misnagdim* (opponents, protestants) was coined by the *Hasidim* and reflects their perspective. It has subsequently been accepted by their opponents, the followers of the Ga'on of Vilna, who emulated his scholarly ideals in the Lithuanian-style yeshivahs.

A striking instance of the acceptance of a hostile epithet is the widespread use of the name orthodox as a designation for Jewish traditionalists in the post-Emancipation era.

The word orthodox was derived from a Christian context and was first applied to Jews with ironic derision in 1795 by a Reform polemicist.

Rabbi Samson Raphael Hirsch, the outspoken leader of the traditionalist forces in Germany, reacted indignantly to this epithet in an essay written in Frankfurt in 1854. And yet the same rabbi, barely thirty years later, established a Free Union for the Interests of *Orthodox* Judaism!

I doubt that the above tendencies are unique to the Jewish experience. I have often suspected, for example, that the oddly phrased word cowboy (as distinct from, say, cattleman) originated in some such derogatory usage, though I have yet to find confirmation for this theory.

If the above hypothesis appears overly cynical, then we must recall that *cynic* (doglike) was also originally an insult intended to ridicule the allegedly uncouth mannerisms of that ancient philosophical school.

SUGGESTIONS FOR FURTHER READING

Cohen, Shaye J. D. (1987). *From the Maccabees to the Mishnah*. Library of Early Christianity, ed. Wayne A. Meeks. Philadelphia: Westminster Press.

Mendes-Flohr, Paul and Jehuda Reinharz, ed. (1955). *The Jew in the Modern World: A Documentary History*. 2nd ed. New York and Oxford: Oxford University Press.

Rudavsky, David. (1979). *Modern Jewish Religious Movements*. New York: Behrman House.

Sanders, E. P. (1992). *Judaism Practice & Belief 63* B.C.E.–66 C.E. London and Philadelphia: SCM Press and Trinity Press International.

17

ॐ

What Does the Talmud Say about Power Walking?*

*A*lthough my editor does not often let me out for exercise, I do try to indulge in modest regimens of running and walking.

Traditional Jewish sources provide us with some useful tips on the proper ways and times for pursuing those activities.

Thus, the Talmud teaches that a crucial time for taking a walk is right after eating. This routine was recommended by the third-century Babylonian sage Samuel, who was also a respected physician.

Though Samuel had great confidence in his effectiveness as a medical practitioner, he admitted that he was at a loss to offer

---

*"Taking It All in Stride." *The Jewish Free Press*, Calgary, May 9, 1996, pp. 13–4.

any assistance to the reckless persons who endangered their health by neglecting to walk four cubits at the conclusion of a meal. Such ill-advised behaviour was certain to have fatal effects upon one's health.

Another talmudic passage is more specific in spelling out the consequences of such conduct: Those who eat without walking the requisite four cubits will cause the food to decay in their bowels, which will produce unpleasant effects on their breath.

For those who were inclined to rest right after their meals, the Talmud recommended positioning an extra cot in the dining room at a specified distance from the table, in order to force the diners to stretch their legs, if only for a few paces.

In issuing their medical advice, the talmudic rabbis were echoing the view of Aristotle who had opined that a walk after a meal is among the indispensable prerequisites of a good physical state. The Athenian philosopher is further reported to have observed that an after-dinner stroll has the power to renew the body's warmth and vigor.

However, not all the ancients were in agreement about the benefits of walking after eating. According to Plutarch, there were people who feared that the exertion might interfere with the workings of the digestive tract and, therefore, preferred to remain stationary for a while before leaving the table.

There was one point, however, upon which virtually all the authors, Jewish and Greek, agreed, namely that napping immediately after eating will have a deleterious effect on the body.

Indeed some of the talmudic commentators understood Samuel's original advice in this light. Rashi, for example, explained that the main purpose of walking after a repast is to prevent one from dozing off right away. A mere four cubits was felt to provide sufficient exertion to avert any ill effects.

Not all forms of walking were considered praiseworthy. In fact, the rabbis took care to discourage certain styles of gait as being either physically unhealthy or morally unseemly.

A frequent target of rabbinical criticism was the practice of "heavy stepping" (*p'si'ah gassah*) The Talmud warns that "heavy stepping can diminish one's eyesight by one five-hundredth."

From some passages it seems that the reference is to a sort of power walking at an accelerated speed. For this reason it is permitted to eagerly heavy-step towards the synagogue, but not when leaving it.

In this assessment, the rabbis were again confirming an observation that had been made by Aristotle, that too much physical exertion can be injurious to one's vision. The philosopher was not entirely certain how to account for the phenomenon, but surmised that it might have something to do with the effects of dehydration on the pupils.

From the Jewish sources, which limit their condemnations of heavy walking to certain situations or personalities, we may deduce that their concern with accelerated walking was not entirely of a medical character.

Thus, the avoidance of heavy-stepping was recommended primarily to scholars. In another context, the midrash relates that Joseph issued specific warnings against taking rapid strides when advising his brothers how to conduct themselves on their journey to Egypt.

From all this, it would appear that an indelicate gait was regarded as a symptom of arrogance and disdain, attitudes to which scholars were particularly susceptible. Similarly, visitors to foreign countries, as were Joseph's brothers, were urged to make especial efforts to avoid demonstrations of superiority.

In this matter as well, the Jewish sages were sharing attitudes that were current in classical antiquity. The orator Demosthenes informs us that a rapid gait was looked upon with disfavor by the Athenians, and defendants who were observed racing about the courthouse could seriously jeopardize their cases. Such uncouth behaviour warranted an apology to the judge, including an assurance that it was not intended contemptuously.

Truly, walking can be a very serious activity. If done properly, it is far healthier than sitting idly in front of a newspaper article.

SUGGESTIONS FOR FURTHER READING

Hallevy, E. E. (1979–82). 'Erkhei ha-aggadah veha-halakhah. Tel-Aviv: Dvir.

18

↝

What Did the Talmud Learn from Construction Workers?*

Like many legal systems, the Jewish *halakhah* must deal in minute detail with questions related to construction and home improvement. In particular, the rabbis had to keep a vigilant eye on cases when renovations to an existing structure might impinge upon the convenience of neighbours, whether by obstructing a view or restricting their privacy.

Indeed, so deeply rooted were these rights in Jewish tradition that in reading Balaam's blessing, "How goodly are thy tents, O Jacob," some of the talmudic sages visualized the heathen prophet being overcome by admiration for the Israelites' scrupulous consideration in not aligning their doors opposite one another, so as to prevent people from peeking into each other's homes.

---

*"The Yarmulke and the Hard Hat." *The Jewish Free Press*, Calgary, June 6, 1996, p. 14.

Although the regulation of such laws demanded intimate familiarity with construction methods, there is little explicit evidence that the rabbis made a habit of consulting with experts in the field. Often, in fact, their typical approach was just the opposite: When called upon to determine empirical facts, the Talmud usually prefers to cite passages from the Bible or oral tradition rather than consult experts or collect experimental data.

Among the exceptions to the above generalization are some passages in the Palestinian Talmud in which the opinions of "builders" are cited in the course of discussions about Jewish law. The information supplied by those ancient builders enriches our knowledge of daily life in the Land of Israel during the talmudic era.

One such discussion deals with the obstruction of access to a neighbor's windows. The Talmud quotes these unidentified builders as stating that if the original window did not overlook an open space, but only a *stoa* or colonnade, then we may assume that the window did not exist for the sake of its view, but merely to allow sunlight to enter the house. Hence, a neighbour who intended to erect a structure in front of that window was obliged to leave only enough clearance for the continued entry of sunlight, but need not worry about interfering with the view.

The premises of the discussion may appear strange to us today, since we generally assume that all windows are designed to provide a view. However, in the ancient world, when the manufacture of large units of sheet glass was rare and expensive, windows tended to be much smaller and restricted to specific purposes. Archeological evidence teaches us that the ancient window was usually no more than a cluster of tiny round holes in the wall. Some were for ventilation; others, for light; and some, for view. Ancient building codes took these factors into account in determining whether or not it was permitted to build a structure opposite somebody else's window.

The Talmud observed that, according to Jewish law, any window that does not provide direct access to an open space must have been built to provide light, not view, and hence, a potential builder must leave only a token distance in front of that window. In support of this distinction, the Talmud makes reference to the customary practice of the builders who follow a similar policy when determining the appropriate distance between an old house and a new one.

The Talmud's account of the builders' opinion is corroborated by a compendium of local Palestinian building procedures that has survived from the early Byzantine era, composed by an architect named Julian. Like the Jewish sources, the municipal bylaws cited by Julian distinguish, for purposes of determining the minimal distances between buildings, between windows that are intended for light and those designed for view. Any view that is fragmentary, indirect, or at an angle is not guaranteed by the law.

The cooperation between yarmulke and hard hat extended to some additional issues as well. For instance, disputes arose over how to distribute the expenses for repairs to multiowner dwellings. How are we to determine which repairs benefit the inhabitants of the individual dwellings, and which serve the interests of the entire building. Here again the testimony of the builders was adduced in order to establish that the costs of repairs to the foundations are customarily shared by all the tenants, whereas improvements to the walls of an individual apartment are paid for only by the inhabitants of that unit.

All this reminds me of the following classic anecdote about a rabbi who volunteered to design a house for a member of his community, to whom he offered assurances that all his construction methods were derived from the Talmud.

A week after the structure was completed, the Jew approached the sage and morosely asked him why his new house had collapsed almost immediately after it was built.

The learned rabbi pored through his Talmud for a moment, and then his eyes lit up with satisfaction.

"How remarkable!" he declared. "Rashi asks exactly the same question!"

SUGGESTIONS FOR FURTHER READING

Lieberman, Saul. (1971). "A Few Words on the Book by Julian the Architect of Ascalon, The Laws of Palestine and Its Customs." *Tarbiz* 40, 4: 409–417.

19

ᘒ

What Can You Do about Bad Financial Advice?*

*W*hen one individual offers advice about how other people should spend or invest their money, this can raise some perplexing legal and ethical issues. It is ultimately the investor who must bear the consequence of any bad advice, and those consequences can at times be costly.

In the days of the Talmud, the economy was less complex than it is today, and the range of available investment opportunities was limited. For Jews, the possibilities were even more restricted, owing to the Torah's stringent prohibitions against the taking of interest.

Nevertheless, there were occasions when individuals would seek expert counsel concerning financial matters, and the ques-

---

*"A Bad Business." *The Jewish Free Press*, Calgary, January 23, 1997, pp. 8–9.

tion arose whether the consultants bore any legal accountability for bad advice.

One financial domain that was more complicated in former times was that of coinage. In our times, it is only on rare occasions that doubts arise with respect to the value or legality of currency. However, in ancient times many doubts attached to coins, relating to their worth or their political acceptability. Money used to derive its value from its actual metallic content; the relative worth of the different metals could fluctuate, or become debased with age, or by intention. Furthermore, ambitious political leaders would often mint coins as a demonstration of their newly declared independence. Of course, the public would be cautious about accepting such currency, lest the independence—and the value of their money—turn out to be short-lived.

When questions arose concerning the wisdom of accepting dubious currency, they would normally be directed to the local money changer. In Hebrew such an individual was known as a *shulhani*; literally, a table keeper, a term that is akin to banker (or bench keeper) of European languages.

The *shulhani* was concerned primarily with exchanging coins between large and small denominations, an area of expertise that demanded intimate familiarity both with the coins themselves and with the changing economic and political circumstances.

The best way to keep up to date with developments in the market was to keep constantly in practice. The midrash used this truth to illustrate symbolically the difference between a sage who is truly wise and one who is merely understanding. "A wise man may be likened to a wealthy money changer, who examines coins not only at the request of a client, but also examines his own money when he has no clients. However, an understanding man is like a poor money changer who can only examine coins when working for a client, but must otherwise remain idle."

It was therefore common to consult successful money changers about the wisdom of prospective investments.

Some talmudic rabbis were involved in such professional activity. Thus, it is related concerning Rabbi Hiyya, who was an accomplished merchant, that a woman once approached him with a *denar* that had recently been offered to her. Based on the rabbi's assurances, she agreed to accept the coin, only to discover to her dismay afterwards that no one wanted to take it from her.

Rabbi Hiyya consented to compensate the woman for his unsound advice. The Talmud was of the opinion that Rabbi Hiyya did not really have a legal obligation to compensate the woman, but that he acted as he did out of moral scruples. Their reasoning was that he was such a virtuoso at his occupation that any error that he might have committed must have been on such an esoteric point that it must be considered unavoidable—perhaps because the currency had been removed from circulation only very recently.

The exemption extended by the Talmud to first-class financial experts puzzled the commentators, since no such concession was given to other professionals, no matter what their qualifications.

Rabbi Solomon Ibn Adret (the *Rashba*) suggested that this followed naturally from the nature of the profession; for, unlike other crafts that demand complex skills and therefore provide varied opportunities to mess up, a financial consultant's vocation consists solely of expertise and keenness of observation. Hence, it is more reasonable to assume that the ill-advised judgment must have resulted from truly unavoidable circumstances.

Medieval authorities were nevertheless uncomfortable with a situation where a financial consultant could be let off the hook for professional shortcomings. Therefore, they explained that the Talmud exempted Rabbi Hiyya only because he had offered his services gratis; however, advisors who accept payment for their opinions, or have been explicitly informed that their advice will be used as the basis for an investment, can be held financially liable when they cause their clients a loss.

Perhaps the issue was most astutely summed up by Rabbi Hiyya himself. At the conclusion of the talmudic anecdote, as he was taking the money from his purse to pay the aggrieved lady, he ordered his assistant—his young nephew Rav, who would later achieve renown as one of the foremost talmudic sages—to add a sardonic note to the margin of his ledger: "This was a bad business"!

SUGGESTIONS FOR FURTHER READING

Beer, Moshe. (1974). *The Babylonian Amoraim: Aspects of Economic Life.* Ramat-Gan: Bar-Ilan University Press.
Gulak, Asher. (1981). "Banking in Talmudic Law." *Tarbiz* 2, 2: 154–171.
Warhaftig, Shilem. (1982). *Jewish Labour Law*. 2nd, revised ed., Publications of the Faculty of Law, University of Tel-Aviv, Jerusaelm: Ariel United Israel Institutes and the Harry Fischel Institute for Research in Jewish Law.

20

⌒

How Would You Compose
a Letter of Reference
to Maimonides?*

$\mathcal{M}$y duties as an academic frequently involve the reading and evaluation of application forms, especially from students seeking admission to the various programs offered by our department.

The art of composing applications and curricula vitae has become a business for professionals; and reading them has correspondingly come to demand subtle skills of critical analysis.

Earlier eras also knew of competition among students to be accepted into prestigious academic faculties or professional schools, and some letters of application have been preserved from earlier centuries.

As scholars of Jewish history have come to expect, the most promising source of such documents is the Cairo *Genizah*, that inexhaustible repository of books and documents that was maintained for

---

*"The Elegant Art of Letters of Reference." *The Jewish Free Press*, Calgary, September 4, 1997, p. 8.

centuries by the Egyptian Jewish community, whose contents have been scattered among libraries and museums throughout the world.

One such letter was composed in twelfth-century Cairo by the father of an aspiring medical student, addressed to a distinguished physician in hope that the latter will accept the petitioner's son to be trained under his tutelage.

In keeping with the spirit of the times, the letter was far more elegant than the standardized applications that pass by my desk. It is introduced by carefully selected biblical verses extolling the virtues of humility and peace, and then proceeds to proclaim the glories of the recipient. The physician is addressed in very personal terms, as the hope is extended that he will live to see his only son married and continuing in Papa's learned footsteps. The letter even includes holiday greetings for the upcoming Passover—which will hopefully be celebrated in the rebuilt Temple of Jerusalem!

The applicant then digresses into a philosophical discussion about the inherent striving of the human soul for self-improvement.

Only now that the groundwork has been carefully prepared does the letter come to its main point. Having heard that a vacancy has recently been created, will the esteemed teacher consider accepting his brilliant and eager son for the position?

And just in case the student's qualifications are not sufficient of themselves to guarantee his acceptance into the programme, the father assures the master that he will be willing to pay a considerably higher tuition than his previous student . . .

We can better appreciate the eagerness that emerges from the letter if we keep in mind that the addressee was not just any Professor of Medicine. Although it is not stated explicitly, all the circumstantial evidence points clearly to the identity of that individual—"Rabbi Moses the prince and noble . . . the judge distinguished in all matters"—as being none other than the great Maimonides!

I do not know how Maimonides reacted to the application, though I strongly suspect that it would have been with liberal sprinklings of sodium chloride. For then, as today, the real students did not always live up to the images projected by their letters of reference.

This truism is aptly illustrated by another letter contained in the *Genizah*, written by a certain medical student to his chums. In it, Natanel Hallevi ben Moshe, a member of an affluent family, apologizes for the fact that he will be unable to socialize with his companions for the foreseeable future, because he has been severely "grounded" until his studies showed improvement.

The "grounding" in this instance had a positive side to it since it was reinforced by a sizable bribe from his father. At any rate, the unfortunate student does appear to have resigned himself with equanimity to his imprisonment, in spite of his tendency to fill his letters with quotations from Job. He reports that he is devoting himself to his studies—in medicine, grammar, Talmud, and theology—and only occasionally sneaks out to an illicit rendezvous with his companions.

We do, in fact, hear from this student in later documents. He grew up to serve as the head of the Yeshivah of Eretz Israel (which at the time had relocated in Cairo) from 1160 to 1170. Concerned parents, take note!

Aspiring physicians in Cairo could not obtain employment in their profession without producing a police certificate of good conduct. Admittedly, this was probably not so much an indication of their unsavory reputation as it was of the grave responsibilities that they bore. At any rate, the *Genizah* records suggest that those certificates were often obtained through bribes and connections.

The high spirits that we now associate with the student lifestyle are not encountered as frequently among European Jews, perhaps because they did not indulge in secular studies; but some testimonies do exist.

What appears to be a Hebrew drinking song—a modest Jewish "Carmina Burana"—survived in some Ashkenazic prayerbook in the guise of a Hanukkah hymn. Its lyrics consist of lively exhortations to continue feasting and drinking day and night, even if it requires the selling of house, field, and cattle.

Well, I must conclude this column now since I have to compose some imaginative letters of reference for my students.

SUGGESTIONS FOR FURTHER READING

Ginzberg, Louis. (1958). *Students, Scholars and Saints.* New York and Philadelphia: Meridian and Jewish Publication Society of America.

Goitein, S. D. (1962). *Jewish Education in Muslim Countries: Based on Records from the Cairo Geniza.* Jerusalem: The Ben-Zvi Institute and The Hebrew University.

———. (1967–). *A Mediterranean Society.* Berkeley, Los Angeles and London: University of California Press.

✌

What Does the Talmud Say about Weight Loss?*

Our contemporary propensity to equate beauty and good health with slimness seems to be of recent vintage. To judge from talmudic sources, earlier generations held diametrically different positions on these questions.

The ancient rabbis more often took pride in their corpulence. Thus, it was related of two famous sages (apparently with some satisfaction) that when they stood opposite one another, a team of oxen could pass under their bellies without touching them.

Conversely, the Talmud often regarded thinness not as a mark of physical beauty, but as a symptom of such diseases as consumption, dehydration, or dysentery.

There are a handful of traditions that allude to efforts at weight loss, whether through exercise or other means. However, it is clear

---

*"Sweatin' to the Oldies." *The Jewish Free Press*, Calgary, May 15, 1997, pp. 18, 20.

from those passages that they do not reflect an attitude that "thin is beautiful."

Efforts at weight reduction are mentioned only in connection with unusual circumstances and occupations.

For example—wrestlers:

The Mishnah (Shabbat 22:6) refers to a type of physical exertion that it calls *mit'ammelin* as being forbidden on the day of rest. The Hebrew word was generally understood as a reference to a calisthenics-like regimen, as described by the tenth-century North African commentator Rabbenu Hananel: "They flex and unflex their arms in front and behind, and similarly bend their legs from their hips, leading them to work up heat and perspiration. This is considered medically beneficial." Based on the above interpretation, the term was adopted as the modern Hebrew word for exercise.

However, as recent scholarship has demonstrated, a careful reading of the passage in light of its context and manuscript variants reveals that it is speaking of a very specific form of physical activity. For the same Mishnah includes references to anointing the body, massaging the belly, inducing vomiting and "going down to the *peloma*." This last-mentioned word is apparently a Greek designation for a mud-filled arena used by wrestlers. An alternative textual tradition reads *keroma*, another well-known Greek term for a wrestling arena. All these activities, including those intended to evacuate the combatants' bowels and stomach to control their weight, were part of the athletes' normal training.

It is evident that such procedures would not require rabbinic regulation unless Jews were actually involved in them—and, after all, are we not descended from no less a wrestling champion than the patriarch Jacob!

It is unlikely that the chief purpose of exercise was esthetic, so much as to enhance the individual's athletic prowess.

Similarly, concern for beauty was clearly not the main motivation behind the following remarkable episode from the Talmud:

The third-century sage Rabbi Eleazar ben Simeon had been hired as a detective by the Roman government, who had recognized (long before Harry Kemmelman!) that talmudic deductive reasoning can make valuable contributions to police investigations. Though he took care to limit his arrests to those who were unquestionably guilty of felonies, Rabbi Eleazar—whose father Rabbi Simeon ben Yohai was notorious for his opposition the Roman regime—continued to be plagued by doubts that he might have inadvertently been responsible for handing over innocent Jews to the despised occupation authorities.

In order to put his mind at ease, Rabbi Eleazar contrived a way to test the purity of his actions: He declared that if his deeds had been consistently sinless, then his innards should be impervious to natural decomposition.

The rabbi then swallowed an anesthetic and had himself carried into a marble chamber, where his belly was surgically opened and the fat removed. Baskets full of fat were removed from his body and placed in the sun on a hot summer day; but miraculously they proved immune to putrefaction.

The results of the experiment satisfied Rabbi Eleazar that he had not compromised his righteousness, even unknowingly. He saw in this sign a fulfillment of the words of the Psalmist (16:9): "My flesh too shall rest and confidently dwell in safety."

When I mentioned this early report of a liposuction operation to various physicians, they assured me that there must be some mistake, and that the procedure had only come into use in recent decades. The fact is that the first-century naturalist Pliny described an almost identical operation that was performed on the son of the Roman consul Lucius Apronius Caesianus, though, in that case, the surgery was for purely cosmetic purposes.

At any rate, most Jews in talmudic times were neither wrestlers nor detectives. Nor, for that matter, were they subject to the temptations of fast foods or remote-controlled televisions, so that undernourishment was probably more of a threat to them than obesity.

And who knows? Maybe there is some hope that society will eventually revert to those fleshier models of beauty that prevailed in earlier times!

SUGGESTIONS FOR FURTHER READING

Lieberman, Saul. (1942). *Greek in Jewish Palestine*. New York: The Jewish Theological Seminary of America.

Preuss, J. (1978). *Julius Preuss' Biblical and Talmudic Medicine*. 2nd ed., Translated by Fred Rosner. New York: Hebrew Publishing Company.

22

❧

Is the Star of David
a Jewish Symbol?*

*W*hat pictorial symbol would you choose to represent Judaism?
If you were living in ancient times, it would probably be an
image connected with Israel's most revered religious shrine, the
Jerusalem Temple. Thus, when we survey the ornamentation on
coins and funeral memorials from the Second Commonwealth era,
we encounter representations of the Temple gates, incense burn-
ers or musical instruments, and an occasional lulav and etrog. It
was the seven-branched candelabrum that would emerge as the
most widely accepted image of Jewish faith and peoplehood.

Conspicuously absent from the above list is the six-pointed star
that is now referred to as the Magen David, the Shield of David.
Indeed, our ubiquitous Magen David has only a dubious claim to

---

*"Seeing Stars." *The Jewish Free Press*, Calgary, November 20, 1997,
p. 8.

authenticity as a Jewish symbol. It was not until well into the medieval era that anyone would have dreamed of associating it with Judaism—and the nature of that association was not necessarily a favourable or complimentary one.

The earliest known incarnations of the Star of David are not found in Jewish sources, but in Christian and Muslim traditions, albeit in works that borrowed freely from Hebrew prototypes. In those sources, the shield is not associated with King David, but with his son, Solomon. And the star in question has five points, not six.

According to a popular legend related by Josephus Flavius and in the Talmud, Solomon was able to exercise control over the demonic realms by means of a magical ring. The legends about King Solomon's ring were elaborated in extensive detail in *The Testament of Solomon*, a Greek pseudepigraphic work of undetermined date. Several versions of this work contain precise descriptions of the ring, and in some of them it is described as a *pentalpha*, a star composed of five interlaced *A*'s. The pentalpha reappears in several Byzantine amulets.

Stories about the Seal of Solomon were also mentioned by Arabic writers, and through them they became known to Jews. The twelfth-century Karaite scholar Judah Hadassi was apparently the first to allude to this magical sign by its alternative name, the Shield of David, a usage that might have originated in the *Qur'an's* depiction of David as a fashioner of armor.

For the most part, references to the shields of Solomon and David, and their use in occult practices, are found in non-Jewish sources, and they frequently reinforce the medieval stereotypes of a Jewish predilection for sorcery. This is not to say that Jews were totally removed from the practice of magic. Like everyone else in those times, our medieval ancestors made ample use of protective amulets, mezuzahs, and the like. Variations on the star shape—including the six-pointed kind—appeared with some frequency in those contexts. However, there was nothing uniquely Jewish in such superstitions.

The earliest known appearance of the Magen David as a specifically Jewish icon was on the official emblem of the Prague Jewish community in the seventeenth century. By then, the shield's association with King David had became sufficiently established for it to serve as a symbol of national pride. In the eyes of many gentiles, it presumably confirmed their suspicions that Jews were generally involved in the dark arts. In truth, however, it was the Christian adepts of alchemy and the occult who were most likely to draw upon Hebrew images, real or imagined, in order to lend their work an aura of authoritative mystery. This tendency gave rise to a widespread impression among outsiders that the Kabbalah was primarily a system of magic.

Nonetheless, the popularity of the Magen David spread rapidly over the subsequent years. The Jews of Vienna adopted it in 1655 to symbolize their own community and, following their expulsion in 1755, they bore it to their new homes in other central European towns. It did not take long for it to achieve immense popularity as a motif of synagogue ornamentation.

Of course, in the eyes of Jews, the figure of King David has a special significance as the paradigm of national glory and the ancestor of the Messiah. In the latter part of the seventeenth century this motif was cultivated by the devotees of the mystical messiah Shabbetai Zvi, and the Shield of David would appear as a secret sign on amulets produced by the faithful, particularly after they had gone underground.

Thus, there is no small measure of irony in the fact that, when nineteenth-century Jews were looking for a recognizable trademark to serve as the equivalent of the cross or crescent, their choice was a symbol whose associations with Judaism owed more to anti-Jewish stereotyping than to any meaningful links with our national or religious values.

However such is the vigor of symbols that, whatever their original purpose, they can be infused with profound and inspiring meaning. For Jewish nationalists, this occurred when the Zionist movement positioned it at the centre of their new flag. In the domain of the spirit, the imagery of the six-pointed star stimulated Franz Rosenzweig to formulate a brilliant religious philosophy in which the realms of God, Humanity and the World are linked together through the religious axes of Creation, Revelation, and Redemption.

Notwithstanding these development, my overall feeling is that the Magen David makes a poor choice of symbol. It has no tangible roots in Jewish tradition and even evokes some themes that are antithetical to healthy Jewish values.

Let me therefore take this opportunity to issue a call to my readers to forgo the Star of David in favour of more authentic Jewish images the next time you are in the market for an item of jewelry or a wedding invitation. Perhaps the change can be accomplished if enough of us rally behind its banner—a banner that will, of course, display a menorah and not a Magen David.

SUGGESTIONS FOR FURTHER READING

Charlesworth, James A., ed. (1985). *The Old Testament Pseudepigrapha.* Garden City: Doubleday.

Glatzer, Nahum N. (1951). *Franz Rosenzweig: His Life and Thought.* 2nd, revised ed., New York: Schocken.

Scholem, Gershom. (1971). *The Messianic Idea in Judaism and Other Essays.* New York: Schocken.

——— (1974). *Kabbalah.* Meridian ed., New York: New American Library.

Trachtenberg, Joshua. (1970). *Jewish Magic and Superstition.* First Atheneum ed., New York: Temple Books.

23

᠕

Why Were the Rabbis So Eager to Invest in Real Estate?*

Though I cannot claim any particular expertise in matters of high finance, I can recognize the soundness of the advice contained in the words of the third-century Rabbi Isaac Nappaha when he declared: "A person's assets should be divided up into three parts: One third should be invested in land, one third in trade, and the remaining third should remain available for immediate use." The result would be a diversified portfolio of the kind that is encouraged by contemporary financial advisors.

The ancient rabbis held a variety of views about which kinds of investments should be most recommended. Rabbi Isaac's statement seems to be typical of the opinions prevalent in Israel and other Mediterranean lands, where commerce was hailed as the key to economic security. This perception was inspired by

*"Dreams of Fields." *The Jewish Free Press*, Calgary, January 29, 1998, pp. 11–12.

the sad state of agriculture under the Roman administration, when more and more lands were expropriated from their original owners, whose status was transformed thereby into that of hereditary serfs enslaved to the absentee landlords. When their situation was ameliorated later under Arab rule, Jews indeed became full partners in a trading enterprise that extended from Spain to India.

A different attitude prevailed among the Jewish sages of Babylonia, as reflected in many teachings and anecdotes in the Talmud. For them, the purchase of real estate was unquestionably the most desirable of investments. The folios of the Babylonian Talmud are filled with accounts of the aggressive measures taken by individuals to acquire available real estate, with the demand far exceeding the supply. In several of these episodes, the courts were called to adjudicate between competing claims by squatters and purchasers to the ownership of available properties. In some of these cases, individuals who already possessed estates of their own would elbow aside less fortunate persons who were trying to get their first foothold in land ownership. Symptomatic of the frenzy for land acquisition was an occasion on which a rabbi, who had been given money with which to purchase property on behalf of a colleague, went and bought the land for himself.

There was a widespread perception that reliable credit could be established only by land holdings, rather than by possession of cash or movables. It was assumed that nobody would sell their fields voluntarily; such a move could only be a result of financial distress in the face of creditors or the tax collector.

Unlike our own times, the land that was attracting so many aspiring buyers was not situated in cities, nor was its value related to its potential for mineral or energy resources. What people were so eager to possess was agricultural land.

This attraction seems somewhat anomalous when we consider that the talmudic sources had a very realistic awareness of the arduous character of rustic life, noting, on occasion, that in order to succeed, farmers must become enslaved to their fields.

Notwithstanding that the livelihood of the merchant was likely to come more quickly and with less exertion, the Babylonian Jews shared with their Persian neighbours a conservative outlook (as reflected in Zoroastrian religious texts) that equated moral virtue with traditional ideals of agricultural industry. Several rabbinic texts speak pityingly of those unfortunate souls who must rely for their sustenance upon the vagaries of the marketplace, as compared with the favored persons who could eke out an independent subsistence from the soil. Indeed, throughout history social prestige has been commonly equated with the possession of real estate; all the more so in antiquity, when *landed* and *aristocracy* were inseparable concepts.

From my perspective as an academic, I should note that, according to the Talmud, land ownership is particularly crucial for us scholars. Thus, a story is related about a rabbi who questioned his students about the progress they were making in their studies. When they responded that they had indeed mastered the assigned material, they added that their success was directly related to their recent acquisition of a small field.

This episode must be contrasted with several others in which scholars' academic performance was impaired by their financial straits. As Rabbi Johanan once summarized his own distress, "all the limbs depend on the heart, but the heart depends on the purse."

If only my employers would pay careful heed to those words of wisdom!

SUGGESTIONS FOR FURTHER READING

Beer, Moshe. (1974). *The Babylonian Amoraim: Aspects of Economic Life.* Ramat-Gan: Bar-Ilan University Press.
Sperber, Daniel. (1978). *Roman Palestine 200–400: The Land.* Bar-Ilan Studies in Near Eastern Languages and Culture. Ramat-Gan: Bar-Ilan University.

24

❧

Is There a James Bond
Adventure in the Talmud?*

A colleague of mine who specializes in the study of ancient Jewish preaching likes to remind me that in talmudic society the synagogue sermon functioned as the central form of entertainment for a Jewish community that was deprived of television or cinema, and was discouraged from attending the theatre or circus. This desire to spice instruction with amusement accounts for some of the more poetic, as well as the bizarre and sensational elements, that find their way into works of "aggadic midrash," a literary genre that is composed largely of snippets from ancient sermons. Not all of our contemporary preachers have proven as skillful in packaging their words in such an attractive form.

The recent screening of a festival of James Bond thrillers on cable television got me to pondering how well the ancient rabbis would

---

*"The Name is David—*King* David" *The Jewish Free Press*, Calgary, February 12, 1998, pp. 8–9.

have succeeded in competing with such exciting fare. Predictably, it did not take me long to come to the conclusion that the standard 007 format was in fact invented by the ancient Jewish sages, and examples of it are found in the pages of the Talmud.

If you find this claim difficult to accept, allow me to cite in evidence the following story. It is translated almost verbatim from the Babylonian Talmud (Sanhedrin 95a), in a story that is in itself an expansion of two verses in the Bible (2 Samuel 21:16–17). Other than a few words of my own enlightening commentary, all that I have added are some headings to call your attention to basic ingredients of what will later be regarded as the standard formula for a James Bond thriller. The swashbuckling hero of the talmudic adventure is none other than King David.

Element #1: The formidable villain: This role is filled by the Philistine Ishbi-benob, brother of the notorious (and deceased) Goliath. Ishbi possesses a horrendous arsenal of destructive weaponry (2 Samuel 21:16: "the weight of his spear weighed three hundred shekels of brass in weight, he being girded with a new sword"), and is determined to wreak vengeance upon his brother's slayer.

Element #2: The hero's briefing with his Superior Officer: Since this is a Bible story, David gets his orders not from a mortal "M," but from the Supreme Commander, the Almighty himself. The session begins with a chastising of David for the recklessness that has led to unnecessary loss of life. His present mission: to penetrate the headquarters of Ishbi-benob.

Element #3: Getting all those neat gadgets from "Q": Well, this is not actually described in the midrash, but from later episodes we can deduce that David has been issued a number of astounding bits of high-tech (or miraculous) weaponry. These include:

- A miniature earth remover.
- A secret communications system to signal his accomplice.

- A warp-speed mule.
- An antigravity device.

Element #4: Getting captured by the arch-villain: David is inadvertently drawn to the headquarters of the Philistine enemy while tailing what he believes to be a simple deer. It is in fact, none other than Satan in disguise.

Element #5: Hero is cruelly imprisoned, rather than killed, by the villain: Ishbi binds David and buries him in the earth under a heavy olive-press beam. Painful death is so certain that Ishbi does not make allowances for:

Element #6: Hero's last-minute escape from death, using gadget #1: Miraculously (literally), David is able to dig himself out of his earthy grave. He makes an appropriately wry comment (predictably, a quotation from the book of Psalms [18:37]): "Thou dost enlarge my steps under me and my feet have not slipped."

Element #7: He calls in reinforcements, with the help of gadget #2: The sidekick here is David's cousin, Abishai ben Zeruiah. The red alert is communicated through one of the following two coded signals:

- by injecting bloodstains into Abishai's hair conditioner.
- by having a distressed dove appear before Abishai.

The impetuous Abishai immediately speeds to David's rescue, but his pace is slowed by the stuffed-shirt bureaucrats. He wishes to drive on David's super-fast mule (gadget #3 above), but first needs official permission from the rabbis for this extraordinary use of His Majesty's property. Once the permission has been approved, he zips over to Ishbi-benob's lair, to encounter. . . .

Element #8: The villain's exotic hit man: In this case, it is a hit woman, Ishbi's mother, Orpah, to be exact. He meets her as she is, in apparent innocence, spinning away at her spinning wheel. Quickly he realizes that her spindles are in reality deadly weapons that she can hurl at her victims with great agility.

Element #9: Villains always miss. Heroes hit their mark on the very first shot: Her first needle misses him. She asks Abishai to return it, but he takes advantage of her error to throw it at her head, killing her instantly.

Realizing that he is now outnumbered, Ishbi plots certain death for King David. He throws David up in the air (remember that he is Goliath's brother), and plants a sharp spear in the ground to skewer David on his descent.

Element #10: When the situation seems hopeless, the hero is saved in the nick of time by his partner: Abishai employs Gadget #4, the antigravity trick, to suspend David in midair.

Element #11: The heroes escape from the villain's stronghold: With Ishbi hot on their heels, David and Abishai flee (after letting the king alight safely to earth, of course).

Element #12: Each stage of the struggle is accompanied by ironic humor: In the present tale, the heroes employ puns based on the names of the villages through which they pass on their way out of Philistine country. At Kubé they say to each other *"Kum beh"*—Stand up to him! At "Be-Trei" they quip "With two [be-trei] whelps they killed the lion." Finally the two take advantage of the villain's weakness, his love for his belligerent mother. In the midst of the struggle, they invite him to join Mom in the grave. In that moment of emotional frailty, David and Abishai are able to overcome and execute him.

That is the story, pretty much as it appears in the Talmud. I believed that my contention is irrefutably demonstrated, that it contains the original prototype for the classic James Bond formula.

Nevertheless, I am sure that there are some among you who are not entirely satisfied. There is still something missing:

Element #13: The gorgeous women: Folks, remember with whom we are dealing here. This is King David, paramour of Bathsheba; a monarch whose romantic escapades rivaled even those of an American President!

No doubt, such stories succeeded in drawing large audiences into the synagogues, even as their current imitations fill the contemporary cinemas.

⟁

Jewish Weddings

25

୬

What Is the Purpose of a Wedding Ring?*

In most respects the Jewish wedding ceremony is a very different affair from its Christian counterpart. Neither the *huppah*, the *ketubbah*, nor the traditional breaking of the glass have any equivalent outside Jewish practice. There is however one element that does seem to cross over religious and cultural boundaries, and that is the use of a ring in the ceremony.

In the Biblical and talmudic sources, we find no explicit mention of betrothal by ring. The Mishnah rules that the betrothal is given legal effect by the groom's transferring a sum of money or some other item of value to the bride or her representative. Cases cited in the Talmud make reference to all sorts of objects that were used for that purpose, including fruits, cups, and jewelry, as well as cash—but not rings.

---

* ". . . With this Ring." *The Jewish Free Press*, Calgary, Feb. 15, 1991, p. 11.

By the Middle Ages, the use of the wedding ring had become a known practice among some Jews, and was identified as a custom which distinguished the Jews of the Land of Israel from their Babylonian cousins. This development is a natural one, since the Holy Land was then under Roman occupation and the exchange of wedding rings was an established Roman practice, described by ancient writers like Pliny and subsequently inherited by the Christians as well.

As in many similar instances, the Jews unconsciously adopted the customs of their environment. For the majority of world Jewry who lived under the Persian or Arab rule, this was viewed as an exotic local idiosyncrasy. Over the years, the use of rings became the norm throughout the diaspora, until it was almost unimaginable to have a wedding without the groom reciting the familiar formula "Behold you are betrothed unto me with this ring, according to the law of Moses and Israel."

Now, Jews have rarely drawn clear borders between their past and present. We like to portray the events of our history in terms that are familiar to us. This last observation also applies to descriptions of Jewish weddings in ancient sources.

In Jewish tradition, the marriage ceremony par excellence was the revelation at Mount Sinai. Midrashic accounts dwell lovingly on the details: God was the groom and Israel the bride, standing beneath a *huppah* of clouds. The Torah is the eternal marriage contract, to which the heavens and earth are called to serve as witnesses.

One version of this story, an Aramaic embellishment of the Biblical account, waxes poetic: "The earth danced and the heavens sang, as the Lord betrothed the daughter of Jacob after liberating her from Egypt. Upon her fingers he placed five rings of light" [symbolizing the five books of the Torah].

Indeed, a later mystical work, the *Tikkunei Zohar*, claims that it was the circular emanations of divine power that came forth from God on that day that served as the model for the rings that are given to brides in subsequent Jewish marriages.

Though we have seen that the use of wedding rings by Jews is a relatively late institution copied from a Roman model, the authors of the above passages took it so much for granted that, for them, God himself could find no more suitable a way of expressing His eternal covenant with the people of Israel than by the symbolic gift of a ring.

SUGGESTIONS FOR FURTHER READING

Lewin, B. M. (1972). *Otzar Hilluf Minhaqim: Thesaurus of Halachic Differences between the Palestinian and Babylonian Schools.* Reprint ed., Jerusalem: Makor.

26

֍

Why Are Jewish Weddings
Held Under a Canopy?*

$\mathcal{T}$he most distinctive feature of any Jewish wedding is the *huppah*. This term is taken from the talmudic stipulation that a marriage does not take legal effect until the bride has entered the *huppah*. We are all of course familiar with the object being referred to. It is a canopy-like structure consisting of a piece of cloth, sometimes a *talit*, that is held aloft on four posts and beneath which the couple stand during the religious wedding ceremony.

While this might be obvious to us today, the definition of the *huppah* was not always so clear. As one reads through medieval works of Jewish religious law, it becomes evident that our rabbis entertained serious uncertainties about what, precisely, the Talmud was thinking of when it spoke about the *huppah*.

---

*"The Huppah: from Eden to Today." *The Jewish Free Press*, Calgary, Feb. 14, 1992, p. 8.

According to many authorities the *huppah* was the groom's house, or at any rate an actual room or building other than the bride's parental home. By entering it, the woman was declaring her official independence from her family and accepting the protection of her husband. Various rabbinic scholars debate whether for this purpose an actual house is required, or whether the requirement can be fulfilled through some sort of symbolic structure or act.

Much of that original function of the *huppah* has now come to be embodied in a separate portion of the marriage procedures that we call *yihud*, (isolation), which involves leaving the newlyweds alone in a room together after the conclusions of the public celebrations, so as to visibly demonstrate their new status as a couple.

In most early sources it was this secluding of the bride and groom that was designated the *huppah*, and attention used to be paid to ways of physically indicating the groom's ownership of the chamber, often through special ornamentation. Rabbi Isaac ben Abba Mari of Marseilles, writing in the twelfth century, relates that it was customary to decorate the designated room with colourful cloths and tapestries or to fashion a kind of *sukkah* adorned with myrtle leaves and roses.

Rabbi Isaac also mentions another custom—one of which he disapproves—namely that of spreading a cloth or a *talit* over the heads of the couple during the recitation of the marriage blessings. This closely approximates our current practice, though Rabbi Isaac did not consider it acceptable. By the sixteenth century, we encounter the earliest references to the four-posted *huppah* with which we are now familiar. Initially, it was accepted with some reluctance, but it is now in universal use among Ashkenazic Jews.

In addition to its technical function in the formalizing of the marriage, the *huppah* was endowed with many beautiful symbolic associations. For example, the midrash relates how the very first wedding in history was accompanied by a *huppah*—in fact, according to one legend, God himself made ten *huppahs* for Adam and Eve, each of them fashioned of gold and precious gems, while the angels entertained the first couple with song and dance.

There was one event in Jewish history that was considered the paradigm of all weddings: the revelation of the Torah at Mount Sinai. In the biblical account of the marriage between God and the people of Israel, our sages also discovered allusions to the presence of a *huppah*, whether in the enveloping cloud of darkness that hovered over the people, or in the fact that the Israelites, about to enter into their marriage with God, were made to stand *"beneath the mountain"*—just as the bride stands beneath the sheltering *huppah* on her wedding day.

SUGGESTIONS FOR FURTHER READING

Zevin, S. J. et al., ed. (1978–). *Talmudic Encyclopedia*. Jerusalem: Talmudic Encyclopedia Institute.

27

∽

What Should You Sing to a Homely Bride?*

*I*t is generally acknowledged that there exists a religious obligation in Judaism to bring joy to the heart of a new bride. Although some authorities regard it as an expression of gratitude for having been invited to the wedding, most view it as a distinct mitzvah in its own right.

According to the Talmud, the obligation is fulfilled by singing the bride's praises—a requirement that is not mentioned with respect to the groom. One commentator explains this gender imbalance by noting that the main purpose of the compliments is to reassure the hesitant young husband about the correctness of his decision. Since women are less demanding in their choice of mates, they have no urgent need for that kind of encouragement.

---

*"Gladdening the Bride." *The Jewish Free Press*, Calgary, February 17, 1994, p. 16.

It was thus common at Jewish weddings to celebrate the beauty of the bride. This practice gave rise to the hypothetical question: What are we expected to sing when the lady in question is not a spectacular beauty? Must we maintain strict standards of honesty at all costs? Should we at least be diplomatically selective in singing her praises? Or are we allowed to lie blatantly in ascribing to her physical charms that we do not really see?

The above question of wedding etiquette is discussed in a well-known passage in the Talmud:

"How are people supposed to sing about the bride as they dance before her?" The School of Hillel states that each and every bride should be extolled for her charm and grace, whereas the School of Shammai insists that she be described exactly as she is, for Judaism can never countenance even the slightest deviation from the unvarnished truth.

The commentators are in some disagreement about the precise limits of both positions. One authority, for example, paints a picture of the wedding dancers, following the strict view of the House of Shammai, belting out a rousing rendition of the lyrics "O bride, as you really are!" The meaning would be that even if her beauty is not apparent to our superficial appreciation, we recognize that her new husband must discern in her many attractive spiritual qualities, for otherwise, he would not have married her. After all, did not the wise Solomon teach us that "Favor is deceitful and beauty is vain; but a woman that feareth the Lord, she shall be praised"!

Rashi paraphrases the School of Hillel's view so that the emphasis is on charm rather than beauty. He subtly alludes to the midrashic tradition that Queen Esther was gifted with a "thread of grace" that caused her to be admired in spite of the fact that she was in reality a homely and sallow ("greenish") creature. Presumably the idea is to focus on the bride's strong points ("She has a great personality and all her friends like her!"), but not to overtly focus on her deficiencies.

The Tosafot, on the other hand, argue that even the School of Shammai would presumably not insist that we be so insensitively honest as to serenade the couple with a list of the bride's blemishes or deformities. Since the Shammaites must also permit some degree of delicacy and discretion, the School of Hillel must be advocating a much more permissive position, allowing for unrestrained compliments, even if they are made at the expense of overt misrepresentation. Anything less than that—even diplomatic silences—would embarrass the bride by calling attention to the glaring omissions in the accolades. It is this interpretation that has been accepted as normative practice by the *Shulhan Arukh* and other law-codes.

The whole issue would not arise at all if we were to follow the stringent position of some rabbis who strictly forbade all those present, out of considerations of modesty, to gaze upon the bride's face. The most that these authorities would concede is that we may peek at her ornaments in order to verify that she has, in fact, been married!

But the issue, as I have described it, is surely a hypothetical one. I am, after all, quite certain that I have never set eyes on a bride who did not radiate beauty on her wedding day.

28

༄

What Can We Learn from Old Marriage Contracts?*

$\mathcal{A}$t most of the Jewish weddings that I have observed in recent years, not much emphasis was placed on the reading of the *Ketubbah*, the traditional Jewish marriage contract. The prosaic legalisms that make up this contract do not always conform to the mood of sentimental spirituality that we consider appropriate to a wedding ceremony, and they are often mumbled cursorily from a standardized text that is written in an incomprehensible Aramaic dialect.

At the heart of the *Ketubbah* is the stipulation of monetary amounts to be paid by the husband in case of divorce. As practical as this matter might be, it is considered an awkward topic to

---

*"Ketubbah Texts Reveal Clues of Ancient Values." *The Jewish Free Press*, Calgary, February 16, 1995, p. 22.

be introducing under the *huppah*. Usually, the financial obligations are enumerated as a generic number of "pieces of pure silver"—though at Israeli weddings it is still common to mention (and haggle over) units of real currency.

Originally the *Ketubbah*'s chief purpose was to deter the husband from impulsively divorcing his wife. However, since the medieval enactment that prohibits divorcing a woman without her consent, the institution of the *Ketubbah* has become something of a ritual formality.

Although stereotyped uniformity characterizes the wording of almost all current *Ketubbahs*, this situation has not always been the case. *Ketubbahs* produced in other ages and lands demonstrate greater flexibility and creativity in the formulation of the clauses and conditions of the marriage contract.

Indeed, texts of *Ketubbahs* have been unearthed in just about every important trove of ancient Jewish manuscripts. The earliest known *Ketubbah* dates from fifth century B.C.E., and is contained in an archive from the island of Elephantine in the Nile, which housed a colony of Jewish mercenaries in the employ of the Persian emperor. From the *Ketubbot* and other records that were preserved there, it is possible to reconstruct a vivid picture of the life of that lost society.

Other *Ketubbah* texts are included among the archeological remnants of Simeon Bar-Kokhba's revolutionary headquarters, including that of the remarkable "Babata, daughter of Simeon," a second-century Jewish woman who left us an invaluable purse full of assorted bills, receipts, and other documents. Several marriage contracts are also included among the tattered fragments of the Cairo *Genizah*.

Many of these documents reveal surprising departures from the versions that are in widespread use today. The Elephantine *Ketubbot*, for example, include separate clauses to deal with the termination of marriages at the initiative of either the husband *or the wife*. One such text contains the following stipulation of penalty clauses for the party that asks for the divorce:

If at some time Ananiah should stand up before the assembly and declare: 'I reject my wife Jehoshama. She shall not be my wife!' then he is obligated to pay divorce money . . . And if Jehoshama should reject her husband Ananiah and declare before him 'I reject you and will not be your wife!' then she shall be obliged to pay the 'divorce money'. . . .

The prospect of the wife divorcing her husband would be considered impossible by later Jewish law. However, *Ketubbah* clauses that define the wife's rights to compel the husband to issue a divorce are cited in the Jerusalem Talmud and were written into most of the Genizah *Ketubbah* texts, which emanate from Egypt and the Land of Israel. The wording in those documents bears an uncanny resemblance to the formulas found in the Elephantine contracts composed 1500 years earlier and indicates a continuous evolution throughout that time.

In general, the wording of the texts from the Cairo *Genizah* expresses a different approach towards marriage from the one that characterizes our conventional *Ketubbot*. The latter speak only from the husband's perspective, as the one who is acquiring a wife and accepting obligations towards her, while the wife passively consents to the terms. The Palestinian tradition, on the other hand, placed an emphasis on the mutuality of the relationship. Thus, the marriage is referred to not as *nissu'in* (literally: carrying, taking), but as a *shutafut*, a partnership, or a *b'rit*, a covenant. Some Karaite *Ketubbot* call the bride a *haverah*, a companion. In addition to the groom's commitment to "nourish, provide for, honour, and esteem," the wife in turn promised to "serve, attend, honour, and esteem" her spouse.

The study of the Jewish marriage contract thus opens a fascinating windows into the lives and worldviews of previous generations.

SUGGESTIONS FOR FURTHER READING

Friedman, Mordechai A. (1974). "The Ethics of Medieval Jewish Marriage." In *Religion in a Religious Age*, ed. S. D. Goitein. pp. 83–102. Cambridge, MA: Association for Jewish Studies.

————. (1980). *Jewish Marriage in Palestine: A Cairo Geniza Study*. Tel-Aviv and New York: Tel-Aviv University and the Jewish Theological Seminary of America.

Goitein, S. D. (1967–). *A Mediterranean Society*. Berkeley, Los Angeles and London: University of California Press.

Porten, Bezalel. (1968). *Archives from Elephantine: The Life of an Ancient Jewish Military Colony*. Berkeley: University of California Press.

Yadin, Yigael. (1971). Bar-Kokhba: *The Rediscovery of the Legendary Hero of the Last Jewish Revolt against Imperial Rome*. London: Weidenfeld and Nicolson.

29

࿏

Why Is the Groom
Trying to Step on
the Bride's Foot?*

$\mathcal{T}$he traditional wedding ceremony, like other significant rites of
passage, is carefully defined by the norms of Jewish law and custom, so that very few of its details are left to chance. Some features, like the text of the Seven Blessings that are recited under
the canopy, or the breaking of a glass in memory of the destroyed
Temple, are rooted in ancient sources. Other practices have
evolved through the conventions of individual communities.

Where the bride and groom are to stand under the *huppah* is
one of those areas that came to be governed by local usage. Sources
from the mediaeval era report that the prevailing custom in
Ashkenazic communities was for the bride to stand at the groom's
right side, a procedure that was supported by a Biblical proof text:

---

*"Starting Off on the Right Foot: Power and Position under the
Huppah." *The Jewish Free Press*, Calgary, February 22, 1996, p. 12.

"Upon thy right hand did stand the queen in gold of Ophir" (Psalms 45:9). In other localities, the order appears to have been reversed. As long as Jews adhered to the practices of their own communities, everything should have continued harmoniously.

This innocent question of wedding protocol became the focus of a controversy in an episode that occurred in Rome in 1528. When doubts arose over what the correct practice ought to be in their city, a prominent local sage, a certain Rabbi Judah, insisted that the bride must stand on the left. As the disagreement progressed, Rabbi Judah made it clear that he would have taken this position even if the local precedent had been otherwise, and that, in his opinion, the long-standing Ashkenazic custom was indefensible.

In order to appreciate the vehemence of his argument, we must note that the Rabbi in question was also a Kabbalist. For proponents of this mystical philosophy the concepts of right and left are fundamental to the metaphysical structure of the universe, reflecting the tension between the divine attributes of justice and mercy. According to the imagery of the Kabbalah, the merciful, masculine aspect of God is identified with the right side, and the just, female side with the left.

In the eyes of the Jewish mystic, human actions are a mirror reflecting the celestial creative forces. The joining of male and female humans is thus, in a profound sense, essential to their being created in the "image of God"—for gender divisions originate in the divine realms. Therefore, it is only fitting that the woman position herself to the left of the man. To do otherwise would be a reversal of the proper order of creation and might be fraught with dire metaphysical consequences.

By insisting that halakhic decision-making be subordinated to mystical theology, Rabbi Judah had raised some sensitive issues about the borders and priorities of law and theology in Judaism.

However, not all questions about where to stand under the *huppah* were of such weighty dimensions. Some related more immediately to the personal relationships between the new couple.

Thus, the seventeenth-century mystic Rabbi Abraham Azulai observed that the balance of power in the marriage will be affected by where the bride and groom place their feet during the ceremony. If the husband succeeds in positioning his right foot upon his wife's left foot while the blessings are being recited, then this will establish the pattern for the future marriage, and she will continue to submit to his authority. But if she puts her left foot on his right, then she will, thereafter, wield the power in the home.

Rabbi Azulai tells of an occasion when a certain bride came out the loser in the foot-stamping competition at the *huppah*. Distressed, she reported the incident to her father, who revealed to her a solution to her dilemma: Just before the consummation of the marriage, he advised, she should ask her husband to bring her a glass of water. This well-timed drink would shift the power back into her hands.

The learned Kabbalist, writing in seventeenth-century Jerusalem, was probably unaware that the procedure he was describing bore an uncanny resemblance to a well-known folk belief still current among the people of Cornwall. According to a local legend, the waters of the famous well of St. Keyne possess the ability to bestow domestic authority upon the partner who is first to drink from them after the wedding ceremony. A popular English ballad expresses the dismay of a fresh bridegroom upon his discovery that his new bride had the foresight to secretly carry a bottle of the wondrous waters to the wedding, giving her an unbeatable advantage.

Such intense competitiveness at the threshold of married life suggests that neither husband nor wife were truly putting their best foot forward.

SUGGESTIONS FOR FURTHER READING

Abrahams, Israel. (1969). *Jewish Life in the Middle Ages*. Temple Books, New York: Atheneum.

Deane, Tony and Tony Shaw. (1975). *The Folklore of Cornwall.* The Folklore of the British Isles, Totowa: Rowman and Littlefield.

Katz, Jacob. (1984). *Halakhah and Kabbalah: Studies in the History of Jewish Religion, its Various Faces and Social Relevance.* Jerusalem: Magnes.

30

୬

Are Matches Really Made in Heaven?*

I believe it was the sardonic seventeenth-century author Robert Burton who first coined the English adage that "matches are made in heaven." However the idea underlying that adage has enjoyed a much longer history in Jewish tradition.

The Talmud observed that forty days prior to conception a divine voice is already declaring which mates are destined to be joined in conjugal life. This perception of a foreordained match is encapsulated in the Yiddish word *bashert*.

The ancient Jewish sages were aware of the myth—familiar to many of us from Aristophanes' speech at Plato's *Symposium*—that men and women were originally a single androgynous being that was split into two, so that in seeking their ideal mates, they are really striving to reunite with the missing portions of their selves.

---

*"Matches Made in Heaven." *The Jewish Free Press*, Calgary, February 20, 1997, p. 16.

This reciprocal aspect of a successful union was voiced in rather archaic terms by Ogden Nash when he spoke in praise of "incompatibility"—when he has income and she is pattable (feel free to switch the gender designations).

The preparation of a proper match is no easy matter, even for the Almighty. Rabbi Yohanan observed that, in the Talmud, the task ranks in its difficulty alongside the splitting of the Red Sea.

When a Roman matron asked Rabbi Yosé ben Halafta how God has been occupying himself since completing the creation of the universe (reflecting the widespread view among ancient philosophers that after setting the world in motion, the Creator withdrew from active involvement in the affairs of that world), the Jewish sage was quick to reply that God has his work cut out for him preparing suitable matches for his creatures.

The lady countered that this seemed a trivially simple task for an omnipotent deity, upon which Rabbi Yosé dared her to try her own hand at it. Taking up the challenge, the matron convened a mass wedding for the male and female slaves of her household.

However, the honeymoons were cut short since, by the next day, most of the newlyweds were bruised and bleeding. The matron was compelled to concede the wisdom of Rabbi Yosé's words!

The talmudic traditions about destined matches came to be interpreted by Jewish thinkers in the light of the new theological ideas and social realities that arose in later generations.

Thus, the medieval mystics interpreted the matchmaking process from the perspective of their own distinctive doctrines. Some Kabbalists observed that a good *shiddukh*, like all other holy handiwork, is fashioned by means of permutations of the sacred letters of the Hebrew alphabet. This, explains Rabbenu Bahya bar Asher, is why the Torah decreed that a marriage can only be dissolved by means of a written document of divorce.

Other Kabbalists, including the author of the *Zohar*, depicted supernatural matchmaking in accordance with their belief in reincarnation: Thus, it sometimes happens that people's transgressions prevent them from finding their destined mate in their current lifetime, and the matter must be deferred to a subsequent existence.

The medieval Jewish philosophers were bothered by this implied suspension of free will. Maimonides addressed this weighty question in a responsum to Obadiah the Proselyte, insisting that the rabbis' statements about preordained marriages should not be taken at face value since they challenged the foundations of moral autonomy. Perhaps, Maimonides suggested, the Talmud meant only to say that God rewards or punishes people by yoking them to worthy or disagreeable mates.

Some ingenious twists on the belief in preordained matches are preserved in the *Sefer Hasidim* (*The Book of the Pious*), that remarkable collection of Jewish lore from twelfth-century Germany.

One passage in *Sefer Hasidim* tells of a bridegroom who was forced into an unwanted—but lucrative—union. In the course of the wedding ceremony, he recited both the *Barukh dayyan ha-emet* blessing which is usually recited over a tragedy or bereavement, and *Barukh ha-tov veha-metiv*, the blessing for good fortune! He justified his strange practice by citing the talmudic traditions about the Almighty's role in the selection of his mate.

New heights of chutzpah are suggested in another passage from *Sefer Hasidim* where an adulterer is said to have evoked the talmudic traditions in order to justify his illicit liaison with a married woman: "If matches are made in Heaven," he deduced, "then it was God who made me do it!"

Needless to say, the rabbi who discussed this argument was less than impressed by its cogency.

Notwithstanding such occasional misuses, the fundamental notion that God has a hand in the selection of a compatible union is hopefully to be regarded as an expression of the feelings of the couple, that an enduring marriage is such a remarkable achievement that it can hardly be credited to chance or human agency.

31

℘

Why Does the Bride
Circle the Groom?*

*D*ifficult as it is to recall all the details of my wedding, which occurred almost a quarter-century ago, one memory that does still emerge through the mists of time was my bride's determination to observe the practice of walking around her groom seven times under the marriage canopy. At that time and in our straightlaced community, this was not a familiar part of the ceremony, and I imagine that the rabbi and guests regarded it as yet another example of our fundamental eccentricity. They were probably right.

I believe that since those days in the hoary past, the custom of circling the groom, like many other obscure and exotic Jewish customs, has achieved more widespread acceptance, often among young couples whose parents or grandparents would never have

---

*"Voyage Round a Bridegroom." *The Jewish Free Press*, Calgary, February 26, 1998, p. 18.

heard of the practice. The standard pattern seems to be that the more exotic and bizarre a custom is, the more fervently will it be touted as an essential expression of authentic Judaism, especially by individuals whose acquaintance with Jewish tradition is of recent vintage.

By Jewish standards, groom-circling can not lay claim to any impressive antiquity. The earliest known reference to it is in a biblical commentary composed by a certain Rabbi Dosa the Greek in the early fifteenth century. Rabbi Dosa cites the custom, which consisted of three rather than seven circuits, as that of Austria. In subsequent centuries, as many central-European Jews migrated eastward, we find the practice mentioned in connection with Hungary, Galicia, Poland, and Russia. Not untypically, we note that similar customs were also attested among non-Jews in Slavic and Balkan lands, and it is not always clear who was copying whom.

The precise details of the custom vary in the early sources. The older texts generally speak of three circuits. In some versions the bride is escorted on either side by a bridesmaid bearing a candle. Several communities accompanied the ceremony with the singing of traditional hymns, or with the humming of a wordless melody.

As is often the case with Jewish customs, there is no consensus about its fundamental purpose or origins.

The favorite biblical text most often cited as the source for the custom is Jeremiah 31: 22: "for the Lord hath created a new thing in the earth, A woman shall compass a man."

In the original context of the prophet's allegory, the woman symbolizes the people of Israel who will initiate the reconciliation with her beloved, the Almighty. Although, in the human realm, such forwardness in a woman was considered an unprecedented novelty, on the religious plain, God anticipates it eagerly. The Hebrew phrase that is translated compass—*tesovev*—is used here to designate a courtship, rather than actually walking around. However, the advocates of the custom found, in the literal translation of the passage, a convenient Biblical precedent.

Indeed, Jeremiah's imagery seems more propitious than that of another biblical passage that was adduced by some interpreters, that of Joshua circling the walls of Jericho seven times until they crumbled to the ground. For all that the theme was understood in a favourable sense, as representing the breaking down of divisions and barriers between the new couple, we may expect that the image would give rise to discomfort among some prospective husbands.

Not all the rationales cited biblical texts. Some scholars proposed interpretations that built more directly upon the elements of the custom.

According to one very practical approach, the whole ceremony was designed to provide the groom ample opportunity to observe his prospective mate from all possible angles, just to make sure that nobody had tried to substitute an impostor in her place. Presumably, the lessons of Jacob's unfortunate deception by Laban have not been lost on his posterity. At any rate, one wonders why this objective could not have been accomplished more effectively by having the man walk around the woman.

However, most authorities prefer interpretations that are less practical and more symbolic. For example, some commentators suggest that the groom is being compared to a king surrounded by the adulations of his ceremonious retinue. This opinion would be more convincing if it were the guests, rather than the bride, who were doing the surrounding.

A more spiritual symbolism was introduced by Rabbi Dov Ber of Lubavitch who explained that, in walking around her spouse, the wife is demonstrating how she will bask in the benevolent influences that radiate, so to speak, from his person.

A variation on this symbolism is that it represents how the groom will now be encompassed by the luminescence that issues from his bride. The seven circuits are required to penetrate the seven shells of solitude in which the soul has been encrusted.

For all the charm or insight that we find in such explanations, none of them strikes me as altogether convincing. Their sheer number arouses the suspicion that their authors were just guessing at the source for a custom whose original reasons were no longer known.

The most convincing theory is that the practice originated as a protective measure against the demonic hosts, whose envy tends to be kindled on festive occasions. The bride's walking around the groom might be a variation on a similar procedure, described in a work from the early nineteenth century, in which the wedding participants encircled him with a cushion into which had been stitched a gold coin. Similar prophylactic devices are widespread in world folklore.

Whatever its original purpose, I have it on reliable authority that the effects can be quite enduring, and that some husbands have been known to remain dizzy for years after the wedding.

SUGGESTIONS FOR FURTHER READING

Ahrend, Aaron. (1991). "Bride Going around the Bridegroom—Study of a Marriage Custom." *Sidra* 7: 5–11.

PART III

In the Community

32

⁓

What's the Difference between Fund Raising and Fund Taking?*

$\mathcal{A}$s has been noted in the pages of recent issues of *The Star*, we are currently marking a number of anniversaries commemorating the beginnings of the Jewish community of Alberta (the centenary of Jewish settlement) and, in Calgary, the eightieth anniversary of Congregation House of Jacob, the oldest Jewish institution in the province.

The establishment of Jewish communities and institutions has always struck us as a remarkable achievement, involving delicately balanced combinations of vision, sacrifice, and practical ability.

The designated readings from the Torah over the next few weeks tell of what was perhaps the first communal building project in Jewish history, the construction of the *mishkan*, the portable

---

*"Fund Raising and Fund Taking." *The Jewish Star*, Calgary/Edmonton, Feb. 17–March 2, 1989, pp. 4, 11.

sanctuary that was to serve as the center of worship during the people's wanderings through the wilderness, until it was replaced by the permanent Temple built by King Solomon in Jerusalem.

Needless to say, the biblical passages describing this event have a lot to teach us about the nature of communal involvement and the skills and attitudes required for the building of successful Jewish institutions.

The sages and rabbis of previous generations were wont to interpret the scriptural verses in the light of their own concerns and to find in them useful models for their own congregational life.

THE FIRST FUND-RAISER

As with any Jewish communal endeavour, the building of the *mishkan* was preceded by a fund-raising drive. The talmudic sources already recognized that this first fund-raiser was to serve as a model for subsequent efforts: "This campaign was run by Moses; but in future generations it would be administered by treasurers, officers, and financial controllers."

A community such as ours, that is hard-put to keep its synagogues and schools on a solid financial footing, has much to learn from this earliest of Jewish "appeals."

The wording of the biblical passage is inherently enigmatic: God orders Moses to tell the people "that they shall *take* for me an offering, of every man *whose heart makes him willing* you shall take My offering" (Exodus 25:2). On the one hand, emphasis is placed on *taking* the contributions, without regard for the willingness of the donors; the commentators have called attention to the surprising fact that the normal Hebrew words for giving are virtually absent throughout the relevant chapters.

On the other hand, the very same verse also underscores the *voluntary* character of the contribution, as the people's hearts motivate them to give to the cause.

The approaches of traditional Jewish interpreters to this ambiguity can serve as indicators of their attitudes towards larger questions of religious philosophy and human psychology.

MOTIVATION VS. OBLIGATION

Most of the commentaries tend to prefer one or the other of the two options. Those whose purpose is to stress the importance of sincere motivation in philanthropic activity (such an attitude is typical of hasidic homilies and other moralistic tracts) may read the verse as saying that donations should not be accepted from those whose motives are suspect.

Others, however, take the opposite stance: the commitment to supporting community institutions should not be left to the fickle and unpredictable vagaries of spontaneous inspiration but should be grounded and regulated in legal obligation. Such an approach underlies the explanation of that "arch-Litvak" Rabbi Naftali Zvi Yehudah Berlin (the Netziv of Volozhin) to Exodus 39:22: "And the children of Israel did according to all that God had commanded Moses; so did they do."

According to the Netziv, the verse should be understood as saying: "In spite of their enthusiasm at the moment, which might have inspired them to go beyond what God had ordered, the people restrained themselves and obediently restricted their activity to a precise fulfilment of God's commands, and no more."

One of the tensions which the talmudic rabbis perceived as having arisen in the *mishkan* building project involved the relationship between the wealthy donors and the average Israelite-in-the-street who could only afford to contribute his few pennies to the cause.

As related in talmudic legend, the tribal princes (*nesi'im*) were quick to respond to Moses' call, offering to pay for the entire project. Moses rejected the offer as running counter to God's intention (Exodus 25:2–3): "Of every man whose heart makes him willing you shall take my offering."

In the creation of Jewish institutions, the purpose was not simply to get the job done as efficiently as possible; getting the people involved in the project was perceived as an end in itself.

In later generations this principle was to inspire a heated controversy between the Pharisees—who refused to allow communal offerings to be donated to the Temple by wealthy individuals—and their Sadducee opponents.

The Pharisaic approach has generally been upheld by subsequent generations of Jewish fund-raisers (including the various Israel appeals) who have recognized the importance of reaching out to the 85% of the population who are responsible for only 15% of the donations.

By the time we reach the end of the campaign (Exodus 36:5–7), the generosity of the people has surpassed the actual requirements of the Sanctuary, and Moses has to issue orders to stop accepting donations.

THE GOLDEN CALF

In the intervening chapters, the Torah has related a considerably less complimentary event, the people's fashioning of the golden calf. This project, too, had to be financed by voluntary donations, and the people willingly contributed their jewellery to the cause. The Talmud *Yerushalmi* notes, with a certain sardonic wonder, the indiscriminate character of some Jewish generosity: "Said Rabbi Abba Bar Aha: It is impossible to figure out the nature of this people—when asked to contribute for the golden calf, they give; when asked to contribute for the *Mishkan*, they also give!"

That is to say, from their earliest history, the Jews could be identified as willing contributors to any appeal, without always looking carefully into the target of their generosity.

SUGGESTIONS FOR FURTHER READING

Liebowitz, Nehama. (1975). *Studies in Shemot*. Translated by Aryeh Newman. Jerusalem: World Zionist Organization, Dept. for Torah Education and Culture in the Diaspora.

33

ॐ

Is Judaism Compatible with Democracy?*

*W*hether we look to Canada, the United States, or Israel, the air is filled with election campaigning.

At first glance, this might appear like an entirely modern, Western phenomenon. Antidemocratic forces in Israel have even argued that the idea of democracy is inherently opposed to Judaism. The familiar political structure of ancient Judaism was generally monarchical, or even theocratic, a term originally coined by the first century Jewish historian Josephus Flavius to describe the priest-dominated government of the Second Temple era.

Actually, even though as influential an individual as Maimonides asserts that the Torah commands us to appoint a king, the biblical sources (e.g. Deuteronomy 17:24–20; I Samuel 8) are ambivalent about the subject. The talmudic rabbis, moreover, were far

---

*"Judaism's Democratic Tendency." *The Jewish Star*, Calgary/Edmonton, Oct. 21–Nov. 3, 1988, pp. 4–5.

from certain that the Torah viewed monarchy as an ideal political structure.

It has been argued that Judaism does not actually recommend any particular political system. Provided that the leadership is guided by suitable religious and moral ideals, Jewish tradition has sanctioned a number of different political models.

A JEWISH CITY-STATE

Among the most venerable of the Jewish political structures is the *kehillah* (community), a town-centered institution whose roots date back to the beginnings of the Second Temple era.

Talmudic sources describe the extensive authority exercised by the *kehillah*, and by its constituent members, the citizens or *b'nei ha'ir*, in such areas as the allocation of funds for welfare, education, and defence, as well as the supervision of weights, measures, and prices, the fixing of salaries, and more.

Some historians have argued that the *kehillah* originated as a Jewish response to the Hellenistic ideal of the *polis*, or city-state, which was the dominant expression of Greek culture in antiquity. Jews, at once accommodating themselves to the prevalent world order and reacting to its pagan character, produced their own counterpart which, typically, outlived all the Greek-style cities.

In enumerating the far-reaching responsibilities of the *kehillah*, the Talmud refers only to the "citizens," meaning adult male residents—never to the king, patriarch (*Nasi*), or even to the rabbinic court. In general, subsequent Jewish tradition has accepted these guidelines at face value and, with certain qualifications, assigned legislative and executive authority to the town's lay citizenry.

Though the Talmud speaks at greater length of authoritarian structures involving rabbinical courts, a *Nasi*, and a king (to which it is often hostile), it is clear that, in reality, it was the local communities which constituted the dominant form of government. The relative silence regarding the *kehillah* has been attributed to the fact that the Mishnah and Babylonian Talmud were edited at times when there was a strong (but unsuccessful) move towards centralized authority.

Nonetheless, it is evident that in *Eretz Yisrael* throughout the talmudic period and afterwards, and in Spain, Italy and Germany thereafter, the democratic communal tradition continued to thrive long after the Roman Empire had become feudalized and the centralized rule of the Babylonian *yeshivot* had declined.

Characteristic of the authority entrusted to the *kehillah* is the fact that various privileges which the Talmud allotted only to official religious courts were transferred by medieval scholars to the lay community leaders. Accordingly, the community was assigned absolute control over its citizens' property, an authority which the Talmudic sources restricted to the recognized rabbinical courts.

MAJORITY RULE

Basing himself on this analogy, the renowned thirteenth-century Spanish Talmudist Rabbi Solomon Ibn Adret (Rashba) summarized the principle that communities should be governed by majority rule:

> As regards the decisions of the people of a specific locality, the law is that whenever the majority agree to enact a law, and accept this law, we pay no attention to individual opinions, since the relation of the majority in each town to the individuals of the community is equivalent to the relationship of the Great Court to the entire Jewish people: Whatever they decree shall stand, and whoever disobeys is to be punished.

DISSENTING MINORITY

At least one important medieval Rabbi, the noted French scholar Jacob ben Meir Tam (known as Rabbenu Tam), denied the power of the majority decisions to obligate the dissenting minority.

Rabbenu Tam's view remained itself a dissenting minority position. One of his most distinguished successors in Germany, Rabbi Asher ben Jehiel (the Rosh, or Asheri) rejected the view, arguing, among other things, that unless we accept the principle of majority rule, no community will ever be able to come to any decisions.

REPRESENTATIVE DEMOCRACY

Another principle which is accepted universally in Jewish communal law is that of representative democracy, that is, that the actual management of the community cannot always be carried out by the whole population but is placed, instead, in the hands of a small governing body.

The Talmud speaks of an institution called *shiv'ah tovei ha'ir,* the "seven leaders of the town." Rabbi Solomon Ibn Adret, in explaining this term, observes as follows:

> The "leaders of the city" mentioned in the sources are *not* men of exemplary learning or wealth or honour, but rather seven men whom the community has appointed as executives to oversee its affairs. . . .

Elsewhere he explains that this institution exists not by virtue of any intrinsic superiority of the leaders, but merely because it would be too cumbersome to bring every question to a vote.

> Otherwise [he writes] no community would ever be able to do anything—plan a budget or pass legislation—without assembling all the taxpaying citizenry (in questions that entail expenditures), until a consensus can be reached—a consensus which would have to include the women as much as the men, since how can anyone dispose of their money without their permission?

This has been only a small glimpse into the rich and vibrant world of Jewish political life. It should, however, be sufficient to demonstrate that such modern inventions as majority rule, representative democracy, and executive responsibility all have long and distinguished roots in Jewish history and tradition.

SUGGESTIONS FOR FURTHER READING

Baer, I. (1960). "The Foundations and Origins of Jewish Communal Organization in the Medieval Period." *Zion* 15: 85–121.

Blidstein, Gerald J. (1983). *Political Concepts in Maimonidean Halakha.* Ramat-Gan: Bar-Ilan University Press.

Elon, M. (1973). *Jewish Law: History, Sources, Principles.* Jerusalem: The Magnes Press.

Morell, S. (1971). "The Constitutional Limits of Communal Government in Rabbinic Law." *Journal of Jewish Social Studies* 33: 2–3: 87–119.

34

ᘐᕀ

What Are the Origins of Jewish Journalism?*

The birth of a new Jewish newspaper is, we are justified in hoping, an occasion to be celebrated. While Jewish journalism is of course a relatively recent phenomenon by Jewish standards—mere centuries old—it is a channel of expression that has come to occupy an important and cherished place in most of our communities.

The first Jewish journals in Europe were not newspapers, nor was their chief purpose to inform their readers about the latest events in the world or in their communities. The editors were out to *educate* their public and to expose them to new ideas.

---

*"Jewish Journalism: Continuing the Tradition." *The Jewish Free Press*, Calgary, Nov. 15, 1990, p. 12.

THE GATHERER

The first important Jewish journal to make its appearance in Europe was the monthly *Ha-Me'assef* (*The Gatherer*), whose first issue was published in Königsberg, Germany, in 1784. This pioneering periodical was founded by disciples of the father of modern Jewish Enlightenment, Moses Mendelssohn of Dessau, and was devoted to the promotion of his ideas among the Jewish masses.

A distinctively Jewish complication that had to be dealt with was the choice of a suitable language for the publication. It was not enough to simply compose the articles in the language most easily understood by the readership. Had the editors of *Ha-Me'assef* taken that seemingly logical course, they would probably have chosen some form of Yiddish, the spoken language of most German Jews of the time.

CHOOSING A LANGUAGE

This option was abhorrent to Mendelssohn and his Enlightened followers (the *Maskilim*) who had nothing but disdain for Yiddish, regarding it as a crude corruption of "real" German. Indeed a major plank in the Enlightenment platform involved weaning Jews away from Yiddish and teaching them proper German, which would facilitate their entry into mainstream German society.

Given this outlook, we might have expected them to compose their publications in German. This, however, was not possible because their target audience was not yet familiar enough with that language and would, inevitably, be reluctant to pick up anything written in a non-Jewish tongue.

SCRIPTURAL PURISM

The only alternative now remaining was Hebrew. Traditional Jews would be likely to open the issues of *Ha-Me'assef* expecting to find conventional religious texts, the only type of material normally composed in the sacred tongue. Hopefully, by the time they caught on, they would already have been won over to the ideology of Enlightenment.

While many of the *Maskilim* involved in the publication of *Ha-Me'assef* might have accepted Hebrew as merely a second-best alternative, they also had a positive agenda in promoting the sacred tongue.

For the most part, they disapproved of the neglect of Biblical studies that prevailed in the traditional yeshivah curriculum, which was overwhelmingly slanted in favour of talmudic learning. Rabbinic Hebrew was, to most of the *Maskilim*, akin to the despised Yiddish, an impure version of the classical Hebrew of the Bible. The writers of *Ha-Me'assef* strove to replace the talmudic Hebrew jargon with a stately, but inflexible, scriptural purism.

LIKE A *SHTREIMEL*

From these beginnings, the Jewish journal or newspaper, in whatever language, quickly became an inseparable part of the communal landscape. Each ideological faction had its own organ of expression.

In such a context, moderation was not necessarily viewed as a virtue. Thus, the Warsaw Yiddish daily *Moment* (whose name has since been resurrected for a respected American-Jewish periodical) was often criticized for its lack of editorial backbone. According to one quip, the newspaper would not offend a fly—out of fear that the fly might one day scrape up the two kopeks to buy the paper!

Another such barb expressed its wonder that the paper could continue to appear in spite of its indolent and lifeless staff. The strange phenomenon was explained by comparing *Moment* to an old *shtreimel*—When you put the tattered fur hat on a table, it moves by itself, powered by the lice that inhabit it. . . .

BUT DON'T READ IT

In this polarized world of nineteenth-century Judaism, the emerging Orthodox movement soon found that it had to publish its own newspapers in order to counter those of their opponents. Some of the important rabbis of the day took part in the publication of those newspapers.

Nonetheless, in at least one instance a rabbi had to warn his students not to waste their time reading his newspaper, since this would constitute *bittul Torah*, an unwarranted break from their religious studies.

The combination of strict orthodoxy and journalism could lead to some strange results. For example, Israel's foremost ultra-Orthodox daily, *Ha-Modia*, has a strict policy of excluding all things sexual.

In a recent instance, a report about a new drug that cures skin diseases happened to mention that the diseases in question were often sexually transmitted. The newspaper's internal censor did not catch the offending sentence until the type was already set and ready for printing, when only the most minor changes could still be introduced.

The result: A single-word emendation, according to which the diseases in question were *commercially* transmitted!

Indeed, there will always be problems and challenges that are peculiar to being a *Jewish* newspaper. We wish the *Free Press* the best of luck in ably continuing the colourful traditions of Jewish journalism.

SUGGESTIONS FOR FURTHER READING

Sachar, Howard Morley. (1977). *The Course of Modern Jewish History*. Updated and expanded ed., New York: Dell [Delta].

Sadan, Dov. (1952). *Ka'arat Tsimmukim*. Tel-Aviv: Newman.

35

❦

Why Do Jews Love Guests?

The classic medieval Jewish disputation literature usually followed a conventional pattern of refuting the misinterpretations of Biblical passages which the Christians would cite in evidence of the truth of their religion. The twelfth-century *Book of the Covenant* by Rabbi Joseph Kimhi of France is largely devoted to this kind of bookish debate over scriptural exegesis.

In his defense of Judaism, Kimhi argues eruditely against the claims of his Christian opponent, but adds a few new points based on contemporary comparisons of Jewish and Gentile moral standards: Jewish decency, modesty, and piety were observable facts which even hostile Christians had to acknowledge.

In this connection Kimhi notes that:

> whenever a Jew stops at the home of his fellow for a day or two— or even a year—he will take no payment for food from him. This is so with all the Jews in the world who act toward their brethren with compassion.

The universal practice of hospitality to travellers and transients was indeed a well-known feature of traditional Jewish societies. The midrash traced it back to Abraham's elaborate preparations for his three unexpected angelic visitors.

The Jews of Calgary have faithfully continued this tradition. In an average summer my synagogue, the House of Jacob-Mikveh Israel, processes over a hundred requests from tourists and visitors in search of kosher meals and Shabbat home hospitality.

These visitors are a variegated assortment, and most veteran members of our community have collected anecdotes about their experiences with the Shabbat guests. Several have assured me that these anecdotes could easily fill up books.

The overwhelming majority of the guests have been charming people whose presence enriched our community. Some were rabbis or cantors, who offered to contribute their skills to the synagogue services. Many have been young Israelis on their customary post-Army international jaunts.

Others, however, have been of a more problematic nature, inspiring their hosts to keep watchful eyes on the family silver. Our family's most memorable experience of this sort was the case of the disappearing guest who went out for a walk after Friday night dinner and has not been seen since . . . We discovered subsequently that this particular individual would spend his days travelling around Canada living off the generosity of local Jews, then vanish when moved by the urge to travel on.

A special category of visitors are the *meshullachim* who show up annually collecting contributions for yeshivahs. While some are pious and learned men, others tend to be lacking in social graces and expect to be honoured as a matter of course (like the one who, without asking, pulled the host family's laundry out of the washing machine and put in his own).

A few years ago my father-in-law was visiting Calgary, staying in the house of some vacationing friends. One morning, a *meshullach* showed up at the door and greeted my father-in-law by the owner's name as if he were a familiar old friend—irrespective of the fact that he did not even know him well enough to recognize his face!

On another occasion, the police found a bearded figure wandering about the Glenmore Reservoir shouting out incomprehensible ravings at the top of his voice. They had learned by now that such odd strangers were likely to be guests of Rabbi Peter Hayman, to whom they promptly returned him. The individual in question was a visiting *meshullach*, a Bratslaver Hassid, who had been indulging in the mystical meditations peculiar to his sect.

The idea of hospitality is indeed an esteemed mitzvah in Jewish tradition. In addition to its religious merit, it adds much color to the lives of the host community.

SUGGESTIONS FOR FURTHER READING

Talmage, Frank, ed. (1972). *The Book of the Covenant of R. Joseph Kimhi.* Toronto: Pontifical Institute of Medieval Studies.

CHAPTER

36

⤙⤙

Should We Pray for the Government?*

There is nothing quite like an election campaign to bring home to us the complex responsibilities that are imposed upon us by the democratic system. In earlier times government was a simpler business. There was a king who did as he pleased, and the common people had little say in choosing either the sovereign or his policies.

Some echoes of the transition from absolutism to democracy are preserved in the Jewish prayer book. Since medieval times, it has been customary to include in the Sabbath services an official prayer for the king. The earliest mention of this custom is found in Rabbi David Abudraham's commentary on the liturgy, composed in fourteenth-century Spain. He describes the custom of

---

*"Praying for the Government is a Jewish Tradition." *The Jewish Free Press*, Calgary, Oct. 28, 1993, p. 9.

including a blessing, a *mi shebberakh*, attached to the Torah reading, in which the congregation expressed its hope that the monarch would be victorious in battle and merciful in his treatment of the Jews. The standard "Prayer for the King" which is recited in most Ashkenazic communities, continued to develop those themes, always referring to the local monarch.

With the decline of monarchy in the western world, the printers of prayer books generally left the traditional text intact, merely substituting the name of the highest officer of government for the king in the original. Thus, many American *siddurim* direct the blessing (whether in English, Hebrew, or Yiddish) to the president and perhaps the vice president. One author who lived under less stable administrations advised the printers of the prayer books to avoid mentioning their rulers by name, lest the next coup d'état result in the banning of the book.

All in all, those of us who do not have contact with royalty and nobility will not appreciate the full significance of the "Prayer for the King." I was made aware of this fact while I was living in Oxford, England, in 1977–8. It was customary there for the benediction to be recited by the local noble, the late Lord Samuel Segal of Wytham (no relation). Lord Segal would make a point of entering the sanctuary after the reading of the Torah, so that the *gabba'im* would not feel obligated to call him to an *aliyyah* as a Levi. To his otherwise traditional recitation of the text, he would introduce one change: Instead of the phrase "and Israel shall dwell in security" at the end of the passage, he would invoke the blessing upon "Israel and Esau." It is the kind of liberty that a lord can take.

My own synagogue uses a precisely formulated version of the prayer which appears to have been composed by a team of experts in constitutional law. It meticulously itemizes the levels of "original and delegated authority" to which the blessing is intended to apply. In recent months some subtle alterations have been introduced into the prayer. I have not been able to fully appreciate the significance of these changes, but I suspect that they emanate from a desire to exclude certain elements of the government, such as bureaucrats or appointed senators.

This phenomenon raises some intriguing questions about the wisdom of our praying for *just any* government. Should we not be more discerning about which legislators really deserve divine favours? To put it another way: How corrupt does a regime have to be before we stop including it in the congregational prayers?

Some interesting conclusions can be drawn from a study of the ancient sources from which the "Prayer for the King" was derived. The prophet Jeremiah urged his fellow Jews to seek the welfare of the Babylonian empire to which they were being exiled, in spite of the fact that this very empire had destroyed their homeland and Temple. A similar sentiment was expressed in the Mishnah by Rabbi Hanina the Deputy Priest: "Pray for the welfare of the government, since were it not for the fear of it, people would swallow each other alive." Rabbi Hanina was presumably referring to the same Roman government which, during his own lifetime, destroyed the second Temple, in which he himself officiated. Any government, he seems to be saying, is better than none at all.

These views were not shared by all the Jewish sages. Rabbinic literature is replete with condemnations of the Roman "kingdom of wickedness," the antithesis of the "Kingdom of Heaven" to which we must give our exclusive allegiance. The sources reflect a continuing controversy over the relative merits of resisting or cooperating with tyranny.

Fortunately, we do not have to worry about such issues. In our free and democratic society, our prayers should ultimately be for ourselves, that we be granted the intelligence to cast our votes wisely.

37

ℑↄ

Why Was the UJA in Trouble—in 1707?*

𝒰nfortunately, there have been few eras in recent history when the Jews of the Land of Israel have not been forced to rely on contributions from their coreligionists in the Diaspora. Since the establishment of the State of Israel, this situation can be blamed on the heavy economic burdens created by her security needs. In earlier generations, the finances of the Holy Land communities were often depleted by cruel and rapacious rulers, by natural and humanly caused disasters, and by the otherworldly pursuits that were the principal concern of most of the Jews who dwelled there.

The gathering of donations for the populace and institutions of Israel was, therefore, a constant source of concern. The wandering emissaries from yeshivot and charitable foundations be-

---

*"Collecting for Israel—circa 1707." *The Jewish Free Press*, Calgary, March 17, 1994, p. 9.

came a familiar feature of diaspora life. Many distinguished rabbis donned the cloak of the mendicant, journeying through the Jewish expanses in search of material sustenance for their communities. In fact, special manuals would be composed to advise the fund-raisers how to make useful contacts in the various cities and effectively present their cases before the prospective donors. These handbooks provide us with some engaging insights into the dynamics of Jewish communal life.

One of the most ambitious of the emissaries' manuals was the *Sefat Emet* by the Jerusalemite Rabbi Moshe Hagiz, which appeared in Amsterdam in 1707. From this book we can learn of the difficulties that frequently obstructed the fund-raisers of the time. Rabbi Hagiz devotes much space to the refutation of common criticisms and accusations that would be leveled against the collectors. For example, to the charge that the needs of the recipients appear to be insatiable, he responds with a detailed financial report of the community's expenditures and growing debts. Nonetheless, it was charged that they would use the revenues to "drink coffee and chew tobacco, and scribble whatever comes to mind so they can publish it." Some communal leaders were arguing that priority should be given to pressing local needs. Others were even claiming that Jews had no business living in Eretz Yisrael before the advent of the Messiah!

Hagiz has harsh words for the reluctant philanthropists who prefer to waste their money in the "conspicuous consumption" of fancy homes and vehicles and extravagant social lives, but treat the visiting emissaries with scorn and disrespect. He accuses them of giving more generously to local gentile charities than to their own needy brethren.

One issue raised by Rabbi Hagiz strikes me as particularly noteworthy. He mentions that in some of the larger European Jewish communities such as Amsterdam, Venice, and Livorno, there were in circulation *private* lists of worthy candidates for charitable donations. Such individual lists counteracted the established policy of having the funds collected and distributed by a centralized authority. Hagiz himself was opposed to this development which threatened the fairness of the allocations and weakened the authority of the recognized institutions.

Hagiz does not make it clear how this state of affairs arose. Perhaps it was the consequence of widespread suspicions regarding the efficiency or trustworthiness of the central agencies. It is also possible that political considerations played a part. The Jewish world in Eretz Yisra'el and abroad was, at that time, in the throes of a fierce struggle between the aggressive followers of the messianic pretender Shabbetai Zvi and his opponents over the control of Jewish religious and communal institutions. Under such circumstances, potential contributors would take special care to assign their donations only to like-minded individuals and organizations.

As usual, the issues confronted by the Jews in eighteenth-century Amsterdam have a distinctly familiar ring to them, and the intervening centuries have not diminished the resonance of the venerable Hebrew tomes.

SUGGESTIONS FOR FURTHER READING

Carlebach, Elisheva. (1990). *The Pursuit of Heresy: Rabbi Moses Hagiz and the Sabbatian Controversies.* New York: Columbia University Press.

38

‮܂‬

How Many Students Should There Be in a Class?*

$\mathcal{B}$eneath the foreboding clouds of the reductions to Alberta's education budgets, some Jewish members of the University of Calgary community have been convening over the past academic year to learn about Jewish attitudes towards public education as they emerge from selected passages in the Talmud, its commentaries and codes. The participants in the seminar were frequently astonished to discover how aptly the ancient Jewish sources anticipated issues that we had hitherto presumed were unique to our own era. Some of the items that we discussed might be of interest to the larger body of *JFP* readers and might be read with profit by our representatives in Edmonton and the local Community Council.

---

*"The Jewish School: Yesterday and Today." *The Jewish Free Press*, Calgary, May 19, 1994, 8–9.

The first remarkable fact that should be emphasized is that a system of universal elementary Jewish education has existed since the era of the Second Commonwealth. According to that ordinance, which remained revolutionary for centuries after its adoption among the Jews, schools must be established in every community to ensure that all Jewish children (at least, the males) have access to formal instruction.

The rabbis recommended six or seven as the age at which a child should begin attending classes, depending on his health and intellectual development. The sources delineate several stages for introducing the pupils to the world of formal learning: Initially, the student is gently encouraged to learn; later, he is "stuffed" with information in a non-coercive way; eventually, he is compelled to apply himself to studies even where this conflicts with his own inclinations.

Although the Talmud is quite explicit in discouraging the admission of children below the age of six, later generations of rabbis strove to reinterpret the sources so as to sanction a lowering of the minimum age to five years or less. They were probably trying to justify the prevailing practices in their own communities.

The Talmud has very precise ideas about the optimal ratios of students to teachers that the community can be forced to support: A single instructor can effectively teach twenty-five students. For forty children, an assistant must be hired (usually an advanced member of the class who can help his fellows with reviews and the like). For fifty pupils, a second teacher must be appointed. There is disagreement among the commentators about whether these numbers represent minimums, maximums, or averages. By all interpretations, they invite some instructive comparisons with the prevailing standards in both public and Jewish schools.

Some parents and educators will sympathize with the words of Rabbi Samuel Kidnover, writing in seventeenth-century Poland, when he laments that in his generation even ten students cannot be managed properly by one teacher, and that the Talmud's ra-

tios must be adjusted in recognition of the spiritual decline that
has occurred over the generations!

Closely related to the issue of teacher–student ratios are such
questions as: What happens if a community has too few school-
age children to warrant their own school? Under what circumstances should they be transported to an institution outside their
town or neighborhood? What consideration must be given in that
decision to the children's comfort and safety?

Another associated problem retains its contemporary and
local relevance: What happens if neighbours object to the establishing of a school in their vicinity on the grounds that it will create excessive noise or otherwise impair the esthetic quality of the
neighborhood?

Here the Jewish position is unmistakable: Although such considerations would normally justify the inhabitants of a residential
community in obstructing the establishment of businesses or other
institutions, in this case the pivotal importance of Jewish education overrides all other objections and the school must be permitted. Regrettably, this principle has not always been appreciated by some elements in our own community.

For those whose curiosity has been aroused, the Talmud and
its commentators deal with many other timely issues related to
elementary education, including: the use of corporal punishment;
tenure and grounds for the dismissal of teachers; the relative
merits of memorization *vs.* critical analysis, and much more.
Hopefully, some of you are already scurrying to your libraries to
learn more about the subject. For the others, I may return to the
subject in a future column.

39

Was Napoleon the Messiah?*

*A*s they mourn the recent passing of their beloved Rebbe, the Lubavitch Hasidim are also struggling to interpret the impact of their loss on the conviction upheld by many of them that Rabbi Schneerson was the Messiah. It is still too early to discern what directions the movement is going to be taking in the coming days.

This is not the first time in history that hasidic groups have been convinced of the Messiah's imminent advent. The best-known precedent was that of Rabbi Nahman of Bratslav, an enigmatic figure whose life was filled with torment and controversy. Rabbi Nahman is most vividly remembered for his legacy of allegorical stories, several of which involve quests for lost princesses, exchanged infants, and other images of a reality that has been knocked out of joint. The plots of the tales revolve around attempts

---

*"Rabbi Nahman, Napoleon and Other Messiahs." *The Jewish Free Press*, Calgary, June 30, 1994, 11.

to correct the respective anomalies that symbolize the exile of the Jewish people and of the divine presence, the *Shekhinah*. Some of the stories lack endings.

Most historians now believe that Nahman saw himself as the messianic figure who, through his arduous spiritual struggle, would succeed in setting right the dissonances of the Jewish fate. The devotion of his adherents was so intense that, when he died in 1810, they refused to transfer their allegiance to any successor. To this day the Bratslav Hasidim acknowledge Rabbi Nahman as their only Rebbe and are known as the Dead Hasidim.

The greatness of a Jewish religious leader was not the only factor that could give rise to the conviction that the Messianic era was about to arrive. At times this perception was ignited by momentous historical events. Such were the upheavals of the Napoleonic wars, especially his conquests of Poland and Russia.

In the eyes of some hasidic leaders, the French Emperor himself was identified as the vehicle through whom God would accomplish Israel's final redemption. It is not difficult to understand how such a belief could have arisen, as the Corsican soldier swept through country after country, tearing down the walls of the ghettos and removing the civil and social inequalities under which Jews had hitherto been living. Napoleon had even restored the glory of the ancient Jewish council, the Sanhedrin—though, to be sure, the assembly was exploited as a self-serving means of manipulating his Jewish citizens. He had even marched into Jerusalem proclaiming his desire to reestablish Jewish sovereignty over the Holy Land.

So taken was Rabbi Nahman of Bratslav by Napoleon's greatness that he was moved to argue that his common-born soul had, in reality, been substituted for one of more regal or aristocratic origins. Hasidic legend related that the image of another prominent hasidic supporter of the French emperor, Rabbi Menahem Mendel of Rymanov, could be seen beside Napoleon during his victorious battles.

Most of the Eastern European Jewish leadership—including the founder of the Chabad–Lubavitch movement, Rabbi Shneur Zalman of Liady—opposed the French ruler, whether out of loyalty to their local rulers or because they feared the breakdown of traditional values that would result from the spread of the ideals of the French Revolution.

Wherever their sympathies might lie, the rabbis believed that the terrible campaign between France and Russia was the "War of Gog and Magog" that would precede the ultimate deliverance. This restless mood of impending cataclysm among the hasidic leaders forms the background of the remarkable historical novel *Gog und Magog* (translated into English as *For the Sake of Heaven*) by the young Martin Buber.

The Messianic expectation of those days was reinforced by the imaginative use of numerical calculations (*gimatrias*) based on appropriate Hebrew texts to prove that the Messiah's arrival was preordained for the year 1810 (= the Hebrew year 5570, as intimated in the words "Sound (*TeQa'*) the great horn for our liberation,") then 1812, then 1814. Napoleon's opponents discerned an allusion to his defeat in the sounds of his name, which evoked the Hebrew root for fall (*napol*). It was told that the foremost hasidic masters of the generation once assembled in order to channel the spiritual power of their combined prayers towards the hastening of the redemption. They even declared that the Ninth of Av would henceforth be transformed from a day of grieving to one of joyous celebration.

Historical hindsight tells us that the apocalyptic fervor and anticipation of that age did not bear fruit. As always, we continue to hope that our own generation will enjoy more substantial success.

SUGGESTIONS FOR FURTHER READING

Buber, Martin. (1945). *For the Sake of Heaven*. 2nd ed., Philadelphia: Jewish Publication Society of America.

Minkin, Jacog Samuel. (1971). *The Romance of Hassidism*. New ed., Hollywood: Wilshire Book Co.

Sachar, Howard Morley. (1977). *The Course of Modern Jewish History*. Updated and expanded ed., New York: Dell [Delta].

40

☙

Why are Jews Concerned about Exploding Cows?*

$\mathcal{F}$or several years now, my better-paid colleague Dave Barry has been trying to alert the world to the dangers of exploding cows. In his columns, the Pulitzer Prize–winning writer has reprinted several newspaper reports about the imminent dangers posed by spontaneous bovine combustion.

Like many, I initially reacted to those articles with smug complacency. As an urban dweller and as a responsible citizen—even in a purported cow-town—I considered myself immune from that particular plague. Now, to my chagrin, it turns out that the phenomenon has had a pernicious and divisive effect on the world's Jewish community.

The current crisis originates in the digestive system of the cow, in a condition known to veterinary medicine as "displaced

---

*"Exploding Cows and the Jewish Question." *The Jewish Free Press*, Calgary, Sept. 29, 1994, 9.

abumasum." What this means is that acids released by the displacement of one of the cow's stomachs can lead to its being filled with gasses. The potentially lethal consequences of this condition are best left to the imagination.

Before you call in the bomb squad, be assured that the problem only affects one cow in two hundred fifty.

Fortunately, for the gentle beasts and for anyone who might find themselves in close proximity to them, there is a medical solution to the problem in a surgical procedure that attaches the errant stomach to its proper place.

Thus, all would have lived happily ever after were it not for the hyperactivity of the New York Jewish rumor-mill. In the middle of August this year—which coincides with the penitential month of Elul—word had it in Monsey and Boro Park that the surgical process included the stapling of the cows' stomachs. This, argued the pious gossips, would place the cows in the halakhic category of *tereifah*, suffering from a life-threatening injury. Therefore, the animal itself could not be kosher, nor could any of the dairy products that were derived from it.

As you might well imagine, this rumor ignited udder panic in the observant Jewish marketplace. No dairy item that was certified kosher could now be trusted to be so. Shops and restaurants that depended for their livelihoods on the sale of these products suffered severe financial losses.

On the other hand, dairies that could produce special certification that they used only non-volatile cattle that had not been subject to the offending medical treatment might now charge premium prices for that valuable assurance.

The Jewish religious community was set astir. The August 26 issue of the Yiddish weekly, *Algemeiner Journal*, devoted to the crisis a front-page headline, two editorials, and a cartoon—not to mention the paid official pronouncements by the Orthodox Union and other rabbinical organizations that decorated the pages. This, I might add, was in a newspaper that included not a single reference to the lesser crises in Rwanda, Bosnia, or Cuba.

At the convention of the distinguished Association of Orthodox Jewish Scientists many important topics were discussed—but the one that attracted a packed house was a clinical discussion by Rabbi Dr. Moshe Tendler (who is considered to be the leading authority on medical halakhic matters) about—you guessed it—the Cow Controversy.

Rabbi Tendler assured his audience that this was a nonissue, a problem that had been discussed and resolved by Jewish legal authorities hundreds of years ago. The farfetched allegations could only be accounted for as the results of sheer maliciousness, profound ignorance of the workings of Jewish law, or a blind determination to seek novel stringent rulings in the halakhah.

I am informed that the Jewish public is still suffering from shortages of certified kosher milk and dairy items.

Thus, we are provided with yet another reminder of how intricately our spiritual fates are entwined with those of our ruminant friends and their digestive problems, as was observed by the wise Solomon: *"For that which befalleth the sons of men befalleth beasts; even one thing befalleth them."*

41

⟨꒰

Are We Receiving Supernatural Messages?[*]

I am not normally a credulous or naive individual, and I usually react with a healthy dose of skepticism when I am confronted with alleged reports of supernatural occurrences

Nevertheless, there have been times when I found myself experiencing events that were so extraordinary that they set even a doubter like myself to wondering.

Several such experiences have befallen me over the years, especially in the course of my activities as *gabbai* at Calgary's Orthodox synagogue, House of Jacob-Mikveh Israel. Here I shall describe two such episodes precisely as I recall them. You are free to draw your own conclusions and interpret them as you choose.

---

[*]"Tales from the House of Jacob." *The Jewish Free Press*, Calgary, September 6, 1995, p. 14.

TALE #1: A DREAM FROM MOTHER

We have a congregant at our synagogue who is, to put it diplomatically, not very meticulous about attending the regular Sabbath morning services, although he is very dutiful about observing the *yahrzeit*s (the anniversaries of the deaths) of his parents.

Several years ago I noticed this congregant seated in the synagogue. As I greeted him, I commented to him that I presumed he
had a *yahrzeit* that week. He replied matter-of-factly that, although
today was not a *yahrzeit*, he did have a special reason for coming
to shul today.

It seems that he had a dream on the previous night in which
his late mother had appeared to him and instructed him to attend synagogue and recite Kaddish on her behalf.

Now, the shul kept a calendar in the office on which the rabbi
recorded the dates of all the congregants' *yahrzeit*s. I happened
to go in later to check the calendar and noticed that there was
indeed a listing of a *yahrzeit* for this congregant in question,
penned in our rabbi's handwriting.

When I approached the gentleman with this information, he
assured me that there must be some mistake, since he definitely
did not have any *yahrzeit* scheduled for several months.

I have never established who was right and who was mistaken
in this episode: Had the congregant forgotten the correct date of
his mother's *yahrzeit* (in which case the dream might have been a
reminder issuing from the subconscious levels of his memory);
or had an inexplicable error somehow crept into the synagogue
calendar?

TALE #2: BACK AT SINAI

The revelation of the Decalogue at Mount Sinai is recited twice
in the course of the annual Sabbath Torah-reading cycle: first, in
the Book of Exodus; and later, as part of Moses' final exhortations

to the people in the section *Va'et-hannan* in Deuteronomy Chapter 5. The latter account does not have the full dramatic build-up of the former, but it does also describe the momentous scene of how God spoke the words "*in the mount, out of the midst of the fire, of the cloud, and of the thick darkness, with a great voice.*"

The passage about the Sinai theophany makes up the fourth 'aliyah of the morning's Torah reading.

When the turn for reading *Va'et-hannan* came up two summers ago, the sun rose to dominate one of those wonderfully clear Calgary skies and continued to shine through the beginning of the service.

However, even as the third reader was approaching the reading platform, the sky above was starting to darken forbiddingly. In a few moments, it had become a dark grey and claps of thunder resounded in the background.

Just before the commencement of the fourth 'aliyah, I made a lighthearted observation to the congregation about how appropriate the natural sound effects were to the contents of our Torah reading. As if in reply, there came a sudden flash of lightning. The darkness, the thunder, and the lightning remained with us through to the conclusion of the 'aliyah, and then gradually set to dissipating.

By the conclusion of the Torah service, the sky had been restored to its original blue and not a cloud remained. There remained no visible indication of the remarkable commotion that had dominated the heavens just a few minutes earlier. Furthermore, throughout the entire display of pyrotechnics not a single drop of rain had fallen.

I repeat: both the above stories were presented here precisely as I recollect them. I shall leave it to my wise readers to speculate on their significance.

42

ॐ

Why Do Jews Publish Their Own Newspapers?*

*I*t is hard to believe that five years have elapsed since I graced the premier issue of the *Jewish Free Press* with an article about the tradition of Jewish journalism. On the occasion of this anniversary it appears fitting to return to that topic, surveying some of the roles that have been filled by Jewish periodical publications since their inception.

According to most bibliographers, the title of First Hebrew periodical goes to a collection entitled *P'ri Etz Hayyim* (*The Fruit of the Tree of Life*), whose first issue appeared in 1691 under the auspices of Amsterdam's renowned *Etz Hayyim* Yeshivah. It is hardly surprising that the pioneering Jewish publication, repre-

---

*"Informing and Creating: Historical Perspectives on Jewish Journalism." *The Jewish Free Press*, Calgary, November 16, 1995, p. 8.

senting the values and interests of a traditional religious society, should have been a scholarly journal that served as a showcase for the yeshivah's rabbinical students and their erudite discussions of Jewish law and exegesis.

Almost a century would pass before journalism would become a major force in Jewish public life. The movement for Jewish Enlightenment, under the guidance of Moses Mendelssohn and his disciples in central Europe, found, in the periodical format, an effective vehicle for the promulgation of their ideological objectives.

Mendelssohn and his followers took particular care to establish digests for the education of the masses. In their pages, simple Jews would be introduced to Hebrew summaries of the latest achievements of European culture and science. It was hoped that this educational enterprise would inspire the readers to seek out a more thorough involvement in the cultural life of their home countries, equipping them for the responsibilities of citizenship in the modern world.

The constraints of this medium came to be felt before long. By 1839, the distinguished Reform ideologue and scholar Abraham Geiger, though extolling the importance of Jewish magazines as expressions of the collective spirit of their time and as miniature communities or social movements, admitted that Hebrew journals no longer had much to offer in the way of scientific education for the masses. The ancient tongue was poorly equipped to deal with modern technical subjects and, by Geiger's time, most of his Jewish compatriots were able to access such resources in German. He concluded that Jewish journalism, especially in the Hebrew language, would make a more valuable contribution if it confined itself to exploring specifically Jewish issues.

Indeed, the next phase of Jewish journalistic endeavor excelled in the exchange of ideas and scholarly advances in the fields of Jewish literature and culture.

A milestone was reached in 1856 with the appearance of the

first Hebrew daily, *Ha-maggid,* in Lyck, East Prussia. Under the editorial direction of David Gordon, a remarkable figure equally at home in traditional Judaism and European culture, this publication was initially intended to provide European Jews with information about the world at large, but it quickly evolved into a forum for debate and discussion of the weighty questions confronting the Jewish community.

The choice of Hebrew as the newspaper's language of discourse was at first justified on pragmatic grounds, as the only means to maintain bonds with Jews throughout the Diaspora. However *Ha-maggid's* scholarly supplement became an important instrument in the revival of Hebrew nationalism, which had been suffering grave setbacks under the ethos of the German Reformers. *Ha-maggid's* pages even hosted the first Hebrew novels (by Abraham Mapu and others), setting in motion a process that would facilitate the revival of Hebrew as a modern spoken language.

Between 1860 and 1863, many new Hebrew newspapers began to proliferate throughout the Jewish world, including: *Ha-mevasser* in Galicia, *Ha-karmel* in Vilna, *Ha-melitz* in Odessa, *Ha-levanon* in Jerusalem.

In varying degrees, each of these journals underwent the same transitions in the perception of their editorial mission: Beginning as simple instruments for education and information, they took on the role of Jewish town halls for the communication of opinions on the controversies of the day. The zenith of their success was achieved when they became (sometimes unwittingly) active contributors and participants in the creation of a dynamic new Jewish culture.

It is to be hoped that in its own modest way the *JFP* will follow in the classic traditions of Jewish journalism, providing not only accurate news reports and a place for communal debate, but actually participating in the fashioning of the Jewish culture of future generations.

SUGGESTIONS FOR FURTHER READING

Kressel, G. (1977). "Attempts at Making a Bibliographical Index of the Hebrew Press." In *Sixth Congress of Jewish Studies in Jerusalem.* World Union of Jewish Studies, pp. 425–35.

Salmon, Yosef. (1991). "The Emergence of a Jewish Collective Consciousness in Eastern Europe During the 1860's and 1870's." *AJS Review* 16: 1–2: 107–32.

C H A P T E R

43

⤫

What's in Today's Mail?*

*F*or those of you who may not be keeping count, my previous column was my one-hundredth in the *JFP*. I think that should entitle me to a brief vacation. Unfortunately, even if my editor did not keep me shackled to my desk, I could still not afford to miss an issue, lest my poor children be forced to go another two weeks without food or Nikes.

By way of compromise, I would like to fulfill a long-standing dream of mine, by submitting a column that I do not actually have to write. No, I am not going to offer summer reruns by reprinting old and dated material. Rather, I wish to fill up a page with selections from letters that I have received from my loyal readers.

I do indeed get many letters, mostly via email, in response to the archive of my articles that is now posted on the World Wide Web of the Internet.

---

*"Gone Fishin'." *The Jewish Free Press*, Calgary, May 29, 1997, pp. 8–9.

One peculiar consequence of this situation is that my corre-spondents do not necessarily deal with current material. Often they are reacting to some unguarded comment of mine that was originally published ten years ago and has since been forgotten. In many cases, the writers do not even bother to indicate which of the hundreds of items on my website they are referring to.

My favorites tend to be the most irate. And make no mistake about it, there are plenty of hostile souls lurking about the Internet. You would think that a column like mine, largely devoted to obscure quotations from old Hebrew books, would not have much potential for antagonizing anybody. But remember, I am dealing with *religion*, one of our foremost sources of strife and intolerance.

Thus, we find the following letter, from an obviously learned individual with an Arabic name, reacting to my 1991 article about the Jews of Baghdad:

> it was shown yure jewish is not emportantat to say baghdad from old time its lland for jewish awant to say
> 1 all jewish are layer
> 2 all jewish book is rong
> 3 all jewish are murder

(English translation will be provided on request).

I should note that letters like the above are counterbalanced by others, like the following:

> Hi. I am Muslim and believe that we have all one source and wor-ship the same God, or Allah, or what ever you call him. Thanks for this information. It is realy good to understand your point of view.

Nor is my hate-mail restricted to members of other faiths. Today's Jewish world has enough internal frictions to incite letters like the following one, from an Israeli Orthodox sage who is clearly irritated by something that was said in an old article of mine about Purim:

> I read your Purim Torah on the "development" of Purim. You ex-hibit a profound ignorance of Talmudic method, Jewish history and

just about every other topic you touch on. Or, to put it in words that even a nitwit like you would understand:
you're full of [four-letter word for fecal matter]

An interesting recent trend is for extremely religious Jews to protest my inclusion of more moderate Orthodoxy (of the Orthodox Union or Yeshivah University varieties) as if they were *really* Orthodox.

And, if mere scholarship can rile folks up, imagine what sensitive territory I am treading on when I venture into spoofs and satire! Several readers were offended by a fictitious letter I once composed arguing Pharaoh's perspective on the Exodus story. Others objected to my story about a supposed Israeli sale of unused surplus vowels to Poland. They were expecting (without bothering to read the actual article) that it must be one of those tasteless ethnic put-downs, which, of course, it was not. Alternatively, some alert fans wrote to protest that a similar article is in circulation in the American military about the Croatian language, and that I ought to stamp out that plagiarism.

Of course there are those who turn to me for intellectual guidance and spiritual advice, as in the following:

I will like prices and shipping information on shabbat candles. or if you have a cadalog you can send me.

A bit closer to my competencies is the following:

I have been with my boyfriend for a while and I really want to learn more about his religion . . . His parents are a little strict about my being a Christian. Please help me.

And there are these frequent requests for assistance:

Hello. I am a student at the . . . and I have to write a report on . . . Please send me all the information by Thursday!

The next item evokes some fascinating speculations about the writer's motives:

What exactly goes on in a Jewish wedding? I need to know by Wed.

I have a special weakness for appeals of the following type, which are surprisingly plentiful:

> Can you direct me to a place where I can learn exactly what the Talmud is, and how would it benefit a born-again Christian to learn and/or study the Talmud?

Or:

> Any tips on teaching Passover to 4-years-old Catholic Hispanics?

Well, I have done it. I have let you compose this week's column for me. Just keep those letters flowing in, the angrier the better, and maybe I will be able to extend this vacation by a few more weeks.

44

ॐ

How Did Medieval Synagogues Try to Attract Worshippers?*

*E*ven a relatively small Jewish community like that of Calgary offers potential worshippers a formidable variety of options, covering most of the main North American denominations. The ability to choose a synagogue that fits our religious or esthetic sensibilities is something that modern Jews have learned to take for granted.

In fact, the coexistence of multiple synagogues in a single community has not always been an accepted norm. In the modern era, it is symptomatic of a worldview that regards religious affiliation as a matter of personal choice. Scarcely a century ago, special legislation was needed to allow Samson Raphael Hirsch to withdraw his Orthodox minority from the predominantly Reform community of Frankfurt am Main; even that was decided

---

*"Membership Drives." *The Jewish Free Press*, Calgary, September 18, 1997, pp. 10–11.

with great reluctance and was not followed by most Orthodox Jews in Germany.

Although the Talmud contains occasional references to synagogues that were owned by private individuals, professional guilds, or immigrants from other lands, in most cases the synagogues were owned and administered by the Jewish municipal councils. In medieval times, the policy was even more pronounced. The local communities were usually insistent that their synagogue be the exclusive place of worship for all residents of the town, a situation that frequently demanded moderation and compromise from both the rabbinic leadership and their flocks.

Occasionally, even during the middle ages, there were historical and demographic factors that brought about the toleration of two or more congregations in one town. Such was true in the cosmopolitan Jewish society of Egypt during the eleventh and twelfth centuries. While the historical roots and political circumstances linked them to the Holy Land, the Egyptian communities were situated at the crossroads of a larger international Jewish populace, most of which was subject to the authority of the Babylonian academies headed by the scholars known as the *Ge'onim*. The result was that most of the larger Egyptian cities and towns hosted two synagogues, worshipping respectively according to the Palestinian and Babylonian rites.

Over the years, a competitive spirit came to characterize the relations between the two congregations as each strove to attract worshippers from among the traders and immigrants who moved to their communities. Although the modern institution of dues-paying synagogue membership did not exist at the time, there were felt to be important advantages, in the size of voluntary pledges that could be expected and in the prestige that would cling to the synagogue's leadership, that promoted a phenomenon analogous to a modern membership campaign. Looking back at such bygone rivalries can be both instructive and amusing.

The Babylonians seem to have fired the opening volley in the competition. Invoking the scholarly prestige of the learned

Ge'onim who stood at their helm in Baghdad, they offered to bestow honorific titles, certified by the Ga'on himself, upon new arrivals to their communities.

It did not take long for the Palestinian synagogues to follow suit, invoking the authority of the revered head of the academy of Jerusalem, with all its sacred associations.

The Palestinians had additional tricks up their sleeves. In their possession were some of the most ancient and pedigreed Torah scrolls and Biblical codices in existence, written by the foremost experts on the text of the Hebrew scriptures. Furthermore, they could offer an advantage that always holds an attraction to at least some synagogue-goers: Their services were shorter. This factor was a consequence of their practice of reading the Torah over a cycle that lasted three and a half years rather than in a single year as in the Babylonian custom. The individual readings on each Shabbat were correspondingly much briefer.

To add to their appeal, the Palestinian synagogue leaders permitted children to chant the Torah readings. We all know how effective that can be in drawing proud parents and grandparents into the synagogue.

The Babylonians, unable to challenge their rivals' claim to a quicker service, packaged their own drawn-out services as an advantage. They directed their appeal to those who preferred an intense, well-crafted worship experience. With this in mind, they advertised that those who attended their synagogues could expect to hear the Torah chanted not by inexperienced youths, but by their most accomplished adult vocalists.

SUGGESTIONS FOR FURTHER READING

Goitein, S. D. (1967–). *A Mediterranean Society*. Berkeley, Los Angeles and London: University of California Press.

45

ॐ

Why Is Everybody Upset with the Gabbai?*

$\mathcal{F}$or a longer time than I care to measure, I have been serving my synagogue in the capacity of *gabbai*. As we shall see, the precise terms of reference for this position are not easy to define, but in general they involve making sure that the synagogue is properly set up for services and assigning roles to the participants in those services.

As with several of the terms that we now use to designate communal functionaries, the current usage of the word *gabbai* bears little resemblance to its original significance. The term derives from the Hebrew root meaning "to collect money" and, indeed, in talmudic literature that is how it is employed consistently, whether with reference to tax collectors in the employ of the government, or to administrators of the Jewish communal charities.

---

*"Beadle-Mania." *The Jewish Free Press*, Calgary, October 23, 1997, p. 8.

In either capacity, the ancient gabbai was not the most welcome of visitors. Furthermore, suspicions naturally arose that they might be skimming off the top of their *pushkas* (charity boxes). Even though procedures were put in place to preclude such distrust (for example, by having them work in teams), the Mishnah still advises against accepting personal donations from gabbais and tax collectors for fear that their contributions were not theirs to give.

The gabbai's duties, as currently defined, overlap those of several different functionaries in medieval Jewish society.

In Arabic-speaking communities, the distribution of tasks in the synagogue service, such as the leading of the prayers and the reading from scripture, was usually a prerogative of the *muqaddam*, the official head of the local Jewish community whose authority was acknowledged by the government.

In the hierarchical societies of yore, the privileges of leading prayers or reading from scripture were taken very seriously as confirmations of one's status in the congregation, and the rabbis of those communities were faced with frequent complaints about alleged slights by synagogue officials.

It was not merely a matter of who did or did not get an aliyah to the Torah. Respected individuals were acknowledged in special blessings, and the honorees were adamant that their names be recited along with a full and precise sequence of honorific titles. One prominent donor prepared written texts to insure that he would always be identified as "pride of the priests, delight of the nobles, trustee of the merchants, eye of the congregation, light of Israel and Judah"—in that exact order.

Even in our world of democratic and egalitarian ideals, the synagogue can often serve to highlight distinctions of communal status. A contemporary anthropological study of synagogue dynamics focuses on the gabbai's role as a power broker within the community: "The gabbai, as keeper and dispenser of *kibbudim* [honorific tasks], thus handles what is perhaps one of the group's most essential properties. As such he shares in its power and importance."

On the other hand, some of the gabbai's more menial chores parallel those of the medieval *shammash*, a general factotum (similar to a church sexton) whose list of responsibilities reflects the centrality of synagogue to Jewish communal life. These responsibilities could extend to some unlikely areas, such as that of the town crier who stood atop the synagogue roof to announce items ranging from the decisions of the court to the approach of the Sabbath, punctuating his proclamations with a shofar blast or the bang of a mallet (by virtue of which he was known as the *schulklopfer*).

For all that the shammash occupied one of the more humble rungs in the synagogue hierarchy, the occupants of that office had a reputation for acting like royalty, and in some places, such as the *kloyz* (the elite, small synagogue) of Vilna, individuals would actually pay for the privilege. An Egyptian contract from 1099 had to stipulate that disrespect for the muqaddam or members of the congregation would be considered grounds for dismissal from the office. The frequency with which similar warnings were repeatedly issued by the Jewish councils in Poland and Lithuania demonstrate clearly how difficult they were to enforce.

Astute readers of this column may have noted that all my recent articles have contained references to practices and records from medieval Egypt. Our intimate knowledge of that community, including the behavior of its *shammashim*, is of course based on the thousands of records preserved in the Cairo *Genizah*, which is presently celebrating the hundredth anniversary of its discovery.

It is therefore timely to observe that if the modern successors of those synagogue functionaries had had their way, those precious records might not have survived at all. For when Prof. Solomon Schechter arrived in Cairo to collect the Genizah's manuscripts and ship them to England, he noted that the documents had a tendency to disappear. In an 1887 letter written from Cairo to the librarian at Cambridge, he summarized the lamentable situation:

The beadel & other infernal scoundrels are helping me to clear away the rubbish and the printed matter. I have constantly to bakeshish them, but still they are stealing many good things and sell them to the dealers in antiquities.

As a practicing "beadel," I find it humbling to trace my craft back to such enterprising and colourful scoundrels.

SUGGESTIONS FOR FURTHER READING

Abrahams, Israel. (1969). *Jewish Life in the Middle Ages*. Temple Books, New York: Atheneum.

Baron, Salo Witttmayer. (1972). *The Jewish Community: Its History and Structure to the American Revolution*. Morris Loeb Series, Westport: Greenwood Press.

Goitein, S. D. (1967–). *A Mediterranean Society*. Berkeley, Los Angeles and London: University of California Press.

Heilman, Samuel C. (1976). *Synagogue Life*. Chicago: University of Chicago Press.

Schechter, Solomon. (1996). "Schechter Shares Cairo Secrets." *Genizah Fragments* 32: 6.

46

৵

Why Do Cantors
Have Such an
Unsavory Reputation?*

$\mathcal{A}$s I observed in my previous column, the titles that we customarily assign to synagogue and communal functionaries have undergone some curious transformations over the years. This claim applies as well to the term *hazzan*, which we use to designate a cantor. The word actually means supervisor and originally denoted the lay leader of a community or synagogue, an office approximating that of a modern synagogue president.

At any rate, the current usage has roots that probably hearken back to the days of the Palestinian Talmud, an era when the functions of synagogue administration and leading prayers were carried out by the same individuals.

There were of course other titles that were borne by the ancient cantors, such as *sheliah tzibbur* (representative of the com-

---

*"Cantor-Culture." *The Jewish Free Press*, Calgary, November 6, 1997, p. 8.

munity); *payyat* or *payyetan* (poet); or *karova* (the one who brings people close to God). The latter two expressions, employed primarily in the Land of Israel, refer not only to their bearers' ability to *recite* the prayers, but also to their talent for *composing* poetic renditions of the liturgy that interwove themes from the day's Biblical readings. The immense bodies of literary work that have come down to us from the great *payyetanim* of yore attest to their astounding erudition in all facets of Jewish religious lore.

This favorable reputation was not always inherited by their successors in medieval and modern times. As the Babylonian preference for fixed liturgical texts prevailed over the Palestinian tradition of poetic improvisation, scholarship and erudition ceased to be viewed as indispensable to the cantor's job description. Emphasis was placed on beauty of voice and on musical proficiency.

Ultimately, the cantor came to be an artist, exhibiting many of the virtues and shortcomings that are typical of the artistic personality.

Documents from medieval Cairo testify that, like operatic virtuosi of later generations, some cantors were plagued by a weakness for the bottle. Maimonides had to deal more than once with the problem of inebriated cantors. In one responsum, he was asked what do to about a *hazzan* who was in the habit of staggering into the synagogue, insulting the presiding cantor, taking hold of the Torah scroll, and dropping it. A second query addressed to him dealt with a group of intoxicated cantors who would obstruct the services with rowdy behavior, which persisted even while a distressed child was struggling to recite his *haftarah*.

The inability of some cantors to understand the words of the prayers they were intoning became proverbial. A younger contemporary of Maimonides, the Spanish Hebrew poet Judah Al-Harizi, composed a satirical poem about the bloopers committed by a *hazzan* whose pomposity was matched only by his ignorance. Al-Harizi provides a lengthy catalogue of passages in the prayer book and Bible that were mangled by the cantor's sloppiness and inability to understand what he was reciting, though he was adorned with all the external signs of wisdom and piety, gyrating emotionally with beard and fringes dragging on the ground. The congregation, bored and confused by the drawn-out renderings of cryptic liturgical poems, eventually gave up and went home to sleep, without having fulfilled the essential obligations of prayer.

The same disparagement of the cantor's craft resurfaces centuries later in Poland, in earnest pronouncements by leading rabbinical authorities. Rabbi Solomon Luria lamented the fact that in their quest for esthetically pleasing *hazzanim*, the lay congregational leadership frequently ignored the rabbis' strictures about the learnedness and piety that ought to be indispensable to the position. In a similar vein, Rabbi Ephraim Luntschitz caustically protested the cantors' tendency to devote more energy to artistic pyrotechnics than to conveying the actual meaning of the words that they were reciting.

In 1623, a Lithuanian rabbinical council was impelled to set strict limitations on the number of tunes that could be included in the services. Rabbi Benjamin Solnik described the situation as follows:

> They cannot read even a single verse from the Torah with its correct cantillation and punctuation, since the communities prefer to appoint *hazzanim* on the basis of their abilities in chanting the prayers and *kedushah*s beautifully and at length. . . . The longer the cantor sings, the more they enjoy it, even if he does not know any of the regulations governing the prayers or scriptural chanting. For this reason, the cantors pay no attention to those laws and do not prepare themselves adequately for an expert public reading in accordance with the requirements of the law.

But not all cantors are of that unsavory ilk, as we learn from the following anecdote in the Talmud:

> In a time of drought, the saintly Rabbi Hiyya was invited to lead the congregational supplications for rain. As he recited the words "who causes the wind to blow," a breeze was felt. When he got to

the expression "who causes the rain to fall," rain indeed began to fall. As he was about to conclude with the blessing "who revives the dead," the earth began to quake, and it was only through direct supernatural intervention that the pious sage could be prevented from hastening the resurrection before its proper time.

Such, indeed, is the formidable power of a cantor who can utter the prayer with sincerity and understanding.

SUGGESTIONS FOR FURTHER READING

Goitein, S. D. (1967–). *A Mediterranean Society*. Berkeley, Los Angeles and London: University of California Press.

Schirmann, H. (1966). *Ha-Shirah Ha-'Ivrit bi-Sfarad Uvi-Frovans*. Jerusalem and Tel-Aviv: Dvir and Mossad Bialik.

Shulman, Nisson E. (1986). *Authority and Community: Polish Jewry in the Sixteenth Century*. New York and Hoboken: Ktav and Yeshiva University Press.

47

ॐ

When Does a Movement Become a Sect?*

$\mathcal{E}$ven out here in Alberta, it is not quite possible to remain insulated from the interdenominational factionalism emanating from Israel and the larger Jewish communities.

Through our history, Judaism has been able to tolerate an impressive degree of theological disagreement and personal rivalry. If the disputes were confined to such theoretical issues, then the current contention would probably not go beyond the level of nasty name-calling. Where matters get serious for Jews is when they begin to impinge on religious practice. Thus, the most acute controversies in Jewish public life have very tangible consequences in determining whether individuals may or may not marry into the Jewish community.

---

*"Family Feuds." *The Jewish Free Press*, Calgary, December 4, 1997, pp. 4, 11.

Controversies of this sort have arisen in previous eras of Jewish history and have been handled in different ways. The Talmud, for example, records several instances in which entire towns and provinces were declared unmarriageable because of questions that arose concerning their genealogical purity or their failure to conform to the accepted religious standards. In at least one case, it is reported that the rejected community abandoned their Judaism altogether.

Not all disputes were treated so unyieldingly. A notable case is described in the Mishnah involving the first-century schools of Shammai and Hillel.

The controversy concerned a complex convergence of several features of Jewish family law, including levirate marriage,[1] incest, and polygamy. The upshot was that a certain constellation of circumstances could arise in which the school of Shammai would require a widow to enter into a levirate marriage with her brother-in-law (or undergo the *halitzah* release ceremony), whereas the school of Hillel would forbid such a marriage as incestuous and its offspring as *mamzerim*, forbidden to marry into the Jewish community.

After outlining the controversy between the two schools, the Mishnah proceeds to relate the following: "Even though one school forbids and the others permit, these declare unfit and these declare fit, nevertheless the school of Shammai did not hesitate to take wives from the school of Hillel, nor vice versa. Furthermore, in all their disagreements over purity and impurity, they did not refrain from partaking of one another's pure foods and vessels."

Now this is surely a remarkable instance of halakhic pluralism, where two opposing camps, divided over fundamental issues of marriageability, agreed to acknowledge the legitimacy of positions

---

1. Levirate marriage is the biblical institution, described in Deuteronomy 25: 5–10, in which a childless widow is required to marry her deceased husband's brother, or perform a ceremony of release, or *halitzah*.

with which they personally disagreed, even to the point of permitting unions that would, in their view, produce *mamzerim*. True, the Talmud tempers this liberality when it explains that what the schools were really doing was scrupulously warning one another about problematic family histories of prospective brides, in order to prevent them from transgressing their respective prohibitions. Even so, this indicates a degree of mutual respect that is not easily imaginable in our present religious climate.

A similar example may be cited from a different historical context. Medieval Jewry was split into two main movements: the Rabbinites, who accepted the authority of the oral tradition as embodied in the Talmud; and the Karaites, who rejected the Talmud in favour of direct reliance on the Bible. The disagreements between these two streams extended to every imaginable area of private and communal life.

Both flavors of Judaism were prominently represented in medieval Egypt. From records in the Cairo *Genizah* we obtain a surprising picture: Although the ideological spokesmen of the two factions missed few opportunities to attack the beliefs and practices of their opponents, we find that, in all matters of communal activity and social interaction, there existed a remarkable measure of cooperation.

Then as now, the welfare of the Jews of Jerusalem was a concern that unified Jews of divergent leanings. Several urgent fund drives were initiated in the twelfth century in order to rescue the holy city from its financial plight. For purposes of these campaigns, the Rabbinates and Karaites temporarily set aside their differences and worked in harmony. This magnanimous approach was encouraged by Egypt's foremost rabbinical leader, Maimonides, whose outspoken opposition to the doctrines of Karaism was balanced by his compassion for the Karaites as people and as Jews.

Of particular interest are the marriage contracts (*ketubbahs*) that testify to the relative frequency of intermarriage between the two sects, even in the families of their most prominent leaders. Because of the radical differences in their respective observances, guidelines had to be set out explicitly in the *ketubbahs* so as to minimize violations of the spouses' sensibilities. One clause, for example, stipulates whether the meat that is brought into the house must conform to the *kashrut* stringencies of the Karaites or of the Rabbinites; another insists that no candles be lit on Shabbat, out of respect for the Karaite prohibition against having any fire in the house on the sabbath. Both parties obligate themselves not to desecrate their spouse's holidays (which might fall on different dates). Some documents speak of one of the partners converting to the other's denomination for the sake of the marriage.

When some of these *ketubbahs* were displayed at an exhibition in Israel this year, they raised several eyebrows from both the secularist and orthodox camps. Similarly, when I recently gave a talk about the history of Jewish sectarianism, it did not take long for my audience to ask me about how those precedents ought to be applied to our contemporary denominational disputes: Should the differences between the Orthodox and Reform be likened to those between the Pharisees and Sadducees, or the Rabbinites and Karaites, who utterly rejected their opponents' claim to Jewish authenticity? Or should they be viewed as a "dispute for the sake of Heaven" as between the schools of Shammai and Hillel, or between medieval rationalists and mystics, where differing religious outlooks did not extend to the delegitimization of their rivals?

With characteristic boldness, I replied that I prefer to wait another century or two until I can see the matters in their proper historical perspective.

SUGGESTIONS FOR FURTHER READING

Friedman, Mordechai Akiva. (1980). *Jewish Marriage in Palestine: A Cairo Geniza Study*. Tel-Aviv and New York: Tel-Aviv University and the Jewish Theological Seminary of America.

Goitein, S. D. (1967–). *A Mediterranean Society*. Berkeley, Los Angeles and London: University of California Press.

CHAPTER
48

✺

What Is It Like to
Be Spiritually Rootless?*

$\mathcal{M}$odern religious movements struggle with a delicate tension
between the contemporary focus on individual expression and the
requirements of conformity to standards of orthodoxy. In recent
months, the Canadian public has had occasion to observe such a
struggle over the unorthodox pronouncements by new moderator
of the United Church of Canada.

From my vantage point in an academic department of religious
studies, I try, to the best of my abilities, to avoid personal involvement in such questions. Nevertheless, I find myself approached
with increasing frequency by individuals who have been stirred
to question their received religious traditions. For all my reluctance to missionize or tamper with people's faith, I do not always
succeed in wriggling out of these encounters.

*"The Tragedy of Spiritual Rootlessness." *The Jewish Free Press*, Calgary,
March 26, 1998, pp. 12–13.

A recent interview of this sort involved a young man who was seriously considering conversion to Judaism. As it turned out, he had Jewish ancestry (on his father's side), and had even spent time in Israel, though he had been raised as a Christian. Unable to accept the beliefs in Jesus' divinity or the virgin birth, he had arrived at a realization that his authentic religious identity must be as a Jew. Towards that end, he was ready to take on the yoke of the commandments.

In spite of my misgivings, this situation seemed to hold some initial promise. As our conversation proceeded, however, certain statements started to raise alarms. First of all, he made a sharp distinction between the revealed laws of the Bible, and that oral tradition that he did not acknowledge.

Now this, in itself, was not an insurmountable obstacle. I recalled the Talmud's story about Hillel the Elder, who, unlike his less patient colleague Shammai, had accepted a potential convert on precisely those terms, in the hope (subsequently borne out) that the candidate could eventually be persuaded to accept the authority of both the written and oral Torahs.

However, as we continued our chat, he confided that his rejection of Jesus being the "son of God" did not imply denial of his role as *Messiah*. Once I had established that he was convinced of this point, I told him that the matter was to all intents and purposes closed: No rabbi, knowing of such views, would agree to accept him as a convert.

While this may have neatly answered the immediate question, it was clear that it did not solve his existential personal crisis. After all, he no longer saw himself as a Christian and was unlikely to feel at home in a Christian community. Since religion is not an affair for isolated individuals, I found myself upset by his predicament.

As is my scholarly custom, I tried to think of historical parallels to his situation and was surprised at how readily they came to mind.

There was, for example, the case of the ancient Ebionites. They were mentioned by the fourth-century church historian Eusebius as a pernicious heresy, allegedly founded by an individual named Ebion. Among their eccentric doctrines was a commitment to observe the laws of the Torah, including the Sabbath, and a rejection of the claims that Jesus was son of God or born of a virgin.

Scholars now realize that there was never a person named Ebion. The Hebrew word, which means poor, was in reality used to refer to the simple lifestyle followed by the remnants of the original Jewish–Christian church of Jerusalem led by Peter and members of Jesus' family. While the mainstream of Christianity had followed a different course, becoming an overwhelmingly gentile religion defined by its faith in the godhood of Jesus, this small sect precariously maintained its identity as a movement within Judaism, distinguished only in their belief in the Messiahship of Jesus but rejected by the vast majority of Jews and Christians alike. By Eusebius' time, orthodox Christianity found it unimaginable that a group of that description could be designated Christian at all. Unable to find a place in either Judaism or Christianity, the Ebionites gradually dwindled and were virtually forgotten by history.

Similar tragedies befell some of the Marranos of Spain and Portugal. Though many of them strove stalwartly to maintain their Jewish identities secretly under the threat of the Inquisition, they had no access to authentic Jewish texts or tradition and fashioned the best substitute they could on the basis of their knowledge of the Old Testament.

When opportunities did present themselves for Marranos to flee to more tolerant lands in Italy or Northern Europe, they were frequently shocked by the disparity between their previous expectations of Judaism and what they encountered in living, breathing Jewish communities that did not live solely according to the Bible but according to a venerable historical tradition.

This led to the appearance of spiritually rootless personalities who no longer felt at home in either their old or new religions. The most famous example was probably Uriel d'Acosta (1585–1640), whose unsuccessful attempts to fit in to the Amsterdam Jewish community reportedly culminated in his suicide (a tragedy that has been portrayed in several plays and operas). The excommunication of Spinoza should probably seen, at least in part, as a product of similar circumstances. In fact, historians have suggested that the presence of so many misfits in Europe may have been one of the chief factors in the rise of the Enlightenment in the seventeenth century.

A more recent manifestation of this phenomenon seems to be arising out of the success of the Messianic Judaism movement. Although their message is clearly a disingenuous cloak for a straightforward missionary campaign, they do call for their adherents to embrace Christianity *as Jews*, including a commitment to the religious commandments (particularly those that are susceptible to Christian allegorization). It appears that many of the Jews who have been drawn to the movement have been taking that message much more seriously than was intended by their self-professed "rabbis" whose initial intention was simply to deceive the uninformed into thinking that they were entering a synagogue rather than an evangelical church.

At any rate, this process is leading to the emergence of a distinctive stream on the contemporary Christian scene that affirms the validity of the Jewish covenant as embodied in the observance of the commandments of the Old Testament. The fact that Messianic Jews are observing Shabbat and *kashrut* does not dovetail with the standard Christian notion that the Torah was rendered obsolete with the coming of Jesus. This is clearly not to the liking of many of the conventional Christians who initiated this project, and it is not yet clear whether this will lead to the evolution of yet another orphaned religious movement.

The spiritual statelessness of such groups and individuals—whether they be Ebionites, Marranos or Messianic Jews—is on the whole a tragic phenomenon.

If nothing else, it might inspire us to be more compromising when our individualism causes us to chafe at the restrictions of community standards. For belonging to even an imperfect community can be preferable to not belonging at all.

SUGGESTIONS FOR FURTHER READING

Pritz, Ray. (1988). Nazarene Jewish Christianity: From the end of the New Testament period until its disappearance in the fourth century, Studia post-Biblica; vol. 37. Jerusalem and Leiden: Magnes Press, Hebrew University and E. J. Brill.

Roth, Cecil. (1966). *A History of the Marranos.* Harper Torchbooks, The Temple Library. New York: Harper & Row.

Schwarz, Leo W. (1963). *Memoirs of My People: Jewish Self-portraits from the 11th to the 20th centuries.* New York: Schocken Books.

Wilson, S. G. (1995). *Related Strangers: Jews and Christians, 70–170* C.E. Minneapolis, MN: Fortress Press.

PART
IV

Jews and Others

49

☙

Is Abraham Only
Our Father?*

It is common for Jews to affectionately refer to the first Patriarch as *Avraham Avinu*, Abraham our Father. But is Abraham so certainly *our father* alone?

If we approach the figure of Abraham from the perspective of later Jewish exegesis, we note a number of additions to Abraham's biography that seem peculiar and unwarranted by the biblical text. A more careful examination of the circumstances reveals that some of these added details reflect some very heated controversies that preoccupied the Jewish commentators through the generations in their contacts with competing religious outlooks.

As an example, let us look at an oft-quoted rabbinic tradition to the effect that

---

*"Abraham Our Father—and Theirs?" *The Jewish Star*, Calgary/Edmonton, December 1987, 15—16C.

Our father Abraham observed the entire Torah before it was given
to Israel, as it is written (Genesis 26:5) "Because that Abraham
obeyed my voice and kept my charge, my commandments, my stat-
utes and my laws" (Mishnah, end of *Kiddushin*).

This claim, which was extended to apply to the other patriarchs
as well, gave rise to all sorts of difficulties.

For example, in Genesis 18:7–8, we find Abraham hurrying to
prepare a meal for his guests that consisted of "a calf tender and
good . . . curd, and milk"—hardly an ideal menu for a kosher meal.
Similarly, Jacob's marriage to two sisters should have been prohibited according to subsequent Torah legislation.

It is possible to interpret the verse cited by the Mishnah in a
limited way (as referring, for example, to the basic laws of humanity and justice embodied in the "seven precepts of the sons
of Noah"). The Mishnah, however, insists on applying it to "the
entire Torah." Why did the rabbis insist on making life so difficult for themselves with their sweeping statement?

ABRAHAM IN CHRISTIANITY

A possible explanation might be found in an exposition by a Jew
who wrote towards the end of the first century C.E.

Saul of Tarsus—who was to become known to the world as
Paul, the leading ideologist of early Christianity—made considerable use of the model of Abraham to support his own belief that
the observance of laws is not conducive to spiritual salvation.

As developed in the fourth chapter of his Epistle to the Ro-
mans, Paul points to Genesis 15:6: "And [Abraham] believed in
the Lord and he counted it to him for righteousness." Did
Abraham, Paul argues, not live before the receiving of the Torah?
Since he did, he could not have observed its laws. Nevertheless,
God deems him righteous!

In a typically "midrashic" exposition, Paul notes that the verse
in question was placed before the account of Abraham's circum-

cision precisely in order to emphasize that circumcision (which for Paul represents the totality of ritual observance) is not a requirement for righteousness or salvation, which are earned through belief and trust in God.

In view of such claims made by the early Church about Abraham, it is perfectly understandable that the rabbis would feel it essential to assert that he was a truly Jewish figure who had observed the precepts of the Torah even before they were made mandatory by the revelation at Mount Sinai.

ABRAHAM IN ISLAM

The Christians were not the only group who claimed to be the true successors of Abraham. With the rise of Islam in the seventh century, the Arabs also came to emphasize their descent from the Patriarch.

Interestingly, the descriptions of Abraham's life as found in the Qur'an are strongly influenced by Jewish traditions. They incorporate many events not mentioned in the biblical accounts, such as Abraham's disputes with his idol-worshipping father and his conflict with the wicked king Nimrod who cast him into a fiery furnace. All this provides ample proof that Muhammed had Jewish teachers.

The story of the *akedah* also found its way into the Koran (37:103), where the story conforms in most respects with the biblical version. Later Islamic tradition took it for granted that the sacrificed son was actually Ishmael, the ancestor of the Arabs.

Yet another aspect of the complex interrelationships between Judaism, Christianity, and Islam is demonstrated by the following example.

The covenant between God and Abraham, as described in Genesis 15, is accompanied by a queer ceremony of splitting the carcasses of various animals into pieces. Verse 11 relates, "And the birds of prey came down upon the carcases, and Abraham drove them away."

A medieval Yemenite midrashic anthology, the *midrash Ha-Gadol*, explains this as meaning that "when Abraham laid the halves of the pieces over against each other, they became alive and flew away," this being God's way of demonstrating to him the doctrine of Resurrection of the Dead.

This detail is not mentioned, as far as I am aware, by any talmudic source, though it is alluded to in the Arabic translation of the great tenth-century scholar Rav Saadia Ga'on, who interpreted the Hebrew phrase *vayyashev otam Avram*, normally rendered as "Abram drove [the birds] away," as "Abram revived them."

The earliest attested version of the legend seems to be the following:

> And when Abraham said: "Lord show me how you will revive the dead," He said, "What, do you not yet believe?" Said he, "Yea, but that my heart may be quieted." He said, "Then take four birds, and take them close to yourself; then put a part of them on every mountain; then call them, and they will come to you in haste; and know that God is mighty, wise."

The source for this midrash? It is found in the *Qur'an* (2:262)!

It would appear possible that later Jewish commentators were making free use of an Islamic tradition that provided corroboration for the Jewish belief in resurrection. The desire to find biblical support for the crucial doctrine of resurrection had long preoccupied the talmudic rabbis, and Muhammed's exegesis offered a convenient solution. The interpretation sounded so orthodox that its true origin was eventually forgotten. The possibility should not, however, be discounted that Muhammed himself may have been citing an originally Jewish teaching which was not preserved in our own sources.

It is evident that all three of the great Western religions have laid claim to "Abraham our father." And the intricate web of relationships between these religions—including both conflicts and points of agreement and harmony—can be traced through the examination of their respective interpretations of Abraham's life.

In addition, as has been evident throughout our history, the interpretations Jews have given to the Scriptures often reflect pressing concerns that go far beyond the particular verses that are being expounded.

For this reason, the study of Jewish biblical exegesis offers a most challenging and rewarding way of exploring the development of Jewish thought and history.

SUGGESTIONS FOR FURTHER READING

Ginzberg, Louis. (1909–37). *The Legends of the Jews.* Translated by H. Szold. Philadelphia: Jewish Publication Society of America.

Katsh, Abraham I. (1980). *Judaism in Islam, Biblical and Talmudic Backgrounds of the Koran and its Commentaries: Suras II and III.* New York: Bloch for New York University Press.

Spiegel, Shalom. (1967). *The Last Trial: On the Legends and Lore of the Command to Abraham to Offer Isaac as a Sacrifice: The Akedah.* Translated by Judah Goldin. Philadelphia: The Jewish Publication Society of America.

50

What Does the Bible Really Say about Abortion?*

$\mathcal{J}$ews who are exposed to the public debate over abortion laws (and who can avoid it today?) tend to find themselves somewhat surprised at the degree of certainty with which some of the parties, notably the Roman Catholics and Protestant fundamentalists, are able to express themselves.

This tone is in marked contrast to the statements of our own rabbis, who often hesitate to speak in generalizations, preferring to emphasize the complexity of the considerations in Jewish law. This, by the way, has not been the tenor of the debate conducted in Israel, where the question—like many other religious issues (autopsies are another example)—has become politicized, forcing many rabbis into one-sided public statements.

---

*"A Biblical Text on Abortion." *The Jewish Star*, Calgary/Edmonton, Calgary/Edmonton August 12–Sept. 8, 1988, pp. 4, 8.

While I do not wish to propose a normative Jewish position on the subject, I would like to examine one aspect of this debate, namely the use of biblical sources by Jews and Christians in support of their respective positions.

Let me begin by singling out one of the principal points of contention: Whatever their position concerning the permissibility of abortion, virtually all Jewish authorities would agree that abortion is not to be legally classified as murder.

This thesis seems to be spelled out quite clearly in the Torah. Thus, in Exodus 21:22–23 we read, "If men strive and hurt a woman with child so that her fruit depart from her, and yet no mischief follow, he shall be surely punished, according as the woman's husband will lay upon him; and he shall pay as the judges determine. And if any mischief follow, then thou shalt give life for life."

The text (presented here according to the non-Jewish King James translation) makes it clear that the causing of a miscarriage where it does not involve the death of the mother ("mischief") is not to be treated as a capital offense; nor even as manslaughter, for which an entirely different procedure would be invoked, involving the exile of the culprit to a "city of refuge." Rather, it is perceived as a civil offence involving nothing more than a monetary compensation to the husband.

TRANSLATIONS DIFFER

So, given the fact that Christians accept the same Bible as we do, how can some of them argue with such certainty that the Bible regards abortion as murder?

The answer to this question involves a little-appreciated fact: namely, that the Christian Bible is *not* always identical to the accepted Jewish one.

In this particular instance, the text used by the Roman Catholic church is actually based on a different reading of the text, as found in the earliest Greek translation of the Hebrew Bible, the Septuagint. This translation was prepared in the Egyptian city of Alexandria in the third century B.C.E.

Though incorporating much authentic Jewish interpretation and referred to with reverence in talmudic literature, the rabbis came to realize that this translation had come to differ to a considerable extent from the Judaism that was developing in the Land of Israel. The Septuagint was eventually abandoned by the Jews in favour of other translations into Greek and Aramaic that were more in keeping with what had become the Jewish orthodoxy.

The Jewish abandonment of the Septuagint was also facilitated by the fact that it was by then the official version of the nascent Christian church.

The Biblical passage in question is rendered in the Septuagint as follows: " . . . if there is no *form*, then he shall be fined . . . but if it has a form, then you shall give life for life."

According to this reading, the verse deals only with the fate of the fetus and is concerned with distinguishing between an undeveloped and developed fetus, a distinction that is recognized by *halakhah* and, for that matter, by the old Canadian law. It establishes that the penalty "life for life" is to be inflicted upon one who destroys a developed fetus.

This version of the passage became the source for the subsequent Roman Catholic positions on the subject—though it does not quite help us to explain similar statements made by Protestant groups who do not accept the Septuagint tradition. These latter groups generally base their positions not so much on specific Biblical texts as on broader positions vis à vis permissiveness or the family.

Those Protestant theologians who do take the Exodus passage into account relate to it in a number of different ways. In a 1969 symposium on the subject of abortion, several participants used the verse to justify liberal positions—including at least one who, during the course of the conference, became persuaded by it to alter his previously held pro-life views.

Other participants resorted to alternative interpretations, construing the word *mischief* to refer to the fate of the fetus as well as of the mother (this was cited in the name of the distinguished Jewish biblical scholar Umberto Cassuto).

Still others argued that, on this point, the text, like much of biblical law, was to be superseded by other quotations in both the Old Testament and Christian scriptures that seem to refer poetically to the existence of souls before birth.

A favorite citation of this sort is Jeremiah 1:5: "Before I formed you in the womb I knew you for my own." Taken literally, this verse could extend the life span of the fetus to *before* conception!

DEAD SEA SCROLLS

All this should not make us forget that the Septuagint is in fact a Jewish translation and reflects traditions that were once held by Jews, whether in the Land of Israel or in Alexandria.

The discovery of the Dead Sea Scrolls had greatly increased our knowledge of the range of views that were current at the time. The authors of these writings also took a very rigid approach to the status of the fetus. For example, Leviticus 22:28 prohibits the slaughtering of an animal and its young on the same day. The *Temple Scroll*, one of the most important sources of our knowledge of the Dead Sea sect's laws (published for the first time in 1978) perceived this as a prohibition against slaughtering pregnant animals, a prohibition which does not exist in rabbinic law.

It is of the essence of religious differences that they can rarely be discussed in simplistic terms of right and wrong. If we trace an issue far enough, we often find that it rests upon unprovable axioms of faith or accepted tradition.

In this particular instance, we might suitably adapt the well-known observation of George Bernard Shaw and recognize the extent to which Judaism and Christianity are separated by their common Bible.

SUGGESTIONS FOR FURTHER READING

Biale, Rachel. (1995). *Women and Jewish Law: The Essential Texts, Their History and Their Relevance for Today.* New York: Schocken.

Bleich, J. David. (1997–). *Contemporary Halakhic Problems.* Library of Jewish Law and Ethics, New York: KTAV.

Feldman, David M. (1974). *Marital Relations, Birth Control, and Abortion in Jewish Law.* New York: Schocken.

Yadin, Yigael, ed. (1983). *The Temple Scroll.* Jerusalem: Israel Exploration Society.

51

ᴄᴪᴐ

Was Jesus a Feminist?*

$\mathcal{A}$s a staff member of the Religious Studies Department at the University of Calgary, my duties include the teaching of introductory courses in Western religions, including Judaism, Christianity, and Islam.

Coming to North America with a specialized Israeli training in Jewish Studies, I was at first quite daunted by the prospect of having to teach Christianity to classes that consisted largely of Christians. In a reputed Bible Belt like Alberta I anticipated some friction with fundamentalist students, and I recall assuring my first class that since I could not expect to avoid offending somebody, I would at least try to offend everybody in equal proportions.

---

*"Jesus on My Mind." *The Jewish Star*, Calgary/Edmonton, Aug. 25–Sept. 7, 1989, pp. 4, 8.

In researching the material for my courses I became more and more overwhelmed by the feeling that, as a Jew, I had a different perspective on the text than was standard in the Christian world. I felt that these records were largely internal Jewish documents, saturated in the realities of first-century *Eretz Yisrael* and full of allusions to a variety of political, religious, and *halakhic* questions.

The subjects are familiar to those who have been brought up in the literature and lifestyles of talmudic Judaism. But could they possibly mean anything significant to someone from outside the fold of traditional Judaism?

Closely related to these thoughts was the conviction that Jesus was after all a Jew, no less so than any of the other assorted Jewish sectarians, reformers, and revivalists who proliferated during the Second Temple era, and had relatively little connection with the religion that was to build up around him.

I was aware that the above approach, which draws a sharp division between the actual teachings of Jesus and the religion called Christianity, is fairly conventional in historical studies of early Christianity, which have long distinguished between "the historical Jesus" and "the Christ of faith." I was, however, unsure to what extent such a perspective had filtered down to the level of the undergraduate classroom.

SHARING A JEWISH VIEW

In the three years that have elapsed since those initial hesitations, I have come to realize that much of what I had thought was a peculiarly Jewish slant on Christian history has come to be part of the standard presentation current in universities and liberal seminaries.

Christians have also become very sensitive to several points that have given offense to Jews. Thus, it is now common to find non-Jewish writers employing the neutral dating system B.C.E. / C.E.

(Before Common Era / Common Era), rather than the theologically loaded B.C. / A.D., which translate respectively as before the Messiah and year of our Lord and presuppose the messiahship and divinity of Jesus.

Our Bible is also referred to in these circles as the Hebrew Bible, or even *Tanakh*, rather than as Old Testament, which implies the existence of a superseding new testament.

On a more substantive level, the first generations of Jewish Christians are depicted as a "Jesus movement" within Judaism, rather than as a distinct religion. A possible indication of this tendency to distinguish between the teachings of Jesus and the religion of Christianity is to be found in the fact that textbooks on Christianity rarely devote more than three pages to Jesus' life or teachings. Christian scholars have been taking the trouble to study the classics of rabbinic literature in order to understand Jesus against the background of his contemporary Jewish society.

In general, then, Christian scholarship has been very careful to dissociate itself from the more glaring anti-Jewish versions of Jesus' life. The most virulent attacks, they argue, should be seen as reflections of the intense rivalries between Jew and Christian in the generations following Jesus' time when the Gospels were being composed. The Gospel of John, perhaps the most vocally anti-Jewish work in the New Testament, is sometimes regarded as an embarrassment to liberal Christians, and we rarely hear them making sweeping references to "the Jews" as a monolithic entity.

Ironically, in trying to minimize the differences between Jesus and his Pharisaic contemporaries it is not uncommon for scholars to veer to the other extreme. Having combed talmudic literature and discovered hundreds of rabbinic parallels to Jesus' teachings, scholars find themselves at a loss to discern any significant difference between the two. If Jesus was really so much like the Pharisees, then why the big fuss about him?

THE POOR CARPENTER

In spite of this general willingness to discard traditional anti-Semitic stereotyping, there are a number of details that have attached themselves to Jesus' biography that make assumptions about Jews and Judaism that are much more subtle, though no less disturbing. In some cases, we have become so accustomed to these details that they strike us as perfectly innocent—until we see the uses to which they are put (as I have learned from listening to my students and reading their essays).

For example, who is not familiar with the description of Jesus as a poor carpenter? Taken by itself this assertion sounds perfectly obvious and harmless. Beneath the surface, however, lurk some troubling implications.

The first problem that comes to mind is that the New Testament itself does not indicate anywhere that Jesus was regarded as poor. In the context of Galilean Jewish society at his time—a community composed largely of small olive and grape farmers and seasonal field workers—a carpenter would have been considered a very comfortable and mobile profession.

The fact that such an unfounded *aggadic* detail is added to the traditional Christian perception of their founder need not trouble us of itself. It certainly is in keeping with other documented aspects of Jesus' teaching that emphasize his appeal to the lower classes and social outcasts.

But here, too, we must recognize that, from the perspective of Jewish society, outcasts were not necessarily poor. Quite the contrary, Jesus seems to have been antagonizing his contemporaries largely because of his over-familiarity with the wealthy tax farmers (publicans), Jews who became rich off the sufferings of their countrymen and collaborated with the Roman occupiers.

Jesus' alleged poverty takes on more disturbing overtones when used in such contexts as, "the learned Jewish scribes did not wish to listen to the preaching of this poor carpenter from Galilee."

The implication is clearly that a Pharisaic scholar could not have been a carpenter, poor or otherwise.

Aside from the fact that this is simply untrue—the Jewish sages at this period in history were normally craftsmen and field workers, and Jewish law then prohibited accepting payment for religious instruction—one wonders what the authors of such statements imagined that the Pharisees *did* do for their livings.

From my own experiences with students, I have often discovered that beneath such innocent-sounding sentences is likely to be lurking a classic medieval anti-Semitic stereotype. The Pharisees, according to the unarticulated presumptions of otherwise well-meaning Christians, must have been wealthy bankers, business executives, or (Lord preserve us!) university professors!

PIONEER FEMINIST?

A similar cliché that I have been encountering quite frequently (and not only from students) has it that "The Pharisees were shocked that Jesus spent so much time in the company of women." Once again the implication is that "real" Jews were hostile to women and that Jesus thereby takes on the appearance of a pioneer feminist.

Here again, the least of the difficulties with this thesis is the fact that it is not supported by any New Testament sources. Christian scripture is not reticent about listing Jewish objections to Jesus and had this been an issue, it would undoubtedly have been mentioned somewhere.

It is evident that what we have here is another instance of twisting the evidence in order to present Judaism in a disadvantageous light. The truth is, of course, that neither Jesus nor the Pharisees seem to present a very consistent picture as regards their attitudes to women. In either case, one can easily produce texts or interpretations to support both sexist and egalitarian readings.

The above instances should alert us to how deep and complex are the roots of Christian anti-Semitism—and I do not wish to imply by any means that equivalent factors do not color our own attitudes towards Christianity. Even with the most sincere of intentions, and even with the progress that has been made, it will prove very difficult to eradicate the unconscious strata of anti-Jewish feeling that have grown up over the centuries.

SUGGESTIONS FOR FURTHER READING

Heschel, S. (1990). "Anti-Judaism in Christian Feminist Theology." *Tikkun* 5:3: 25–8, 95–7.
Kellenbach, Katharina von. (c. 1994). *Anti-Judaism in Feminist Religious Writings*. American Academy of Religion cultural criticism series, Atlanta, GA: Scholars Press.
Plaskow, Judith. (1980). "Blaming Jews . . . for the Birth of Patriarchy." *Lilith* 7: 11–3.

52

✌

What Was the Real Shape of Moses' Tablets?*

*A*sk any child to draw you a picture of the tablets with the Ten Commandments and chances are that they will produce the same familiar picture of two joined rectangles with rounded tops. This is the image which occupies a central place in Jewish ritual art, particularly as a decoration of synagogue arks.

If one examines the many remains of ancient Jewish religious art, one would be hard put to find *any* representation of the tablets of the covenant, let alone the one depicted above. Unlike the *lulav*, the Temple and the seven-branched *menorah*, the tablets were not considered an identifiably Jewish symbol. This surprising situation might reflect the fact that Judaism—unlike Christianity—does not attach special significance to the Ten Com-

---

*"What Did the Ten Commandments Really Look Like?" *The Jewish Free Press*, Calgary, Nov. 11, 1993, pp. 9–10).

mandments inscribed on the tablets, but sees them only as part of the total of six hundred thirteen.

Although we do not possess any ancient Jewish pictures of the tablets, the Talmuds have preserved some discussions of their shapes. The Palestinian Talmud describes them as two separated oblong tablets; whereas, according to the Babylonian Talmud, they were squares measuring 6 × 6 × 3 handbreadths each—very different from any of the portrayals that we are used to. None of these sources speak of rounded tops.

Pictures of the tablets do not begin to show up in Jewish art until the thirteenth or fourteenth centuries, and they do not become widespread until a few centuries afterwards. When Jewish artists sought ways to represent them, they invariably copied models that had been developed over a long period in Christian iconography.

From the earliest days of the Church, it had included the Ten Commandments in its traditional artwork. Ironically, the tablets figured not only in illustrations of Moses and the revelation at Mount Sinai but also (and some would argue, primarily) in contexts that we would regard as anti-Jewish. To take one notable instance, a favorite motif in church art was the confrontation of the Church victorious and the Synagogue vanquished. In these portrayals, the synagogue was personified as a woman with a broken staff holding the tablets of the Law that represented the Jews' stubborn clinging to dry legalism. The image of the two tablets became so identified with Jewish stubbornness and evil that in the thirteenth century it was prescribed as the mandatory shape of the yellow badge that Jews had to attach to their garments as a humiliating symbol of their inferiority.

When Christians drew the tablets, what did they look like? At first, they took the form of two unattached rectangular blocks (like the ones that are held by Michaelangelo's Moses). It was only in the twelfth century that we begin to encounter the familiar joined oblongs with the rounded tops. Scholars now believe that the latter form was inspired by the diptych, a popular type of writing tablet consisting of two waxed boards attached by a hinge that could be closed shut. It was in this shape, which was also used for other forms of church art, that the tablets became familiar to Jewish artists in the later Middle Ages. In time, the unpleasant associations came to be forgotten until the tablets found their way into almost every Torah ark in the western countries.

Not all Jews had forgotten where the tablet image had come from. About ten years ago the Chabad Hasidim began a campaign to eliminate the rectangular tablets from Jewish religious art, arguing that they contradicted the talmudic descriptions and were an imitation of Christian portrayals. Some respected rabbis (including Rabbi Eliezer Shach), while acknowledging the truth of these arguments, insisted initially that the images had become so rooted in the Jewish mind that they had, by now, taken on the status of a venerable Jewish custom.

And indeed, when we see how universally this image has been accepted into our conventional synagogue decorations, it is hard to realize just how problematic it really is.

SUGGESTIONS FOR FURTHER READING

Melinkoff, Ruth. (1973). "The Round-Topped Tablets of the Law: Sacred Symbol and Emblem of Evil." In *Abstracts of the Sixth Congress of Jewish Studies*, D-28. Jerusalem: World Union of Jewish Studies.

53

༄

Was There a Cross on Jacob's Bed?

Chapter 47 of Genesis contains the touching scene in which the aged patriarch Jacob, lying on his deathbed, presses Joseph for a promise that he will not be buried in Egypt. When, at the conclusion of this story, Joseph consents to his father's wishes, the Bible states (verse 31) that *"Israel bowed himself upon the bed's head."*

Commenting on this verse, the *Ga'on* Rabbi Samuel ben Hofni, head of the talmudic Academy of Sura in tenth to eleventh-century Baghdad, makes the following remarkable observation: "The Christian copyists have mistakenly rendered this verse as if it read 'upon the head of the *staff*,' since they confused the Hebrew *mittah* [bed] with *matteh* [staff]."

The textual variant noted by the *Ga'on* had a long history. The translation *staff* is found cited as early as the Septuagint, the earliest Greek version of the Bible, which was composed in Alexandria in the third century B.C.E. The mistake is simple enough to explain, since the two Hebrew words in question are written exactly the same and differ only in their vowels which, in Hebrew, were not written down. This reading *staff* (which is also reflected in the old Syriac Bible translations) stood before the author of the New Testament's "Epistle to the Hebrews" (11:21) which relates that "Jacob, when he was a dying . . . worshipped, leaning upon the top of his staff." The Christian Church later adopted the Septuagint as its official version of the Bible, hence it is natural that Rabbi Samuel ben Hofni should have designated its reading as a Christian one.

Predictably, the Christian reading of the verse was also well-known to Jewish Bible commentators who lived in the heart of Christian Europe. Furthermore, from the writings of exegetes such as Rabbi Hayyim Paltiel (fourteenth century), we learn that the textual variant was not merely of antiquarian interest but that it became the focus of a lively interreligious polemic. For the Christians argued that the staff mentioned in this episode could be none other than a cross, and, therefore, they cited this passage as proof that Jacob himself had been worshipping the chief symbol of their religion. This argument figured prominently in Christian polemical writings such as the *Quaestiones* of Isidore of Seville (sixth–seventh centuries).

Jews, who were secure enough in their own textual traditions, were not particularly disturbed by such arguments. Nevertheless, the Christian interpretation found its way into the various manuals that were composed in order to assist Jews in refuting Christian arguments.

An extraordinary example of how Jewish debaters would respond to such an interpretation is contained in the *Nizzahon Vetus*, a collection of anti-Christian arguments and refutations that was probably composed in thirteenth-century Germany. Purely for the sake of argument, suggests the anonymous Jewish author with tangible irony, let us accept the Christian reading. This would furnish evidence of how seriously Jacob's judgment had been affected by his illness! However (continues our writer), if we follow the Christian argument to its logical conclusions, then we must also recognize that Jacob came to regret his action as soon as his health returned and he came to his senses. For does not the Bible inform us a mere two verses later (Genesis 48:2) that *"Israel strengthened himself and sat upon the bed* (mittah)!" If our Christian disputant is truly consistent, then here, too, he will have to read *staff* (cross), and what greater gesture of contempt could there be than to portray the patriarch as sitting on it!

It is unlikely that arguments of this sort would persuade either Jew or Christian to reconsider their faiths. Nevertheless, the controversy does give us some insights into the complex considerations and ulterior motives that often influenced medieval biblical exegesis. It also provides a surprising picture of the pride and sheer *chutzpah* that Jews were prepared to demonstrate in defending their beliefs, even in an era when such outspokenness could—and frequently did—come at a great price.

SUGGESTIONS FOR FURTHER READING

Berger, D. (1979). *The Jewish-Christian Debate in the High Middle Ages.* Philadelphia: Jewish Publication Society of America.

Greenbaum, A., ed. (1978). *The Biblical Commentary of Rav Samuel ben Hofni Gaon According to Geniza Manuscripts.* Jerusalem: Harav Kook Institute.

Kasher, M. (1927–81). *Torah shelemah (Complete Torah): Encyclopedia of the Pentateuch.* New York: American Biblical Encyclopedia Society, Inc.

Speiser, E. A. (1964). *Genesis.* Garden City: Doubleday.

54

✧

Why Don't Muslims Have a Sabbath?*

$\mathcal{S}$ome delicate legal questions have been raised by the current struggle of Ontario's Jewish community to achieve an official status for Jewish schools. At the same time, Ottawa's Muslims are campaigning for acknowledgment of their holidays in the public school schedule.

As Jews we can readily appreciate how the civil (or secular) calendar that regulates our society is in reality a Christian one and therefore creates conflicts with members of other religious communities. At any rate, the problems involved in the celebration of Muslim holidays are not fully comparable with those confronting traditionally observant Jews. In spite of some interesting similarities between the two religious calendars, there are also

---

*"Days of Rest and Prayer." *The Jewish Free Press*, Calgary, March 30, 1995, p. 8.

some fundamental differences between the festivals of the two faiths.

For Jews, the most striking parallels between the Jewish and Muslim calendars are in the ways they define their months and years: In both systems, the months are determined by the phases of the moon, and hence the Jewish and Muslim new moons normally occur on the same day. For both religions, twelve such months make up a year.

At this point, we encounter the first of the important differences between the two systems. The Jewish calendar is periodically (as happened this year) adjusted through the addition of an extra month in order to keep it from lagging behind the solar year. In the Muslim tradition, no such adjustment is introduced, and therefore, their calendar annually falls eleven days behind the solar cycle.

This is not a mere technical matter, but derives from some essential differences in the characters of the respective religions.

We often take it for granted that Jewish festivals are closely associated with stages in the agricultural year. This is, however, not true about Muslim holidays. Although the Torah sees its typical community as consisting of farmers and peasants living in harmony with the soil and the seasons, the Qur'an was addressing a society of merchants whose daily lives were removed from the cycles of nature.

This basic difference can be discerned in some other spheres as well. For example, the central occasion in the Muslim religious year is the holy month of Ramadan, during which the faithful are obliged to fast throughout the daylight hours. Though this type of fast makes exacting demands on physical laborers, especially when it falls during periods of intensive agricultural activity, it is less of a hardship for people whose work is carried out in shops and offices, or whose timetables are not determined by the seasons of nature.

This premise might account for the fact that the Islamic calendar contains a comparatively small number of holidays and that none of them require resting from work. Once again, the typical Muslim is not perceived to be involved in physical work and, therefore, does not require religiously sanctioned days of rest.

Ironically, it is likely that that original society of merchants for whom Muhammad designed his religion might have been composed largely of Jews, who were prominent in the first Muslim community of Al-Madinah.

The weekly Muslim holy day falls on Friday, which is designated in Arabic as *Yawm al-Jum'a*, the Day of Assembly, and is not defined as a day of rest. Saturday continues to be referred to in Arabic as the *Sabbat,* though it is not observed as such by Muslims. *Yawm al-Jum'a* is a day of public worship in the mosque, accompanied by sermons and other spiritual solemnities, but it is not unreasonable for an observant Muslim to leave the mosque after services and head directly to work or school.

At the root of this difference in approach might lie a deeper theological issue. Remember that our Shabbat commemorates how God ceased from work and rested from the six days of creation. Now, the picture of a God who had to relax from his exertions is one that was unacceptable to the straightforward Muslim conception of divine omnipotence. As it states in the Qur'an: "In six days We created the heavens and the earth and all that is between them, and weariness did not affect us."

Hence, for the Qur'an, the institution of a day of rest was *not* considered a suitable way of celebrating the creation.

This theological difficulty was, of course, well known to the Jewish commentators. One early midrash explains that God had the biblical passages speak loosely of *God*'s resting on Shabbat only in order to encourage *humans* to try to emulate the Creator by relaxing once a week.

Jews living in Muslim countries were sensitive to the implications of these issues, and echoes of the controversy can be discerned in Jewish commentaries that were composed in Muslim lands. Thus, Rabbi Saadia Ga'on's important translation of the Bible into Arabic (tenth century) was probably responding to

Muslim criticisms when he carefully rendered all the offending references in the Creation account as if they said "God allowed the *world* to rest"—but the Almighty did not require such relaxation.

Of course, little if any of this has direct bearing on how Jewish or Muslim holidays should be treated under Canadian law. Hopefully, though, it has enriched our understanding of some unappreciated dimensions of our religious calendar.

SUGGESTIONS FOR FURTHER READING

Lazarus-Yafeh, H. (1982). "Some Halakhic Differences between Judaism and Islam." *Tarbiz* 51:2: 207–25.

CHAPTER
55

࿔

How Has the Story
of Joseph Been Told
in World Literature?*

$\mathcal{F}$ew texts in Jewish literature are as dramatically crafted as the
Joseph story that dominates the latter chapters of Genesis. It is
hard to imagine what could be added to such an elaborately plot-
ted tale.

And yet storytellers over the ages could not resist the temptation to add to the Biblical narrative, filling in, in meticulous detail, the personalities of the protagonists.

JOSEPH AND ZULEIKA

An outstanding Hebrew example of this genre of expanded Bible
is a work entitled *Sefer Hayyashar*, first published in Venice in

*"A Coat of Many Cultures." *The Jewish Free Press*, Calgary, January
2, 1996, pp. 6, 8.

1625. In retelling the stories of the book of Genesis, the unnamed author weaves into the Biblical text all manner of supplementary traditions derived from the midrash, ancient apocryphal works, and other sources.

One episode that clearly caught the author's imagination was Joseph's stalwart resistance in the face of his employer's wife's attempts to seduce him. Whereas the Bible speaks only of an anonymous "wife of Potiphar," the *Sefer Hayyashar* gives her a name: Zuleika.

Against the Biblical narrator's terse and suggestive account, *Sefer Hayyashar* paints a vivid portrait of a woman pathologically obsessed with Joseph's physical beauty. She continually urges Joseph on, whether by enticement, threats, or trickery, and her passion ultimately brings upon her a suicidal state of physical depression.

The *Sefer Hayyashar* illustrates these themes by means of the following episode: In response to the Egyptian women's berating her for her lack of self-control, Zuleika invited them to a banquet at which oranges were served. Joseph entered as the women were peeling the oranges, and they became so distracted by his beauty that they cut right through their hands, drawing blood. This, Zuleika stated, was the kind of temptation she had to put up with day after day!

The name Zuleika is not mentioned in either the Bible or Midrash. As to the incident of the oranges, its origin is unclear. Similar episodes (with variations in the menu) are included in some medieval midrashic anthologies, but the earliest datable attestation is in Muslim tradition: The twelfth chapter of the *Qur'an*, known as "*Surat Yusuf*," is, in itself, an elaborate midrash on the Joseph story, incorporating many elements from the Jewish aggadic tradition.

The name Zuleika also seems to emanate from an Islamic source. Epic poems on this theme circulated widely in medieval times, of which the most popular was the Persian *Yusuf and Zulaikha*, composed in 7,000 Persian couplets by the fifteenth-century poet Jami. The author was a Sufi who regarded the story of Joseph's temptations as an allegory for the mystical striving after divinity.

Scholars are not in agreement about the chronology of the tradition: Were the Jewish authors of works like *Sefer Hayyashar* borrowing Muslim traditions that had originated in earlier Arabic or Persian novels? Or were they in fact repatriating ancient Jewish legends that had, for some reason, been excluded from the standard compendia of midrash?

JOSEPH AND ASENATH

If the situation of Joseph and Potiphar's wife inspires an intrinsic fascination, there is a more urgent difficulty posed by the other woman in Joseph's life: His wife, Asenath.

Asenath is identified in the Bible as the daughter of an Egyptian priest—a *yihus* (pedigree) that comes into conflict with the Jewish prohibition against mixed marriages.

This discomfort was felt most acutely by the Jews of ancient Alexandria, Egypt. While participating in a vibrant and cosmopolitan centre of Greek culture, this community was ardently committed to their ancestral religion. Furthermore, they had a special reverence for Joseph, whom they regarded as the founder of their own community.

It is against the social background of first-century Alexandria that we are to appreciate the composition of *Joseph and Asenath*, one of the most remarkable literary creations of Hellenistic Judaism.

At one level, the Greek story provides a simple solution to the fundamental religious problem: It relates how the chaste Asenath learned to reject her idolatrous upbringing and underwent a sincere conversion to the faith of Israel.

However, *Joseph and Asenath* does not stop there. It makes use of all the conventions and devices of Greek literary art to fashion a readable romantic novel that conforms to the esthetic tastes of

Hellenistic culture. The resulting tale includes such ingredients as love at first sight, a struggle against the unwanted attentions of Pharaoh's son, plenty of swashbuckling swordplay between Joseph's brothers and the royal rivals, and more.

JOSEPH AND HIS BROTHERS

Some years ago I participated in an engagement dinner hosted by one of Jerusalem's most eminent *Rosh Yeshivahs*. As is the custom at such occasions, one of the Yeshivah students delivered a learned discourse on the blessings of marriage. In his *d'var Torah* the student made references to several rabbinic embellishments to the Biblical stories about Jacob and Joseph.

At the conclusion of the discourse, the Lithuanian *Rosh Yeshivah* asked the student if he could identify the source of a *midrash* he had just cited (Some 25 years later, I no longer recall its precise content). The student sheepishly replied that he had heard it at a previous engagement dinner and did not know its original source.

The learned Rabbi smiled and pointed out that the tradition in question is not found in any traditional Jewish text. As far as he could tell, its earliest source is Thomas Mann's historical novel *Joseph und sein Brüder*.

I admit that I was struck initially by the sage's erudition—noting that there are probably few among his younger colleagues who could have made the identification. On a more profound level, however, I was most impressed by the rabbi's attitude. At no point did he suggest that the story's foreign source should be construed as grounds for rejecting it.

I suspect that he saw this as yet another instance of Judaism's genius for drawing upon the esthetic sensibilities of surrounding cultures in order to uphold the vitality and relevance of the Torah.

SUGGESTIONS FOR FURTHER READING

Yohannan, John D., ed. (1968). *Joseph and Potiphar's Wife in World Literature: an Anthology of the Story of the Chaste Youth and the Lustful Stepmother*. New York: New Directions.

Burchard, J. C. (1985). "Joseph and Asenath." In *The Old Testament Pseudepigrapha*, ed. J. H. Charlesworth. Vol. 2. London: Darton, Longman, and Todd.

56

༉

What Kind of Prophet was Balaam?*

$\mathcal{J}$ewish tradition has proposed two principal models for understanding Balaam's job description.

While the Bible designates him clearly as a *kosem*—a sorcerer or soothsayer—there exists a widespread tradition, found most frequently in the midrash, that classifies him as a prophet—in fact, as one of the greatest prophets whose abilities rivaled those of Moses himself!

The commentaries have indulged in considerable speculation about how Balaam went about his work. The midrash, for instance, relates that he possessed a talent for discerning when circumstances would be favourably or inauspiciously disposed towards human undertakings, thereby allowing him to influence a project's

---

*"Prophet of the Nations." *The Jewish Free Press*, Calgary, June 20, 1996, pp. 8–9.

outcome by scheduling it at a particular moment. In this way, his curses and blessings acquired a reputation for effectiveness.

Rabbi Abraham Ibn Ezra, ever an enthusiast of astrology, attributed Balaam's reputation to his skill at reading the stars. Once the horoscope had determined that a catastrophe was about to occur, Balaam would ceremoniously proclaim a curse, creating the fraudulent impression that his malediction had actually caused the disaster.

The thirteenth-century commentator Rabbi Bahya ben Asher asked why, if Balaam's blessings and curses were completely fraudulent and could not truly affect the destiny of the Israelites, did God take such elaborate measures to discredit him and demonstrate the baselessness of his oracles? Let Balaam stand and curse all day! In the long run it won't make any difference.

The answer to this question can be better understood if we realize that the outcome of human actions is not predetermined. As Ibn Ezra suggested, matters could take a course that might mistakenly be perceived as a corroboration of Balaam's curses. It was in order to prevent such a misunderstanding that God took the trouble to discredit Balaam and demonstrate the patent falseness of his pretensions.

Most of the commentators accept some variation on the view that Balaam's sorcery consisted of an insight into future developments. And yet many of these same commentators are equally insistent that Balaam did not qualify as a real *navi*.

Now these interpretations may strike us as puzzling. Are not insights into the future precisely what defines true prophecy? Were not the great prophets of the Bible famous for their knowledge of the divine plans for future history?

Actually, this perception of prophecy is a misleading one, widespread though it may be. It derives largely from alien influences.

In reality, the English word prophet is not an accurate translation of the Hebrew *navi*. Whereas the Hebrew term comes from a root meaning to speak or proclaim, the English one originates in a Greek word denoting the prediction of the future. The concept of Greek prophecy reflects a very different religious culture, in which oracles foretold coming events and had scant interest in moral instruction.

This is definitely not the case among the Hebrew prophets. The *Nevi'im* were not concerned with revealing the course of future events. Their messages were invariably aimed at the here-and-now, to proclaim God's word to their contemporaries.

While it is true that several of the prophets do make declarations about what will befall Israel in days to come, about impending conquests or about the Messianic restoration—these matters are never the principal concern of the message. Rather, they are intended to indicate the consequences of disobedience and moral laxity, or the rewards in store for those who maintain their devotion under conditions of adversity. Except perhaps in the most general of terms, none of these prophetic visions of the future has the character of an absolute or unalterable scenario. Ultimately, they are all conditional upon the people's response.

Balaam's predictions about the fates of Edom and Amalek are of an oracular sort, and the Talmudic Rabbis were quick to distinguish them from the ethical and compassionate spirit that should direct true *nevu'ah*. They were well aware of how the Christian church in their day was ingeniously transforming the Hebrew scriptures into a book of coded prophesies and prefigurations that irrefutably heralded the coming of their savior.

The view that history follows a predictable course is what the Torah ascribes to the *kosem*. Ironically, it is precisely the worldview that in our society is widely identified with prophecy, as anyone will appreciate who has had occasion to listen to the forecasts of Christian televangelists, Israeli messianic extremists, or those who read the Torah as an elaborate supernatural word-search puzzle.

Perhaps this is the crucial point that Balaam misunderstood. He thought he could predict the future by charms or horoscopes and that this would qualify him to be counted in the ranks of the prophets.

Yet if, as we have seen, Balaam was the antithesis of a true prophet, then why do the sages of the Talmud and midrash refer to him so often as a *navi*? This question was asked by Rabbi Isaac Arama in his *Akedat Yitzhak* commentary. He replied by pointing out that Balaam is never referred to simply as a *navi*, but always as the "prophet *of the nations.*"

According to Arama, the Rabbis' purpose was to emphasize the contrast between the opposed perceptions of prophecy in Israel and among the nations of the world. For Jews, the prophet is ultimately a moral figure, whose insights into the future are relevant only insofar as they guide our conduct in the present. For Balaam, on the other hand, humans are playing out a predetermined scenario over which our actions can exert no meaningful control or influence.

Seen this way, the career of Balaam comes to embody a fundamental conflict between the Torah's ideal of *nevu'ah* and "the prophecy of the nations."

CHAPTER

57

❦

Is There a Lamp
under the Bushel?*

*F*rom time to time I receive communications from my Adoring Public in which I am encouraged to seek a broader readership than can be reached through an obscure Jewish newspaper from the Canadian wilderness. Recently, a reader expressed that sentiment by urging me "not to hide my lamp under a barrel."

The quaint expression caught my fancy. It is rarely heard today, and I doubt that many of those who do use it are aware that it originated in Christian scriptures. The author of the Gospel of Matthew has Jesus exhort his disciples not to be shy about spreading their message, since it makes no sense to light a lamp if you are only going to hide it under a bushel. Rather, it should be set up on a stand from which it can provide light for everyone in the house.

---

*"Of Lamps and Bushels." *The Jewish Free Press*, Calgary, August 29, 1996, p. 10.

In our metric world, it should be explained that bushel translates into the Hebrew *homer*, a container used to measure out a standard volume of grain.

The maxim is one of the few expressions from the New Testament to be cited in the Talmud. However, the rabbis cleverly incorporated the citation into a subtle wordplay, as part of an anti-Christian satire that reflects the heated antagonisms between the rival religions in ancient times.

The talmudic passage in question claims to relate an incident that occurred in the late first century. A local magistrate, described as a "philosopher," was known for his Christian leanings. Although he had acquired a reputation for incorruptible honesty, some of his Jewish neighbors suspected that he was not above being swayed by financial inducements.

Imma Shalom, the sister of the Patriarch Rabban Gamaliel, decided to have some fun at the judge's expense. She approached him one day with a fictitious claim that she was entitled to share in the estate of her recently deceased father. To strengthen her case, she brought the magistrate a precious gift: a golden lamp.

Suddenly overcome by egalitarian ideals, the honorable justice acceded to her request and ordered that the inheritance be distributed equally between Imma Shalom and her brother, Rabban Gamaliel.

The latter pointed out that, according to the law of the Torah, sisters are not entitled to inherit when there is a male heir. To this the judge retorted "Since the day when you were exiled from your land, the Law of Moses has been rescinded and has been replaced by the 'Evangelion,' which states that sons and daughters inherit as equals."

Although no such rule is actually found in the New Testament, the judge's argument was very much in the spirit of the Christian doctrine that their new faith had rendered Jewish law obsolete.

The following day, Rabban Gamaliel returned to court. This time, however, he did not come empty-handed, but bore a generous gift of his own: a choice Libyan donkey.

The appreciative judge suddenly became receptive to Rabban Gamaliel's point of view. He piously quoted Jesus' proclamation that he had come "not to destroy the Law but to fulfill it." Hence, he argued, the precepts of the Torah may never be abrogated.

From her seat in the courtroom, Imma Shalom blurted out the words "May your light shine *like a lamp!*" hoping to call the judge's attention to her original bribe—to which her brother quipped cynically:

"It appears that the donkey has come and extinguished the lamp."

To fully appreciate Rabban Gamaliel's gibe we must keep in mind that the Hebrew word for donkey, *hamor*, is a homonym of *homer*, a bushel. Thus Rabban Gamaliel was ingeniously punning on the well known Christian proverb (which happens to be found in precisely the same chapter that had just been quoted by the judge).

The above anecdote is constructed a bit too symmetrically to be fully credible, and it seems to reflect a considerably later stage in the development of Christianity, after it had effectively severed itself from its Jewish roots and evolved its own distinctive scriptural canon. However, it does offer a vivid characterization of the kinds of disputes that could have arisen between Jews and gentile Christians in the third or fourth centuries.

At any rate, it does inspire me to reconsider the wisdom of expanding my readership. While some might view such a course as freeing my light from the constraints of a provincial bushel, others will undoubtedly prefer to discourage this old donkey from plunging any more readers into darkness and confusion.

SUGGESTIONS FOR FURTHER READING

Guedemann, M. (1876). *Religionsgeschichtliche Studien*. Leipzig.
Urbach, E. (1987). *The Sages: Their Concepts and Beliefs*. Translated by I. Abrahams. Cambridge, MA. and London, England: Harvard University Press.

How Did the Story of the Buddha Become a Jewish Classic?*

$\mathcal{W}$hile traversing the corridors of the University of Calgary this year, several people have been taken aback by the incongruous sight of Chinese Buddhist monks, garbed in their traditional robes, absorbed in intensive study of the Talmud and works of Jewish religious law.

I confess that I had something to do this anomalous phenomenon. The monks were students in my graduate seminar on Jewish Legal Literature, preparing their assignments with characteristic diligence.

When the two exotic students made their first appearance in my classroom, I was very apprehensive about the prospects of finding common ground between what I presumed were totally dissimilar

*"The Monks and the Mishnah." *The Jewish Free Press*, Calgary, February 6, 1997, p. 8.

religious traditions. My fears were quickly assuaged when I noted their fascination with certain themes of Jewish ethical and spiritual life and, especially, the ease with which they were able to handle the intricacies of rabbinic logic. As I was to learn, the art of logical dialectic, though directed more to philosophical than to legal questions, was a central component of their religious training.

Although Jewish interest in Buddhism has usually been marginal—typically involving individuals whose inadequate Jewish educations have prompted them to seek spirituality from more exotic sources—mainstream Buddhists have taken an unexpected interest in Judaism. This has been particularly true of the Tibetans, exiled by their Chinese overlords, who have found an instructive example in the Jewish ability to maintain their national and religious identity under adversity and outside their homeland. So intense is this interest that some years ago I saw a picture of the Dalai Lama being instructed in how to wrap a set of *tefillin*.

Many Jews would be surprised to learn that a legend about the Buddha enjoyed immense popularity in Jewish literature in several languages.

The story in question goes under the name "The Prince and the Monk." The Jewish prototype of the story was composed by the thirteenth-century poet Rabbi Abraham Ibn Hisdai of Barcelona. The work is an example of the *makama* genre that enjoyed immense popularity in medieval Arabic and Hebrew literatures. In a typical *makama*, a loosely structured plot formulated in rhymed prose provided the author with an opportunity to link together heterogeneous units, many of which were composed as formal poetry.

The basic plot of "The Prince and the Monk" involves a pagan king who had been cautioned that his son would one day forsake his royal station in favor of a new religion. In order to prevent this from happening, the king placed the prince in total isolation from the world and banished all religious teachers from his realms. In spite of all these precautions, the prince was prompted to ask a number of profound existential questions and eventually was approached by a spiritual mentor who succeeded in secretly instructing him in his new faith, persuading him to exchange his life of opulence for that of a spiritual ascetic.

The motif of individuals turning their backs on material comforts to pursue a course of spiritual fulfillment is a common one in fact and legend; the Jewish Rabbi Eliezer ben Hyrcanos and the Christian St. Francis of Assisi are two familiar instances that spring to mind. It is clear that Ibn Hisdai's immediate source was an Arabic text, though the Hebrew version was an independent and thoroughly Jewish work in its own right. The Arabs had apparently picked up the story from the Manichees of Central Asia, who had, in turn, learned it from Buddhist missionaries.

For the story of the prince and the monk is, in reality, none other than the traditional tale of the enlightenment of the Buddha, the Siddhartha Gautama.

The convoluted wanderings of this story add up to one of the most extraordinary achievements of world literatures. From its origins in India, it entered just about every known Asiatic and European culture. It achieved wide circulation in medieval Europe in its Christian guise as the "Tale of Barlaam and Josaphat." The prince's Latin name, *Josaphat*, is actually a variant of the Arabic *Yudasaf*, which appeared in Manichee as *Bodisaf*, recalling the original Sanskrit title *Bodhisattava*, "the future Buddha [enlightened one]." As Saint Josaphat the Buddha came to be acknowledged as a full-fledged Christian saint, complete with shrines and relics! The legend has exerted a powerful influence on figures like Tolstoy, who was inspired by it to exchange his aristocratic life for a simple, pacifistic one.

In its Jewish version, "The Prince and the Monk" enjoyed immense popularity. It was reprinted dozens of times and ranked among the foremost Hebrew moralistic treatises. A Yiddish edition was published in Lublin in 1874, and reprinted several times thereafter.

Indeed, if the story of the Buddha can be accepted as a source of Jewish ethical teaching, why should we be so startled by the spectacle of my Buddhist monks poring over the Talmud?

SUGGESTIONS FOR FURTHER READING

Schirmann, H. (1960). *Ha-Shirah Ha-'Ivrit bi-Sfarad uvi-Frovans*. Jerusalem and Tel-Aviv: Dvir and Mossad Bialik.
Smith, Wilfred Cantwell. (1981). *Towards a World Theology: Faith and
the Comparative History of Religion*. Library of Philosophy and Religion. Philadelphia: Westminster.
Zinberg, Israel. (1972). *A History of Jewish Literature*. Translated by B.
Martin. Cleveland: Case Western Reserve.

PART V

News and Commentary

59

༫

Why Does the Olympic Spirit Lack a Jewish *Neshamah*?*

News Item: February 1988—Calgary hosts the Winter Olympic Games.

Some time ago a note was circulated to various lecturers at the University of Calgary, including members of my own Religious Studies Department, requesting articles that would reflect the close links between our respective fields of expertise and the values embodied in the ideals of sportsmanship and the "Olympic Spirit."

The simple request made me very uncomfortable. This was not only because of the impossible deadline that would have had to be met (it wasn't), but also because of a gut feeling that, whatever might be the case with respect to other cultures, religions,

---

*"The Olympic Spirit, the Jewish Neshama." *The Jewish Star*, Calgary/Edmonton, September, 1987, pp. 5–6.

and academic disciplines, there exists an essential conflict between traditional Judaism and the world of athletics, and the
conflict is exacerbated when the pursuit of athletics is translated
into a value system.

After giving the matter some more thought, I decided to subject my gut feelings to the scrutiny of scholarship.

GREEKS VS. JEWS

The earliest association I can think of between Jews and athletics is part of the Hanukkah story (the archery practice through
which Jonathan signals David to escape in I Samuel 20 hardly
qualifies as a sports event, especially during wartime).

When the author of the First Book of Maccabees, our main
source for the events, wishes to characterize the wicked Jewish
accomplices of Antiochos' Hellenization program, the first act he
sees fit to describe (I:14ff.) is how the traitors "built a gymnasium
in Jerusalem in the heathen fashion, and submitted to uncircum-
cision, and disowned the holy covenant; they allied themselves
with the heathen and became the slaves of wrongdoing."

E. Bickerman, in his classic study of the issues behind the
Maccabean revolt, writes:

> The "gymnasium," i.e., the sports-stadium, during the Hellenistic
> period formed the symbol and basis for the Greek way of life. Physi-
> cal education was something alien to the Oriental, but a natural
> thing for the Greeks. Wherever Greeks came together, or people
> who wanted to be counted as Greeks, they started athletic exer-
> cises. . . . That meant that when native people participated in the
> athletic contests, they were accepted into the ruling class, and they
> acknowledged the hegemony of the Greek way of life.

Simply put, indulgence in athletics was viewed by the good guys
of the story as tantamount to a denial of one's Judaism. The fact
that this episode has not been universally included in the teaching of the Hanukkah story results in the historical irony that the

name "Maccabee" came to be applied today to (of all things) a Jewish athletic organization!

In a similar vein, Josephus Flavius described at length the Hellenizing activities of King Herod (that archtyrant of Judaea who succeeded in perpetuating his rule by currying the favor of the Roman rulers at the expense of the sensibilities of his Jewish populace). Among other things, Josephus also reports that Herod established his own quinquennial-yearly games on an international scale, in honor of Caesar, to be held in Jerusalem and elsewhere. He even named one of his daughters Olympia.

Josephus' account of Herod's own Olympic games reveals to us a new phase in the development of the athletic worldview of antiquity. Whereas Jewish objections to Greek sports were primarily due to their inherently pagan character (as well as to their immodesty and frivolity), the Romans introduced a new element to the arena: cruelty, which surpassed even that of professional hockey.

The classic examples of Roman viciousness included throwing prisoners (among whom were probably numbered many captured Jewish freedom-fighters) before wild beasts and gladiatorial combat. Herod included such displays in his own games, to the delight of pagan tourists and the indignant shock of his Jewish subjects.

This sadistic side of athletics seems to be the one that figures most prominently in rabbinic writings.

Thus "theaters and circuses" are commonly condemned in the Talmud as places of idolatry and evil, though Jews are permitted to attend the events even on the Sabbath, because they might be able to save the lives of victims (by indicating, through the thumbs-up gesture, their wish that the victim's life be spared).

One noted rabbi, Simeon ben Lakish, was forced by economic difficulties to take up the life of a gladiator. The talmudic legend describes how his eventual choice to embrace the life of the Torah was at the expense of his physical prowess—the two worlds were perceived to be inherently antithetical.

MEDIEVAL FRIVOLITY

As we move into the medieval period, most of the aspects of ancient athletics which had aroused the objections of the Jewish
authorities—especially the pagan connections and the cruelty—
were no longer in force. Most of the writings which discuss sports
seem to bundle them in with other frivolous pursuits. As such,
they are generally frowned upon, though the sources allow for
situations when frivolity is sanctioned.

A homily on the word *ke-dorbonot* (*"The words of the wise are as
goads"*) in Ecclesiastes 12:2 presumes the existence of "girls' ball
games" (*kaddur banot*) to which the transmission of the Torah is
compared. This probably reflects a belief that such pursuits as
games were more appropriate to women. Men indulged only at
special times.

For example, even as the talmudic rabbis had outdone each
other in feats of juggling and so forth during the festive Rejoic-
ing of the Water-Drawing (*Simhat Beit Ha-She'uvah*) on Sukkot,
medieval sources speak of jumping competitions on Purim and
of mock jousting and fencing at weddings. These were occasions
when frivolity was acceptable.

Rabbinic writings that discuss the fine *halakhic* issues involved in playing ball on the Sabbath serve to remind us that
the solemnity of the rabbis was rarely realized in the practice of
ordinary people. Maimonides, in his medical writings, recom-
mends (though not necessarily for Jews) an occasional game of
football as a beneficial form of exercise. These seem to be the
only concessions allowed for sports activities in traditional rabbinic literature.

An argument might be made for the claim that the demand for
competitiveness and play was filled in traditional Judaism by the
aggressive debate that characterizes Talmud study. Conversely,
the fact that the Talmud did succeed in satisfying these needs
may account for the unlikely popularity of Talmud as against such
subjects as Bible or theology.

"PHYSICAL REPENTANCE"

A radical departure from the normative Jewish antipathy towards athletics is to be found in the writings of Rabbi Abraham Isaac Kook, the revered Chief Rabbi of the Land of Israel during the formative years of the Zionist revival in *Eretz Yisrael*.

Rav Kook's Zionist outlook saw that the life of Torah must exist in harmony with nature, and the spiritual redemption promised by the reestablishment of Jewish independence must be accompanied by a corresponding physical rebuilding of Jewish bodies. He even cites the Hebrew equivalent of Juvenal's famous dictum: *Mens sana in corpore sano* ("A healthy mind in a healthy body").

Unique among Jewish religious thinkers, Rav Kook viewed "physical repentance" as an essential condition of the ideal of *teshuvah* that permeated all his writings. The traditional negation of things physical was, according to him, the consequence of the anomalous conditions of exile and the influence of alien religious values, a symptom of a general spiritual imbalance that had to be undone before true redemption could be achieved.

"When the holy people will be physically firm and strong," Rav Kook wrote, "holiness will prevail in the world. When Jewish children will be strong, sound, and healthy, the air of the world will become holy and pure." Clearly, physical achievements (or, for that matter, military heroism) cannot become ends in themselves. They must always be employed as a means to a spiritual goal. Rav Kook insisted that physical education should be an important part of the curriculum of the yeshivah.

In his study of Rav Kook's thought, Zvi Yaron summarizes the issue:

> Since one of the factors that makes possible the fulfilment of "our physical duties" is athletic activity, the Rav comes to the conclusion that there is a great spiritual value to sports. The strengthening of physical prowess is a form of worship. The spiritual power of the most righteous becomes improved through the "exercises practised by the

youth of Israel in Eretz Yisrael in order to strengthen their bodies to
make themselves courageous sons of their nation."

Accordingly, Rav Kook made a special request to the 1927 Zionist Congress in Basle that care should be taken to hold all athletic events, including football games, on weekdays, so that religious youths could participate freely.

As in other aspects of his work and teachings, Rav Kook was going
firmly against the grain of the religious establishment of his time.

Just as the distinguished rosters of modern great Jewish sports
heroes did not pay much attention to Orthodox Jewish law (since
their activity was inherently a symptom of non-Jewish cultural
influence), so, too, traditional Orthodoxy has never really called
for the abolition of Sabbath sports events. This is probably because they presumed that their own youth had no practical interest in sports.

Nonetheless Rav Kook's ideas have proved influential in parts
of the Israeli religious community. They also help to place in clear
focus the borderlines within which traditional Judaism could relate to athletics.

On the one hand, Rav Kook realized well that the objections
raised against athletics in the ancient world—the heathen connotations and the sadistic cruelty—no longer applied to most
modern manifestations.

On the other hand, he does not really extend his favorable attitude to sports substantially beyond the parameters allowed by
the medievals. Athletic endeavor is justified as a means towards
physical fitness. Physical fitness is, in turn, a legitimate instrument for the better performance of a Jew's religious duties, as well
as part of the process of national redemption.

We should not, however, allow Rav Kook's enthusiastic phrase-
ology (which is typical of his admiring reactions to the achievements
of the Zionist pioneers) to lead us to ignore a fundamental feature
of his position: Even he would deny that there is any legitimacy to
the concept of a "spirit" or value system attached to sports.

For it is the belief of traditional Judaism that there is only one value system: the religious worldview of the Torah. Other areas of human life may or may not be in harmony with the teachings of the Torah. Where an essential conflict must exist is when these areas (and this would apply to fields such as art, patriotism, or science, as much as to the "Olympic Spirit") claim to make up autonomous ideologies.

Traditional Judaism—or for that matter, any religious worldview—does not recognize rival value systems.

Thus, speaking from the perspective of Jewish sources (I emphasize that I am writing as an historian, not as a rabbi or theologian), it would be difficult to point to much affinity with any approach which sees athletic activity as more than part of a fitness program.

This premise would tend to discourage spectator sports altogether, except insofar as they arouse our admiration for God's masterful creation of the human body. It would also tend to limit the amount of time a Jew should be devoting to such pursuits.

Professional or full-time athletes (unless it is with a view to teaching or some other justifiable end) would be frowned upon for avoiding their legitimate functions of contributing to the public welfare of the world, a charge which would also be brought against professional gamblers and other unproductive types.

It is when people begin to attach an inherent value, or spirit, to athletic achievement that Jewish tradition must find itself at odds with the secular environment, forced to stand at some distance from the Olympic arena.

SUGGESTIONS FOR FURTHER READING

Bickerman, Elias. (1979). *The God of the Maccabees: Studies on the Meaning and Origin of the Maccabean Revolt.* Translated by Horst R. Moehring. Studies in Judaism in Late Antiquity. Leiden: Brill.

Yaron, Zvi. (1974). *Mishnato shel ha-Rav Kuk.* Jerusalem: [Jewish Agency].

60

ॐ

How Did Moshe Desta Revolutionize the Israeli Army?*

News Item: 1989—Outbreak of a prolonged Palestinian uprising, the Intifada, in territories occupied by Israel.

In reading the troubling reports of the current developments in the Israeli occupied territories, one naturally tries to imagine oneself in the boots of the soldiers who are thrown into such a situation. After being trained in the doctrine of "purity of arms"— which forbids the use of force against civilian or other non-military targets—Israeli soldiers suddenly find themselves today outnumbered by violent throngs of stone-throwing women and children. To complicate the situation, the soldiers are conscious that any overreaction will be eagerly taken up by the international

---

*"A Rock for a Rock." *The Jewish Star*, Calgary/Edmonton, May 27–June 9, 1988, pp. 4–7.

news media. Yet a second's delay by the soldier in responding might result in serious injury.

In short, it is not an enviable situation.

AN INFALLIBLE AIM

Pondering all this, I am reminded of some events that took place during my own basic training in the Israeli Army several years ago.

In accordance with the normal policy regarding draftees whose number comes up when they are older than the normal draft age, I was assigned to a Stage Two unit. There we were given four months of standard G.I. combat training (in my case, for the Engineering Corps) without the usual full three years of regular service.

The Stage Two units consist mostly of immigrants and can serve as a reliable index of the status of *aliyah* at any given point in time. Our unit had representatives from twenty-one different countries.

Our first actual mission (during Hanukkah 1983) involved patrolling in a refugee camp near Bethlehem (a frustrating fifteen-minute drive from my house). Much of our job consisted of marching through the alleys waiting for someone to fling a rock so that we could chase after them. We never caught anybody.

Whoever was not on patrol had to find ways to keep busy. Popular pastimes included housekeeping, endless rounds of Trivial Pursuit, and a circulating copy of *Playboy* supplied by somebody's considerate wife.

One evening when I returned from patrol, I noticed that some of the fellows had set up some tin cans on a rock wall and were competing at trying to knock them down with stones. The game quickly lost its interest when it became clear that one of our soldiers had an infallible aim. He just never missed.

This sharp-eyed stone-thrower was named Moshe Desta. He was one of two Ethiopian Jews in our outfit (we also had one non-Jewish Ethiopian). This was several months before the public revelation of "Operation Moses," the mass transportation of thousands of Ethiopian Jews to Israel. Before coming to Israel, Desta had been a shepherd and had used his skills to chase away threatening predators and to hunt the occasional bird.

Desta's distinctive expertise became evident again, at a later stage in our training, when we were stationed "Somewhere in the Judean Wilderness" practicing at using mine detectors. This was the sort of exercise that only a few can undertake at a time, while the rest stand idly by. Desta employed some leisure moments by taking a stray piece of rope, braiding it in a special way, placing a stone in it, and hurling it as a sling at various targets.

As expected, his accuracy was still infallible.

This aroused the interest of our commanding officer, who started asking him some very specific questions about the extent of his abilities. Desta replied as best he could, with his infectious and proverbial grin. (Our standard instructions when going out on night patrol were to remove all shiny objects so that "nothing should be visible except Desta's smile").

Desta showed our commanding officer how to tie together a sling. He showed him how to swing it so that it made a swooshing sound. He showed him how to turn off the sound.

The CO joked that this would be a great way to throw grenades. Desta replied with a perfectly straight face that, in the Ethiopian army, that *was* how they threw grenades!

The CO could not control himself any longer. He ordered a quick halt to the mine-detecting practice and started issuing strands of rope. Everybody was to gather an arsenal of appropriately-sized stones. Then we went off to the stone-firing range for target practice.

Needless to say, none of us came close to Desta's achievements, but some (not I, to be sure) did demonstrate some potential.

At the time, I wondered idly whether we might, in fact, be seeing the beginnings of a turning point in Israeli military doctrine: the founding of a Rock Corps. Could it be that under the leadership of a new generation of Ethiopian shepherds, this Rock Corps might present an appropriate response to challenges hurled by opponents in Gaza, the West Bank, or Me'ah She'arim?

As the years have elapsed and no such corps has been formed by the Israeli Defense Forces, I still cannot help wondering occasionally how such a special military force would be accepted by the shapers of world opinion.

61

✌

What Does the Talmud Say about Free Trade?*

News Item: June 1993—After heated public debate, the Canadian government under Prime Minister Brian Mulroney ratifies the North American Free Trade Agreement with the United States, which will go into effect in January 1994.

The Canadian free trade debate is by no means without precedent.

The argument over the relative wisdom of protecting local industry or of opening up foreign markets has been with us for millennia. Talmudic literature records a number of instances of such exchanges, many of which sound as if they could have been taken straight out of today's newspapers.

---

*"Mulroney's Persian Predecessor: The Free Trade Debate in Days of Yore." *The Jewish Star*, Calgary/Edmonton, Nov. 18–Dec. 1, 1988, pp. 4, 7.

One of the earliest recorded instances of rabbinical legislation dates back to the time of the Maccabees and consists of a decree declaring that glass is capable of becoming ritually impure.

In a famous lecture delivered at the opening of the Institute of Jewish Studies of the Hebrew University in Jerusalem in 1929, the noted talmudic scholar Louis Ginzberg argued that this measure was originally intended to curb the imports of glass products from Tyre and Sidon (in what is now Lebanon), who, at that point in history, were just beginning to export this novel and desirable product to the Holy Land. Judean technology was not yet capable of manufacturing glass vessels and was at a disadvantage since this material, which is not mentioned in the Torah, was thereby thought to be exempt from the possibility of ritual defilement. Such a claim would have made the product very attractive in a market that was dominated by the Temple and the priesthood.

By declaring that the imported dishes were equally susceptible to impurity, the ancient Jewish sages were, in effect, protecting the local manufacturers of earthenware vessels from what they perceived as unfair foreign competition.

According to Ginzberg, similar motives were at work in a number of other early laws. One generation after that first decree, Jewish sages were arguing that such commodities as Alexandrian wheat, Baalbekian garlic, and metal vessels were all impure or susceptible to defilement. All these decisions can be perceived as attempts to protect local industries.

Other scholars of the time opposed this protectionism; they felt that free international competition would ultimately serve to lower prices, better serving the broader needs of the average consumer.

Ginzberg also notes that the sages of talmudic times were concerned as well with limiting exports of strategic resources, especially the sale of real estate and large cattle to foreign landowners who would use these items to undermine Jewish control over Judean territory.

Ginzberg's interpretations have not been universally accepted by scholars, but they do offer a fascinating insight into the interrelations between Jewish law and day-to-day concerns.

FREE TRADE NEGOTIATIONS

Visitors to Jerusalem may be familiar with the nearby village of Motsa, down the hill on the road to Tel Aviv.

The Arab name for this village was *Qalunia*, reflecting the Roman title of the village as recorded in the Talmud: *Colonia* (or colony), which denoted a status that carried with it an exemption from customs duties. Talmudic tradition fancifully traced the Hebrew name to the same source—*motza* in Hebrew means removed, in the sense of removed (or exempted) from the obligation to pay duties.

At the beginning of the third century we find one of the greatest of talmudic leaders, the Patriarch Rabbi Judah Ha-Nasi (the renowned compiler of the Mishnah) actively lobbying to have the Galilean town of Tiberias declared a *colonia*.

As described in rabbinic legend, Rabbi (as Rabbi Judah was known) was approached by his constant companion, the Roman Emperor Antoninus (possibly the Stoic philosopher–ruler Marcus Aurelius), who sought his advice: "I want my son Severus to succeed me and to have Tiberias declared a *colonia*. If I ask them [the Senate] to allow one request, they will do it; but not if I ask for both." This phenomenon of a head of state facing a hostile senate is not a recent invention.

In those days, too, free trade negotiations were conducted in secrecy. Rabbi Judah, who was obviously in favor of instituting free trade in Tiberias, replied with the following coded message: He ordered to have a man carry another on his shoulders, and the topmost man to carry a dove. The lower figure was to tell the upper to release the dove.

Antoninus understood the symbolism. He asked the Senate to confirm his son's appointment and, in turn, instructed his son to declare Tiberias a free trade *colonia*.

The rabbis would often read their own preoccupations into events depicted in the Bible. For example, when we read the midrashic versions of the Book of Esther we often have the impression that the free trade debate was one of the major themes of the Purim story.

To cite some typical examples: in describing the elaborate decorations for King Ahasuerus' great banquet, mention is made of *dar* and *soharet* (Esther 1:6), generally translated as shell and onyx marble. A talmudic rendering reads this as, "He declared freedom (*dror*) to all who dealt in trade (*sehorah*)."

Similarly, among the various promises made by the king in order to persuade Esther to divulge her nationality, the rabbis include a pledge to reduce duties (as indicated in Esther 2:18 "And he made a release to the provinces").

Indeed, according to the Aramaic version of Esther, the official edict issued by Ahasuerus in support of the Jews is addressed to "all who desire to export goods from one nation to the other, from one people to the other."

The Persian monarch truly comes across in these sources as an oriental Brian Mulroney.

These quotations, cited from among a wealth of materials in our traditional literature, should suffice to indicate, once again, how similar the world of our ancestors was to our own.

SUGGESTIONS FOR FURTHER READING

Beer, Moshe. (1974). *The Babylonian Amoriam: Aspects of Economic Life.* Ramat-Gan: Bar-Ilan University Press.

Ginzberg, Louis. (1955). *On Jewish Law and Lore.* Philadelphia: Jewish Publication Society of America.

62

ر

What Books Have been Banned by Judaism?*

News Item: February 1989—The Iranian Muslim religious leadership declares its determination to assassinate British author Salman Rushdie for allegedly blaspheming the prophet Muhammad in his book The Satanic Verses, *prompting Rushdie to begin a period of prolonged concealment.*

EXTRANEOUS WORKS

The notion of a banned book is not alien to Jewish tradition. In the course of our history, a variety of books have been declared

---

*"Rushdie, Yes; Ayatollah, No." *The Jewish Star*, Calgary/Edmonton, March 31–April 18, 1989, pp. 4–5.

religiously or morally unacceptable, either forbidden for reading or consigned to destruction. The list is a fascinating one.

Talmudic literature speaks of a category of "extraneous" books (*sefarim hitzoniyim*), warning that those who read them will forfeit thereby their place in the World to Come. As an example of such "extraneous" works reference is made to the Book of Ben Sirah, a work composed in Hebrew around 180 B.C.E., very similar in spirit to the biblical Book of Proverbs.

In fact, the work is cited with some frequency in the Talmud, and it is hard to discern anything objectionable in it. Surprisingly, the same talmudic passage that bans Ben Sirah declares that the works of Homer, in spite of their obvious pagan character, may be read for pleasure.

The Book of Ben Sirah has been preserved in Greek translation (usually called Ecclesiasticus). It was Solomon Schechter's identification in 1896 of a manuscript fragment from Egypt as part of the Hebrew original of Ben Sirah that inspired him to recover the remains of the famous *Cairo Genizah* (a centuries-old repository of discarded Hebrew writings), one of the major landmarks in modern Jewish scholarship. Since then, the Dead Sea Scrolls have furnished us with additional portions of this banned Hebrew masterpiece.

Among the earliest works to be condemned by Jewish law were Christian scriptures, including the New Testament itself. Thus, the sages of Yavneh (around 90 C.E.) discuss the proper fate of the *gilyonim* (blank sheets), a derisive wordplay on *Evangelion*: Should they be burned in their entirety, or ought the sacred names of God be removed beforehand? All the authorities are in agreement that the books themselves are to be destroyed.

As we move into the Middle Ages, we find that among the more distinguished Jewish authors of banned books was the great twelfth century rabbi and philosopher, Moses Maimonides. Many of his contemporaries, especially in France, felt that his interpretation of Judaism, in accordance with Aristotelian philosophy, was too radical and threatened to undermine traditional belief. Maimonides' opponents in France denounced the *Guide to the Perplexed* to the Church, which ordered copies to be burned in the public squares of Paris in 1233.

POETIC WORKS FORBIDDEN

The reasons for banning a book were not confined to theological difficulties. Moral concerns also came into play.

For example, in describing the sort of reading that is appropriate for the Sabbath, the *Shulhan Arukh* forbids Jews to read the works of Immanuel. The personage in question is not identified by the standard commentators but is well known to students of Hebrew literature. He is indeed one of the most colourful Jewish figures of the Italian Renaissance, the poet Immanuel of Rome (1261–1330).

Immanuel, a contemporary of Dante, was a typical sort of bohemian poet, wandering about the Italian towns looking for part-time work (often as a synagogue secretary) or—better still—for generous patrons.

He was responsible for introducing the sonnet form into Hebrew poetry. He composed his own Hebrew tour of heaven and hell in the style of Dante's *Divine Comedy*. He also appears to have penned the earliest version of the *Yigdal*, the rhymed version of Maimonides' "Thirteen Articles of Creed" that has become one of the favourite hymns of the synagogue.

In a manner typical of his age, Immanuel had no qualms about mixing the sacred with the extremely profane. Much of his poetic output is downright lewd, going on, at sometimes tedious length, about his erotic conquests, with graphic appreciations of female anatomy. In one sonnet he muses that, given the choice, he would prefer to be sent to hell, because that is where all the beautiful women are to be found.

As noted, Jewish law as codified in the *Shulhan 'Arukh* has forbidden the reading of Immanuel's verse. The fact that such a prohibition was felt necessary does, of course, testify to Immanuel's popularity as reading material for leisurely Shabbat afternoons. To the best of my awareness, however, no Jewish religious authority went so far as to order Immanuel's assassination.

Cultures and traditions are normally judged by the literary works that they have produced and honoured. Nonetheless, it is not entirely inappropriate to characterize them also by those works which they have banned and condemned.

SUGGESTIONS FOR FURTHER READING

Roth, Cecil. (1959). *The Jews in the Renaissance*. Harper Torchbooks ed., Temple Library. New York: Harper & Row.

63

৵

What Does Judaism Say about Ecology?*

$\mathcal{A}$s spring struggles to assert itself in Alberta, I am reminded of the charming blessing ordained by Rabbi Judah the Patriarch, to be recited upon viewing the seasonal blossoming of the trees:

> Blessed are you, our God, King of the Universe, who has left his world lacking in nothing, and has created in it goodly creatures and fine trees to give pleasure to humans.

Nature exists, according to this *b'rakhah*, "to give pleasure to humans." On the surface, this would seem to be a fairly innocuous and inoffensive perception. However, it takes on a more problematic dimension for me when viewed in the light of a recent conversation I had.

---

*"Judaism and Ecology." *The Jewish Star*, Calgary/Edmonton, May 26–June 7, 1989, pp. 4, 8.

One of my students at the University of Calgary approached me some weeks ago visibly concerned over a passage in the Torah.

In the original Hebrew, she asked me, what is the force of the divine order issued to the first man and woman in Genesis 1:28, "... replenish the earth and *subdue* it, and *have dominion over* the fish of the sea, and over fowl of the air, and over every living thing that creeps on the earth."

Are the King James-like "subdue" and "have dominion" stronger than the intention of the original text?

Though I anticipated the reasons for her discomfort, I had little consolation to offer on that particular point. Indeed, the Hebrew roots are considerably more uncompromising than the English, carrying connotations of military conquest and subjugation, even (at least in modern Hebrew) tyranny.

This passage has not been very popular with environmentalists, who have frequently blamed our current environmental plight on such scriptural passages, which they feel arrogantly relegate nature to a role of a plaything to be exploited for the fulfilment of human need or greed.

I recognized that my student, in this instance, was seeking a way of deflecting some of the blame. Restricting myself to the immediate question, I was unable to supply one.

A DIFFERENT REALITY

It could be argued that biblical monotheism saw itself consciously opposed to any theology that overly glorified Nature. The essence of pagan religion was usually revealed in the way that it deified natural forces. The vilified cults of Ba'al, Ashtoret, and their companions were probably more in tune with the rhythms of nature; by contrast the Israelite deity was a God of history and morality who occupied a place above the natural processes.

Having said this, I cannot help but feel that I failed to give my student a sufficiently rounded picture of what is, after all, a complex issue.

Central to any assessment is the recognition that, however wise and relevant our ancient sources are, at times they reflect a reality that is fundamentally different from our own. Here, too, we should take care not to lose our historical perspective.

Our forefathers were an agricultural folk. So, if we do accept as a fact that Judaism is consistent in placing human interests above the natural world and in urging the exploitation of nature for human convenience, this should by no means necessitate a negligent attitude towards either the environment or natural resources. The desire to keep the world clean and fruitful is justified by the most selfish of interests: you cannot exploit what is no longer around.

More importantly, even if one should have wished to ruin the ecological balance, preindustrial technology simply did not have the means to produce such destruction. Until the present century not even the most perverted of intentions would have succeeded in destroying the ozone layer, saturating our food with harmful chemicals, or polluting the Alaskan coastline. The kinds of issues that we associate with environmentalist policies were quite unimaginable two hundred years ago.

Nevertheless, without a great deal of ideological fanfare, Jewish tradition has generally approached these questions with characteristic practicality, often impelled by a hardheaded self-interest.

A PRACTICAL APPROACH

To take a well-known example, Deuteronomy 20:19 orders the conquering Israelite armies, when besieging Canaanite cities, not to needlessly destroy the fruit trees from which they will later have to eat. Out of this practical advice, the talmudic rabbis elaborated the prohibition of *bal tash-hit*, which extends the ban on wastefulness to include other foodstuffs, clothing, fuel, and water, or any other useful resource.

This utilitarian approach to environmental care was particularly pronounced in the area of urban planning. For instance, the Torah orders that the cities of the Levites be surrounded by park areas as well as agricultural lands.

The medieval Spanish *Sefer Ha-Hinnukh* asserts that the biblical provisions for Levitical cities are to be regarded as a divinely sanctioned ideal. Accordingly, the Mishnah insisted that recreational parkland is essential for the "quality of life," and laid down as law that areas that had been designated for parks could not be utilized for residential construction or cultivation. Rashi observes that the aesthetic quality of a city demands the allotment of open recreational areas.

The ancient Rabbis were well aware that in order to make life livable for the citizens of a town, restrictions must be placed upon the types of industries that are allowed to be set up there. Some of the clauses in Mishnah *Baba Batra* have a distinctly modern ring to them:

> A permanent threshing floor must be distanced at least fifty cubits from a town (to prevent damage from the chaff in the air). . . . Carcasses, graves and tanneries must be distanced from the town at least fifty cubits (because of their foul and unhealthy smells). A tannery can only be set up to the east of a town (since in Israel the wind blows almost exclusively from the west) . . .

CAUSING HARM

Talmudic literature over the generations has dealt in great detail with such actual problems as air pollution, often in the form of harm caused by smoke drifting from one person's property into his neighbor's. It has done this in general without much theologizing, but as an extension of the basic laws of damages—nobody has the right to cause unnecessary harm or discomfort to his neighbor's person or property.

There are, of course, instances where acts do not necessarily bother specific contemporary individuals but are judged to threaten the long-term health of the environment or resource supplies. I am not aware of such issues being raised in rabbinic literature (probably because they did not exist before recent times), though I am confident that the rabbis would have dealt with them by extending the above principles to include long-range as well as immediate damage.

In general, Jewish tradition seems quite aware of our dependence on our natural environment and has set down concrete measures for ensuring its physical continuity as well as its quality. All this was done in the consciousness that God did indeed create in his world "goodly creatures and fine trees to give pleasure to humans."

Let's go out and appreciate the creation and ensure that it will continue to be around to give us pleasure.

CHAPTER

64

~

Could Maimonides
Join the Mounties?*

*News Item: 1990—Baltej Singh Dhillon became
the first Sikh officer in the Royal Canadian Mounted
Police to be allowed to wear a turban instead
of the traditional "Mountie" hat.*

It would seem that most Canadian Jews were pleased with the recent decision upholding the Sikhs' right to wear turbans in the
RCMP. After all, many of us also have vested interests in keeping
our heads covered as part of our own traditional religious observances. A skullcap is, of course, easier to accommodate than a turban, as it may be discreetly placed underneath a Mountie hat.

But some of our ancestors were also turban-wearers. As with
many items in Jewish history, this fact continues to affect us in
some surprising ways.

"When Jews Wore Turbans." *The Jewish Star*, Calgary/Edmonton,
April 6–May 3, 1990, p. 9C.

To take a rather simple example: the daily prayers recited by observant Jews include a benediction praising God "who crowns Israel with glory."

Though the common practice currently is to recite this blessing in the synagogue, the original custom was to say it as one was getting dressed. The Talmud says clearly that one was to say it while wrapping the turban around his head. In fact, the commentators make a special point of noting that it is appropriate to make the blessing over other types of headgear as well . . .

Newcomers to Hebrew have to learn that the Hebrew word for to wear (*labash*) can be used for most garments, but a different verb must be used to indicate the wearing of a hat: *habash*. The verb actually means to wrap (and is the root of the word for bandage, for example). Its origin dates back to a time when the only thing a well-dressed Jew would be likely to be wearing on his head was a turban, a long piece of cloth that would have to be wrapped around the head.

It appears that, among the Jews of Babylonia, the turban was felt to have special spiritual efficacy. It is told of one rabbi, for whom the astrologers had foretold a life of crime, that, as a counter-measure, his mother insisted on his wearing a turban at all times. Once during his childhood, when it accidentally unraveled, he found himself unable to resist the temptation to take a bite of someone else's dates.

In general, it seems that the turban was viewed as the distinctive mark of Torah scholars, who saw their wearing such a head covering as a sign of special piety.

With the rise of Islam, the turban came to be considered the crown of the Arabs and the badge of Islam. The honourable status that attached to the wearing of a turban created problems for the Jews of Muslim lands.

Officially, Jews were considered a tolerated minority (*dhimmis*) whose social inferiority was to be enforced by law. In the seventeenth Century "Pact of Omar," which defined the status of non-Muslims in the Islamic empire, the Jews and Christians agreed "not to attempt to resemble the Muslims in any way with regard to their dress, as for example with the . . . turban . . ."

As with similar dress restrictions that were often imposed upon their brethren in Christian Europe, this kind of law would often prove difficult to enforce, since Jews frequently developed amicable personal relationships with individual Muslims. The official authorities often responded to such social mingling by insisting that the Jews don identifiable apparel that would visibly indicate their inferior social position.

The Jewish turbans became a frequent target of Muslim reformist zeal. At times, Jews were required to wear distinguishing marks on their turbans; on other occasions, a limit would be set to the length of winding cloth that could be used for the turban (ten ells maximum, according to a decree of the Mamluk Sultan al-Malik al-Salih in 1354). The sixteenth-century Sultan Murad III forbade the Jews altogether from wearing turbans.

Historians take the view that the frequency with which such regulations had to be repeated indicates how ineffective they probably were in real life.

Perhaps the most familiar turban in Jewish tradition topped the head of Rabbi Moses Maimonides, the noted twelfth-century rabbi and philosopher. The same traditional portrait of Maimonides' stern, bearded visage has been appearing on the title pages of his works since the beginnings of Jewish printing.

In spite of the portrait's widespread acceptance, it has always seemed to me somewhat suspicious. It did not appear until many centuries after the Egyptian sage's lifetime, and it is doubtful that such a picture would have been commissioned by Maimonides himself, who shared his society's rigid disapproval of representational art.

My suspicions seemed to be confirmed a few years back when I visited Jerusalem's L. A. Meyer Museum of Islamic Culture. There among the many fascinating artifacts was sitting a copy of the familiar portrait of Maimonides—except that, according to the caption on the exhibit, it was a sixteenth-century Turkish merchant!

It would seem that the early Hebrew printers in Venice or Constantinople, eager to supply their readers with a tangible likeness of the Egyptian Jewish scholar, had simply pulled out an available piece of clip art that conveyed a rough image of what he might have looked like. That picture has defined our conception of Maimonides ever since.

And to think: If he were among us now, he could join the RCMP . . .

SUGGESTIONS FOR FURTHER READING

Stillman, Norman. (1979). *The Jews in Arab Lands*. Philadelphia: Jewish Publication Society of America.

65

౨౯

What is Baghdad's Importance for Jews?*

News Item: January 1991—Outbreak of the Persian Gulf War. An international coalition led by the United States attacks Iraq in response to Dictator Saddam Hussein's invasion and annexation of Kuwait.

A number of times every winter I am asked about the peculiar scheduling of the petition for rain in the daily service, which the prayerbooks instruct us to begin reciting from 4 December. I usually mutter some confusing reply about talmudic calculations based on autumnal equinoxes and other concepts that are not all that clear in my own mind.

---

*"Baghdad: For Centuries a Major Centre of Jewish Life." *The Jewish Free Press*, Calgary, March 15, 1991, p. 8.

During the fateful days of the Gulf War, the more basic significance of this date comes to mind in all its irony: We are actually praying for an abundant rainfall for Iraq!

Surprising as this might sound in today's circumstances (especially when we keep in mind the terrible drought that troubled
Israel this year), this fact underlines the special connection that
has always existed between the Jewish people and that part of the
world currently known as Iraq. This was the birthplace of Abraham
and the land to which the Judeans were exiled after the destruction of the First Temple. Scholars believe that this was where the
Torah underwent its final redaction.

The fact that Jews throughout the Diaspora continue to define their winters according to the Iraqi climate testifies again
to the decisive influence of the Iraqi (or, as known in other times:
Babylonian, or Mesopotamian) Jewish community. It was the
Babylonian Talmud that was recognized as the highest legal authority for Jews throughout the world, and it occupied a place of
such centrality in their studies that the Babylonian landscape was,
at times, more real for many Jews than their own.

Let me illustrate this vast subject by limiting myself to a few
comments about the Jewish involvement with Iraq's capital,
Baghdad. Now, the history books tell us that the history of Baghdad
did not commence until the year 763, when it was built as a new
military outpost by the Caliph al-Mansur. However, students
of the Talmud are familiar with a third-century Rabbi Hanna
Bagdata'a. For Rashi, writing in eleventh-century France, it was
obvious that this rabbi was a native of Baghdad. Modern scholars are not ready to automatically reject that identification since
Muslim Baghdad was likely built upon an already existent town
that may well date back to talmudic times, as evidenced by its
Persian name.

By the tenth century, the major Babylonian institutions, including the great talmudic yeshivahs of Sura and Pumbedita and the
court of the Exilarch, had all relocated to Baghdad in order to be

closer to the seat of the Islamic Caliphate, which was the most powerful political force in the western world. It was through their official recognition by the Baghdadi Caliphs that the Babylonian Jews were able to impose their religious leadership and their Talmud upon most of the Jewish world.

During the zenith of Iraqi–Jewish dominance, it was inconceivable to many Jews that Baghdad had not always been a major Jewish center, and some talmudic sources were rewritten to reflect that perception. According to one such tradition, Rav, the original founder of the venerable talmudic academy at Sura, had really intended to go to Baghdad but had been tricked into staying by the mother of one of his students, who did not want to be parted from her son. The woman in question had approached the scholar asking how much milk would be needed to cook a portion of meat. Shocked by this display of *halakhic* ignorance, Rav concluded that his presence was needed in such a Jewish wasteland, and so he stayed there.

I recently had a look at a fascinating medieval Hebrew text, which claims to describe how the vessels from the first Temple in Jerusalem had been hidden away prior to its destruction by the Babylonians. "All of these vessels were concealed and interred in a tower in the land of Babylonia, in a city named Baghdad." The source, by the way, states that the hiding places of these vessels were recorded on a copper tablet. This legend is particularly interesting when we note that a copper scroll containing a treasure map indicating the hiding places of Second Temple artifacts (possibly reflecting a plan that was never executed) is one of the most enigmatic documents to be discovered among the Dead Sea Scrolls.

All these sources testify to the strength of the historical Jewish connection to Iraq and its capital, a fact which only serves to intensify the tragedy of the current situation, when a self-styled Nebuchadnezzar has again tried to aim his deadly arrows towards Jerusalem.

SUGGESTIONS FOR FURTHER READING

Jellinek, A. (1967). "Tractat von den Tempelgerathen." In *Bet-Ha-Midrasch*, ed. Adolph Jellinek. Vol. 2, pp. 88–91. Reprint ed. Jerusalem: Wahrmann.

66

⚜

Was Moses
King of Ethiopia?*

News Item: 1984—In "Operation Moses,"
7,000 Ethiopian Jews were brought to Israel.

News Item: May 1991—"Operation Solomon" airlifted
almost all the remaining community to Israel.

None would question the appropriateness of the name that was given to the recent airlift of Ethiopian Jewry: "Operation Solomon." The tale of King Solomon's encounter with the Ethiopic Queen of Sheba is well-known to all readers of the Bible.

Not so self-evident was the name of the earlier 1984 rescue which was entitled "Operation Moses." The biblical connection between Moses and Ethiopia is not a strong one, being limited to

---

*"Moses: King of Ethiopia." *The Jewish Free Press*, Calgary, June 14, 1991, p. 11.

a vague reference to Moses' Ethiopian wife, a mysterious figure about whom we are told very little.

Jewish legend, however, fills in this episode in the prophet's life in meticulous and romantic detail, relating that Moses actually reigned as King of Ethiopia for no less than forty years!

According to this tradition, Moses, in his flight from Egypt following his killing of the Egyptian taskmaster, wandered off first to Ethiopia, where he found himself in the midst of a civil war. It seems that while the legitimate king, named Kikanos, had been off on a foreign campaign, he had entrusted the homefront to the wily Balaam, who took the opportunity afforded by the king's absence to execute a *coup d'état*, fortifying the country against the returning monarch. Moses happened upon King Kikanos as he was laying siege to the capital city trying to recapture it and was instantly appointed commander-in-chief. When Kikanos died soon afterwards, Moses was declared the new king and set to completing the liberation of Ethiopia, a task which had already dragged on for nine long years.

The most formidable of the enemy fortifications consisted of a barrier of venomous snakes and scorpions. Moses defused this minefield by having his soldiers unleash a volley of hungry storks, who immediately swooped down upon the serpents and devoured them, allowing Moses' forces to recapture the capital. As was the custom in antiquity, Moses was expected to contract a diplomatic marriage with King Kikanos' widow, Adoniah. Daunted by the prospect of intermarriage, Moses never consummated the union. Nonetheless, he continued to reign as king of Ethiopia for forty years until his embittered queen aroused the population to remove this foreign ruler. Moses then proceeded to Midian where the biblical narrative resumes.

The story as I have described it is based on a work called the *Sefer Hayyashar*, composed in Spain during the later middle ages. However, versions of the story are found in Greek sources that date back to antiquity, except that, instead of storks, these versions refer to the ibis, the sacred bird of the Egyptians. These versions relate that the Egyptians' reverence for these birds resulted from their association with this episode.

Between "Operation Moses" and "Operation Solomon," we have been witnessing the dramatic conclusion of a long association between the Jews and Ethiopia.

SUGGESTIONS FOR FURTHER READING

Ginzberg, Louis. (1909–39). *The Legends of the Jews*. Translated by
H. Szold. Philadelphia: Jewish Publication Society of America.
Shinan, Avigdor. (1978). "Moses and the Ethiopian Woman: Sources of a
Story in *The Chronicle of Moses*." *Scripta Hierosolymitana* 27: 66–78.

67

❧

Who was the First Rabbi on the Moon?*

News Item: 1991—The comet Levy is visible in the night sky. A more famous comet named for the same American astronomer [Levy-Shoemaker 9] would later attract much attention when it dramatically collided with Jupiter in July 1994.

When a report in the *Calgary Herald* a few months ago announced the arrival of the comet Levy, my personal ethnocentric reaction was one of appreciation that a comet had been given such a fine Hebrew name. As it turned out, the comet was named for its discoverer David Levy, an amateur astronomer who used to live in Canada but now scans the skies from his backyard in Tucson, Arizona.

---

*"The First Rabbi on the Moon and the Long History of Jewish Astronomy." *The Jewish Free Press*, Calgary, July 2, 1991, p. 11.

A BLESSING FOR COMETS

Comets have long been of interest to Jewish sources. The Mishnah prescribes a blessing for their sighting. The talmudic sage Samuel, a noted astronomer of his day, claimed that though he was as familiar with the paths of the heavens as with the streets of his home town of Nehardea, he felt himself ignorant in the face of the mysteries of the comets.

The name "Levy" has been given not only to a comet, but also to a crater on the moon; and not any ordinary Levy, but a Rabbi Levi no less! I presume that the crater in question was named after the fourteenth-century French Rabbi Levi ben Gershom, known to Jews as Ralbag and to other as Gersonides, Magister Leo Hebreus or Maestre Leo de Bagnols. Ralbag is known for his popular commentaries on the Bible. Students of philosophy know him better for his vigorous critique on various views of Maimonides and Aristotle, a critique which eventually paved the way for the radical views of Spinoza.

JACOB'S STAFF

The scientific world has recognized Rabbi Levi's important contributions to the fields of mathematics, astronomy, and navigation. This summer I had occasion to see some examples of his scientific creations in a remarkable exhibition held in Montreal entitled "Planets, Potions and Parchments." This exhibition presented a rich assortment of books and artifacts illustrating the Jewish involvement with science from the Dead Sea Scrolls until the eighteenth century. The excellent catalogue of the exhibition is available at a number of Calgary book stores and makes fascinating reading for anyone interested in either science or Judaica.

Visitors to the exhibition were given the opportunity to operate an instrument known as the Jacob's Staff, a surveying tool consisting of a long rod with sliding plates, used to calculate angular distances with reference to the stars. Credit for the invention of the Jacob's Staff, which became a necessary aid to medieval sailors, was claimed by Gersonides, who placed great emphasis on the need for empirical observation as a basis for astronomical research.

Gersonides' observations caused him to raise serious criticisms against the prevailing astronomical theories of Ptolemy as regards the motions of the moon and the earth. These objections would eventually result in Copernicus' complete overthrow of traditional astronomical theory. These contributions were recognized in the naming of a lunar crater in Gersonides' honour.

THE SCIENCE OF ASTROLOGY

As with many medieval astronomers, Gersonides was a confirmed believer in the scientific validity of astrology. Appropriately, the Rabbi Levi crater on the moon can enjoy the company of another rabbinic crater, also named for a Jewish sage with an appreciation for astrological matters: Rabbi Abraham Ibn Ezra. The twelfth-century Ibn Ezra, who hailed from Golden Age Spain, loved to offer astrological explanations for Scriptural passages. He saw an astrological significance to the timing of the religious festivals and compared the High Priest's jeweled breastplate to the astrolabe, which made it a useful instrument for charting the future.

For Jews, astronomy was rarely a mere academic interest. Some familiarity with the courses of the sun and moon was essential for proper observance of time-defined commands such as daily prayers and the holiday calendar. These calculations could be very complicated.

Some years ago, Yale University Press sponsored a translation of Maimonides' code of Jewish law, the *Mishneh Torah*. When the translators came to the section dealing with the rules for calculating the Hebrew calendar, they realized that this was no simple job of translation, but required specialized knowledge of mathematics and astronomy. One thing led to another and, in the end, the short treatise had to be released as a separate volume with learned appendices by distinguished scientists.

The Jewish interest in astronomy has been a long and fruitful one. When the first Jew arrives on the moon, he will hopefully feel that this, too, is, in some way, territory trodden by his ancestors.

SUGGESTIONS FOR FURTHER READING

Levy, B. Barry. (1990). *Planets, Potions and Parchments: Scientifica Hebraica from the Dead Sea Scrolls to the Eighteenth Century.* Montreal and Kingston: McGill-Queen's University Press for Jewish Public Library of Montreal.

68

~

When Did Moses
Deliver the Mail?*

***News Item: September 1991—The Canadian
Post Office workers are on strike.***

The *Free Press*, like the rest of us, has been learning to cope with
the recent postal strike. Efficient postal service is one of those
things that is essential to modern society but is not appreciated
until it is disrupted.

Those of us who know some modern Hebrew will probably be
familiar with the Hebrew word for mail: *do'ar*. The fact that there
seems to be a real Hebrew word (as distinct from a Hebraized
foreign term) should already suggest that the term goes back to
our ancient sources. The origins of modern postal service, in the
sense of the government-administered delivery of private letters,

---

*"Moses the Mailman." *The Jewish Free Press*, Calgary, Sept. 27,
19091, p. 11.

do date back to ancient times, and it should not be surprising to find that mail service is mentioned in classical Jewish writings.

The word *do'ar* is taken from the Talmud, where it refers to a postal station. For example, a passage in the Babylonian Talmud discusses how much time one ought to allow when sending a letter so that it will be delivered before Shabbat, and distinguishes between whether the recipient's town does or does not have a *do'ar* office. It is evident that the talmudic rabbis who debated the question were used to enjoying the benefits of the Persian mail system.

Ancient authors often spoke admiringly of the elaborate Persian network of mail couriers. In a frequently quoted passage, the Greek historian Herodotus writes:

> There is nothing mortal that accomplishes a course more swiftly than do these messengers. . . . It is said that as many days as there are in the whole journey, so many are the men and horses that stand along the road, each horse and man at the interval of a day's journey; and these are stayed neither by snow nor rain nor heat nor darkness from accomplishing their appointed course with all speed.

There was, however, a negative side to this efficiency. The Talmud makes frequent mention of an institution known as the *angaria*, a forced conscription of pack animals by the government for purposes of mail delivery. The owner of the animal can never be certain that his beast will be returned or in what condition it will be by then. It is as if the Post Office had the right to arbitrarily borrow your family automobile whenever it pleased. Jewish law has to deal with questions such as: Who bears the loss if the conscripted animal is a rented one?

The midrash uses the image of a postal courier to illustrate the story of how Moses shattered of the tablets of the Torah when he saw the people worshipping the golden calf; on that occasion, Moses watched the holy letters flying away from the tablets, signifying that God had removed his sanctity from the tablets:

> Moses [says the midrash] was like a postman who was delivering a royal decree to a certain town. As he was crossing a river the docu-

ments fell into the water and the letters were erased. What did the postman do? He tore them up [since they were no longer of any use].

It seems likely that the midrashic metaphor is rooted in the reality that then, as now, not all letters got delivered intact.

69

◈

What Moral Standards Are Expected of Judges?*

News Item: 1991—The appointment of Clarence Thomas to the United States Supreme Court is accompanied by lengthy Congressional hearings, much of which focuses on accusations of sexual harassment in his past.

During the recent debates over the confirmation of U.S. Supreme Court Justice Clarence Thomas, I found myself in the company of American relatives who remained glued to their televisions throughout. My initial reaction was disdainful; certainly no Canadian would ever develop such a fascination over a judicial appointment.

On reflection, however, I have come to consider the matter from the perspective of Jewish tradition, and my assessment has become much more favorable. Judaism has always prided itself

---

*"'With Righteous Judgment': Jewish Reflections on the Appointment of Judges." *The Jewish Free Press*, Calgary, Oct. 31, 1991, p. 9.

in its legal system and, accordingly, has paid much attention to the quality of its judges. More than this: We have gone so far as to place the *tallit* (mantle) of religious and moral leadership upon individuals whose fundamental qualification is as judges—for this, of course, is the true meaning of title *rabbi*, that the individual so certified is deemed fit to serve as a judge in a religious court. All the other functions that we currently associate with the job of rabbi are either secondary or recent innovations copied from Christian models.

The Torah speaks in several places of the requisite qualities of a Jewish judge. For example: *"They shall judge the people with righteous judgment. Thou shalt not wrest judgment; thou shalt not respect persons; neither shalt thou take a gift . . ."* (Deuteronomy 16:19–20). For Rashi, this was not going far enough. We do not need the Torah to tell us that a judge must be honest and competent in the performance of his duties. What the Torah is demanding must be more than this: that the judge be upright in all aspects of his life.

Maimonides compiled an imposing list of qualifications for members of a Jewish court. In addition to various intellectual achievements (which include expertise in medicine, mathematics, and astronomy), he insists that they must be "free from all suspicion with respect to conduct" even in areas that do not bear directly on their judicial activity.

Thus, the sort of meticulous investigation into a candidate's personal behaviour that characterized the recent American Senate hearings would not have been out of place in a Jewish judiciary.

Who, in a Jewish legal system, would have been responsible for the appointment of the new judge? This was often a source of intense controversy among different factions in the Jewish community, a controversy which was fueled by the dual nature of the institution, which is at once an administrative and a religious one. At various points in history both the religious and the secular leaderships would insist on the right to appoint new members of the court. As a result of such disputes during the talmudic era, it became necessary for a new appointee to receive confirmation from both the head of the Yeshivah (representing the religious branch) and the *Nasi* or Exilarch (representing the secular branch).

With the decline of the centralized administrations of the ancient world, the appointment of communal judges and rabbis came more and more to be a prerogative of the secular communal leadership. Under the new arrangement, the judge was often a salaried employee of the community over which he was supposed to hold authority. This situation produced considerable discomfort among the judges concerned.

We can discern some of these hesitations in the following remarks by Rabbi Ephraim Luntshitz, a noted preacher in sixteenth–seventeenth-century Poland. In commenting on the wording of Deuteronomy 16:18 "Judges and officers shalt thou make . . . and they shall judge the people with righteous judgment," he is bothered by the shift in focus from *thou* to *the people*. Rabbi Luntshitz interprets this as a separate warning to those community leaders involved in the appointment of judges, that they must take care to hire individuals who will exercise authority not only over the general public, but even over those very leaders who hold the power over the appointments. Rabbi Luntshitz bluntly contrasts this ideal with the reality of his own generation, in which communal leaders abuse their authority by appointing judges whom they can hold under their thumbs.

The uneasiness expressed by Rabbi Luntshitz is probably not unlike that felt by American judges in the face of the political pressures that threaten to compromise their authority and integrity.

It seems to me that, as Jews, we do have much to learn from the intense involvement of the American public in the selection of its judges. They have learned the ancient Jewish truth that a society can be judged by the quality of its judges.

CHAPTER
70

❧

What is Clean Language?*

News Item: January 1992—Canadian politicians use
foul language in attacking one another in Parliament.

As bland and inept as they may be in other respects, recent verbal outbursts in Ottawa have proven our Canadian politicians to be among the most foul-mouthed of their breed. The notion of foul language is in itself an intriguing one. I find it curious how different societies define certain words as obscene or dirty, whereas other words having the same objective connotation are, nonetheless, deemed respectable.

The Talmud makes a conscious effort to maintain standards of dignified and clean expression. While there are no topics that were so delicate as to prevent their being discussed, our sages

---

*"Talking Clean—Talking Dirty." *The Jewish Free Press*, Calgary, January 30, 1992, p. 9.

avoided lewdness through the widespread use of euphemisms, which they termed *lashon neqiyyah*, clean language. Thus, when we read the Torah in the synagogue it is customary to replace certain explicit expressions with more polite equivalents. A similar practice governs the wording of talmudic texts. Sometimes the euphemisms are so successful that we remain unsure what they are replacing. A favourite circumlocution, *davar aher* (something else) is used in so many different contexts that students of the Talmud may frequently experience some confusion as to whether it is being employed to mask sexual activity, pork, idolatry, or . . . something else.

On the whole, Hebrew does not lend itself readily to obscene expressions. This is a fact that was recognized by Maimonides. The distinguished Jewish philosopher, consistent with his opinion that Hebrew is a natural language without any inherently mystical qualities, was called upon to explain why the Talmud refers to it as "the holy tongue." The reason, he argues, is that Hebrew lacks a vocabulary for describing the baser bodily functions.

An Egyptian acquaintance recently asked me about Arabic words that had entered into Hebrew. I hesitantly volunteered that Arabic constituted a rich source of obscenities and curses, in which Hebrew itself was lacking. To my relief, my acquaintance was neither offended nor surprised. Arabs recognize that this is one of the distinctive characteristics of their tongue. It is likely that Maimonides, a proficient speaker of Arabic, was conscious of this difference between holy and profane languages.

While Israel's parliamentary culture can hardly be considered more civilized than Canada's, I cannot recall anyone in the Knesset being censured for obscene language per se. There is, however, an episode that springs to mind that may reflect a distinctly Jewish slant on the propriety of political discourse. It concerns an incident some years ago in which an individual was brought to trial for directing an obscene gesture against the head of Israel's Labour Party (consisting of the upward pointing of the middle finger), which is referred to in English as "giving the finger" and in Hebrew—for unexplained reasons—as "the oriental gesture." This case extends the limits of obscene language to include nonverbal forms of communication—appropriate to a people that is noted for accompanying verbal speech with impassioned gesticulations.

By the way, this venerable gesture has a long history to it. According to the Jewish mystical classic, the *Zohar*, it expresses profound metaphysical mysteries and was used by Moses himself in the battle against the Amalekite foes.

We should note that the same Knesset has recently had to cope with another uniquely Jewish question of verbal propriety in politics in its recent decision to ban the use of curses and blessings in election campaigns. This phenomenon arose among religious political parties who promised their supporters the blessings of pious rabbis and the equally efficacious maledictions of these rabbis against those who would (God forfend!) vote against them. The curses in question were, of course, of the respectable variety and bear no resemblance to the curse words being hurled across the benches of the Canadian House of Commons.

SUGGESTIONS FOR FURTHER READING

Matt, Daniel Chanan. (1983). *Zohar: The Book of Enlightenment.* Classics of Western Spirituality, ed. Richard J. Payne. Ramsey, NJ: Paulist Press.

Pines, Shlomo, ed. (1963). *The Guide of the Perplexed—Moses Maimonides.* Chicago: University of Chicago Press.

CHAPTER

71

✌

What May You Do
to Win a Race?*

*News Item: January 1994—U.S. figure skating champion
Nancy Kerrigan is clubbed on the knee by a henchman
associated with rival skater Tonya Harding.*

Imagine this picture: Two eager young men posed nose-to-nose
as they run towards the finish line. They are approaching the last
tense centimeters of the race as one of the youths begins to feel
that he is falling behind. In desperation, he recalls that they are
now ascending a ramp, and that his rival is precariously close to
the edge. A slight push and the other racer falls over the edge with
a broken leg.

The above incident sounds as if it could have come from the
pages of a daily newspaper. In fact, its setting was neither a race-

---

*"Cutthroat Competition Is as Old as the Hills." *The Jewish Free Press*,
Calgary, March 3, 1994, p. 7.

track nor an Olympic arena. It is described in the Mishnah (*Yoma* 2:1) and took place in the Temple in ancient Jerusalem as two priests strove to be the first to reach the sacrificial altar. The prize that awaited the winner was not a gold medal and not a lucrative contract endorsing sports equipment. The glittering attraction that provoked such violence was nothing less than the privilege of cleaning off the ashes from the altar in accordance with the command recorded in Leviticus 6:3.

The original reason behind the establishment of this competition was to make the commandment seem more attractive and to provide the young priests with an opportunity to give physical expression to their eagerness in serving God. As often happens, the primary purpose became obscured, and the competition itself became an overriding obsession to be won even at the cost of injuring one's fellow.

Things could get even worse.

A similar incident is recorded in the pages of the Talmud, except that in that race the losing runner did not satisfy himself with injuring his opponent. This time he pulled out a knife and stabbed the other priest in the heart. To add insult to injury, before the victim expired, his father appeared on the scene and began to express his concern for the possible ritual defilement of the knife!

Once again, the dimensions of this ancient tragedy teach us the truth of Ecclesiastes' observation that "there is nothing new under the sun," and that sometimes there are no lengths to which people will not go to in their ambition to be a winner.

The Jewish sages of that time were shocked into the realization of how skewed some people's priorities can become in the presence of a competitive challenge. They immediately abolished the race and instituted a lottery for the assigning of jobs in the Temple worship.

To the best of my recollection, our sources do not relate whether there were frequent attempts to cheat the lottery.

But matters were not always so bad. The Talmud tells of other occasions when people, especially children, were encouraged to compete for the right to perform a *mitzvah*. For example, according to the Mishnah (*Pesahim* 8:3), it was customary for parents to urge their children to hurry along on the Passover pilgrimage by offering a share in the paschal sacrifice to the first one to reach Jerusalem. I imagine that the alternative to such a practice would have been a persistent chorus of whining "Are we almost there yet?" In this case, the results seem to have been more wholesome, and the triumphant child would generously share his portion with the remaining siblings.

And just for the record: The Talmud informs us that sometimes it was the girls who came out ahead of the boys in the race to Jerusalem.

72

✿

Were There Rigged Quiz Shows in the Talmud?*

News Item: 1994—In his film "Quiz Show," director Robert Redford evokes the scandals surrounding the rigged television quiz shows of the 1950s.

Because I do not get to attend very many first-run movies, I have not yet had an opportunity to see the highly praised new film, "Quiz Show." Though you would not believe it from looking at me, I am old enough to remember (but only barely!) the scandal that is dramatized in that film. I was one of those many viewers who were initially filled with adulation for the fraudulent geniuses whose spurious erudition was earning them huge fortunes on television quiz shows, until it was revealed that they were being provided with the answers in advance.

---

*"A Talmudic 'Quiz Show.'" *The Jewish Free Press*, Calgary, October 13, 1994, 8.

The story called to my mind an incident that is related in the pages of the Talmud, in which an ancient rabbi had to be provided with the answers to a quiz to which he was about to be subjected.

The episode occurred around the middle of the second century in the aftermath of the catastrophic Bar Kokhba uprising. The leaders of that generation were faced with the difficult task of reconstructing Jewish morale and religious institutions that had been shattered in the wake of the revolt and its ruthless suppression by the Romans.

The official head of the Jewish community at that time was the *Nasi* Rabban Simeon ben Gamaliel, who served as the head of the Sanhedrin, the council of sages that was acknowledged as the supreme authority for the interpretation and implementation of Jewish law.

Although he was a well-known scholar and heir to a dynasty of patriarchs that traced its origins to the illustrious Hillel, Rabban Simeon seems to have been a less assertive leader than most of his princely forebears—or than his son, the renowned Rabbi Judah the Prince. Eventually his authority became a source of dissatisfaction among his colleagues.

We do not know precisely what the issue was that gave rise to the questioning of Rabban Simeon's leadership. The Talmud ascribes the conflict to his introduction of ceremonies and protocols that did not give suitable recognition to the senior sages of the Sanhedrin.

Whatever their motives, two of the prominent rabbis on the Sanhedrin became disgruntled with the *Nasi*'s leadership and looked for a way to force him out of office.

They hit upon the idea of quizzing him about an obscure and rarely studied area of Jewish law known as *uktzin* (dealing with the purity of the stems and handles of various plants and foodstuffs). If things went according to plan, then it was virtually certain that the Patriarch would be caught unprepared and would be unable to answer the questions that were posed to him.

The plotters hoped that the resulting humiliation would force Rabban Simeon to resign.

Fortunately for the *Nasi*, one of his supporters, Rabbi Jacob ben Korshai, got wind of the conspiracy. On the night preceding the planned confrontation, Rabbi Jacob (in what might be the first documented use of subliminal teaching procedures) stationed himself outside Rabban Simeon's room and set himself to reciting the texts that would form the basis for the next day's "quiz." The *Nasi*, though puzzled at this exotic choice of subject matter, began to suspect that something might be afoot and decided to spend the night brushing up on the material.

Rabbi Jacob's stratagem accomplished its purpose. When the session convened the next day, the patriarch breezed through the quiz to the amazement of the assembled rabbis and the distress of his opponents. The *Nasi's* authority was reinforced and the rebels were disciplined.

When the full story came to light, it was recognized that the principal blame lay not in Rabban Simeon ben Gamaliel's actions, but in his rivals' readiness to disgrace the authority of the patriarchal office.

Unlike the television quiz show scandal, there is no suggestion that either party in the talmudic dispute was motivated by greed, financial gain, or personal ambition. As has often happened in the course of Jewish history, the animosities arose over differing perceptions about the proper honors that are due to the Torah and its representatives.

73

⨯

Does Jewish Law Recognize Academic Tenure?*

News Item: October 1994—The Ministry of Advanced Education of the Province of Alberta issued its "White Paper on Adult Learning." Among other things, this dealt with the roles of the universities and their faculty members. One of the topics that it raised was the sensitive question of academic tenure.

The Alberta government's recent white paper on adult learning has again spotlighted the issue of academic tenure at postsecondary educational institutions. Although universities were not a part of the traditional Jewish landscape, questions of job security were dealt with in the Talmud and its commentaries, usually with reference to elementary school teachers.

---

*"Sages Also Argued the Pros and Cons of Job Security." *The Jewish Free Press*, Calgary, November 15, 1994, 10–11.

The principal focus for all discussions on the topic is a ruling by the fourth-century Babylonian teacher Rava, who stated that an inferior teacher should not be replaced by a better one lest it lead to indolence. The Talmud records a dissenting view of Rav Dimi of Nehardea who argued to the contrary that "the jealousy of scribes increaseth wisdom," and hence, competition would lead to better performance.

The commentators are not in agreement about exactly whose perspective is being discussed: that of the original teacher or that of the replacement.

Rashi explains that it is the possible indolence of the new, better teacher that is of concern to us: Rava fears that the replacement "will become arrogant in his heart and confident of his unequaled superiority, leading him to behave indolently towards his pupils, since he will have no fear of being dismissed." Rav Dimi, on the other hand, is arguing that the mere knowledge of how his predecessor had been removed would continue to keep him on his best behavior. As Rashi puts it: "He will take special care to teach well, since he will be afraid that his colleague [the teacher whom he replaced] will continue to bear him a grudge for his dismissal and will constantly be looking for opportunities to embarrass him before the townspeople."

A different commentary on the talmudic passage takes the view that the Rava and Rav Dimi were speaking from the perspective of the original teacher, the one who was faced with the possibility of dismissal. According to this interpretation, Rava is arguing that the apprehension that one's job is always under threat of termination whenever a talented competitor appears on the scene could drive a teacher to a state of despondency that would deter him from any effort to improve himself or even to maintain his level of competence. Rav Dimi's view, on the other hand, is that constant awareness of the threat posed by competition will spur a good worker to be ever improving himself, which will ultimately work to the advantage of the educational system.

According to either of the above explanations, the dispute between Rava and Rav Dimi is about whether academic tenure should be perceived as a means of perpetuating idleness and incompetence or as a source of psychological security that would enable responsible instructors to devote their full attention to their teaching.

Subsequent halakhic authorities were not always in agreement over which of the two talmudic views is to be followed. The most widely followed code of Jewish law, the *Shulhan Arukh*, sided with Rav Dimi and against the ideal of tenure. However, this position was not held universally.

Thus, Rabbi Menahem Ha-Me'iri (southern France, thirteenth–fourteenth centuries) states that "Wherever the community has appointed a full-time schoolteacher . . . he may not be replaced by another during his lifetime, unless for idleness, or because of some other gross negligence on his part, such as excessive beatings, etc."

At around the same time, Rabbi Asher ben Jehiel, the Rosh, responded to an inquiry about a man who wanted to dismiss a private tutor in favor of a superior teacher. The Rosh replied that since the teacher had been contracted for a fixed period of time, he could not be dismissed without due cause.

The noted Egyptian Rabbi David Ibn Zimra went so far as to forbid such dismissals, even if the teacher were guaranteed employment in a different field. He also raised the issue of severance pay.

At the other extreme, authorities like Rabbi Jehiel Mikhal Epstein have argued that teachers—who should not be treated differently from any other employees—can be fired without specific grounds in favour of better qualified candidates even in midterm, for (he reasons), if it were not during the term of the appointment, it could hardly be considered a dismissal!

The debate that has been conducted in the pages of talmudic codes and responsa is much more complex than can be conveyed in a short article. Nevertheless, this cursory overview should suffice to demonstrate how much of the contemporary debate was anticipated by the Jewish sages of previous generations.

SUGGESTIONS FOR FURTHER READING

Warhaftig, Shilem. (1982). *Jewish Labour Law*. 2nd, revised ed., Publications of the Faculty of Law, University of Tel-Aviv, Jerusalem: Ariel United Israel Institutes and the Harry Fischel Institute for Research in Jewish Law.

74

⟡

Why Were Jews Indulging in Ethnic Politics?*

News Item: October 1995—Separatist Premier Jacques Parizeau blames "the ethnics and the money" following defeat of referendum to separate Quebec from the Canadian confederation.

The recent Quebec referendum campaign and its inconclusive results have left Canadians with an unpleasant aftertaste. Jews, in particular, felt alarmed at Premier Parizeau's accusations of betrayal by *les ethniques*.

We should recall that there have been similar situations in Jewish communal politics, where the interests of the established citizenry were not identical to those of the more recent immi-

---

*"The Ethnic Vote: Duisburg 1910." *The Jewish Free Press*, Calgary, December 1, 1995, p. 4.

grants. In such instances, Jewish communities have not invariably been altruistic in choosing the highest good.

A case in point: The cultured, native Jews of Germany in the nineteenth and early twentieth centuries were notoriously contemptuous of the uncouth *Ostjuden* cousins who had migrated recently from Eastern Europe, bringing with them the traditional religious outlooks and mannerisms of Polish and Russian Jewry. The clash became even more acerbic when agitated by the emotions of nationalism. The modern German Jews had long defined themselves as a purely religious grouping whose undivided political allegiance was to their European fatherland; whereas the Eastern Jews cultivated deep commitments to Jewish national solidarity.

The spread of Zionism to Germany at the turn of this century challenged many of the ideological assumptions of the liberal Jewish establishment who aspired to complete acceptance and assimilation into the host society. Predictably, the philosophic dispute carried over into the arena of Jewish communal politics, which, in Germany, were kept under the vigilant watch and enforcement of the state.

In several communities, the Zionist activists came to the realization that the only hope they had of obtaining political power in the *Gemeinden* was by forming alliances with other disenfranchised groups. This resulted in electoral cooperation between secular Zionists and Orthodox traditionalists—in a dynamic not unlike the coalition politics common in Israel, where socialist politicians don *yarmulkeh*s and seek to pass themselves off as defenders of religious traditionalism. The hybrid came to be viewed as a conservative party.

In several communities the strategy proved effective, and the conservative lists took over the local community councils. The established Jewish leadership became desperate to hold on to their power base.

The initial reaction was a familiar one: The liberals complained that the balance of power was unfairly held by the Jewish *ethniques*, the recent arrivals from the East who did not share the interests and loyalties of *real* German Jews. They appealed to the government to disenfranchise all Jews who did not hold full German citizenship. The local Zionists were quick to assail the insensitivity of their liberal opponents.

A confrontation of this kind in the tiny Jewish community of Duisburg, Prussia, exploded in 1909–1910 to became a model for similar struggles throughout central Europe. Reacting to the unexpected electoral successes of the Orthodox–Zionist allies, the liberals petitioned the government to have the results overturned on a technicality, arguing that the chief Zionist representative did not satisfy the residency requirements. The governor's decision to disqualify the one candidate without cancelling the whole election frustrated both parties. The veteran residents were barely dissuaded from seceding from the Jewish community council by the local rabbi—a liberal himself, who valued communal solidarity above partisan interests.

By the time of the next round of elections in Duisberg in 1912, the conservative faction captured all eight vacant seats on the assembly. The defeated liberals again sought vainly to have the civil authorities overturn the results. They accused the Orthodox (falsely, it was eventually shown) of buying votes. But more importantly, they argued that their opponents "mostly immigrated in recent years and stand apart from their native coreligionists." It would be unthinkable to allow those foreigners "whose hearts cannot beat in unison for Germany" to decide the future of a loyal German *Gemeinde*.[1] Furthermore, they claimed that the naive immigrants had been stirred into a panic by exaggerated charges of the radical reforms that would be introduced into traditional religious life if the liberals were to control the council.

---

1. From a memorandum issued by the Duisburg Executive Board to the district governor in Dusseldorf, cited by J. Wertheimer, "The Duisberg Affair: A Test Case in the Struggle for 'Conquest of the Communities.'" *AJS Review* 6 (1981), 185–206, p. 193.

Most significantly, the liberals pointed out that the margin of victory had been paper-thin, less than twenty votes. Clearly, if only the *true* German Jews had participated, the results would have been different!

The Zionists, for their part, were quick to capitalize on their rivals' utterances, accusing them of being more despicable and depraved than the gentile anti-Semites. More moderate and responsible Jewish liberal organizations were discredited by the rash behavior of their comrades in Duisburg as the factions throughout Germany became increasingly polarized.

There might be some reassurance in knowing that the *ethnics* were ultimately vindicated: The Prussian Interior Minister declared on May 4, 1914, that full membership in the Jewish community organizations must be extended to all resident Jews, whatever their citizenship.

SUGGESTIONS FOR FURTHER READING

Wertheimer, Jack. (1981). "The Duisberg Affair: A Test Case in the Struggle for 'Conquest of the Communities.'" *AJS Review* 6: 1–2: 158–206.

75

ॐ

Why Did Doña Gracia Impose a Blockade?*

News Item: March 1997—The U.S. passes the Helms–Burton Law. Extending their long-standing boycott to encompass other nations that continue to trade with Cuba, the new legislation permits suits in U.S. courts against companies doing business with Cuba. According to this law, the U.S. can refuse entry to executives of such companies. Canada and other countries object to the law, claiming that the U.S. has no right to impose its foreign policy on them.

Lately we Canadians have been roused to heights of righteous indignation by the American threat to punish foreign firms that violate their economic blockade of Cuba. As Jews, we might be particularly sensitive to the issue, having ourselves been the victims of boycotts declared by assorted enemies.

---

*"Doña Gracia's Blockade." *The Jewish Free Press*, Clagary, April 25, 1996, p. 10.

Perusing the annals of Jewish history, we discover that there was a time when the Jews of the world tried to band together to inflict punitive and retaliatory sanctions on a hostile power.

The episode began in the Italian city of Ancona. During the sixteenth century, Ancona became a haven for Jewish merchants, who were enthusiastically encouraged to settle there in order to enhance the city's status as a free port. Resisting pressures from Jew-baiters in the Church, several Popes guaranteed protection to any Jews who settled in the city. Scores of Jewish traders responded to the invitation, including Marranos from Portugal and the Levant. The situation proved beneficial to all concerned.

Matters took a turn for the worse in 1555 when Pope Paul IV revoked the Jewish privileges and revived several all-too-familiar discriminatory measures, such as the wearing of a yellow badge, confinement to a ghetto, and vocational restrictions.

The refugees from Spain and Portugal found themselves in a particularly dangerous predicament. Since they had formerly been baptized as Christians, they were now subject to the authority of the dreaded Inquisition. It was not long before fifty-one Jews were put on trial, of whom twenty-five were burned at the stake. The Jewish world was stunned and outraged.

At that time there lived one of the most formidable Jewish political leaders since ancient times, the illustrious Doña Gracia Mendes Nasi. Though born a New Christian in Portugal, she had escaped to settle in Antwerp, where her husband was a wealthy jeweler and financier. Upon his death, she took charge of the family business, which also served as a cover for a vast and effective underground railroad whose agents throughout the world were constantly at work smuggling Jews from the Iberian Peninsula to more hospitable shores.

After publicly declaring her Judaism, Doña Gracia was forced to leave Europe to join the thriving community of Sepharadic refugees in Constantinople. There, she devoted her considerable spiritual and material resources to the benefit of the local Jewish institutions. La Señora, as she was called, became the revered patroness of synagogues, yeshivahs, and Hebrew letters. Her control over the communal leadership, strengthened by her amicable ties with the Turkish Sultan, was close to absolute, and she has been described as the most powerful woman of her generation.

Immediately upon hearing of the tragic fate of the Ancona martyrs, Doña Gracia resolved that retaliation was called for. She reasoned correctly that Spanish Jewish merchants made up an economic force of such magnitude that if they were to cease trading with Ancona, transferring their cargoes instead to neighbouring harbors, the duplicitous city could be reduced to financial ruin. The only catch was that, for the plan to succeed, it would have to be supported by all Jewish merchants without exception.

Since so much of international Jewish commerce emanated from Constantinople itself, Doña Gracia stood a reasonable chance of success. True, there were some traders who opposed the boycott, whether out of personal economic interests or because of fear of reprisals against relatives in Christian lands. Several rabbis issued halakhic rulings against the boycott. However, it was a relatively simple matter for "la Señora" to invite the insubordinate sages to her palace and quietly remind them what was likely to become of their yeshivahs or synagogues should she decide to withdraw her generosity. It was an offer they could not refuse.

Initially, the sanctions proved effective. Over time, however, it became apparent that they could have perilous consequences for Jews who remained subject to the Pope's authority. An extensive debate was conducted in the Jewish community over the painful question of whether it was worth endangering fellow Jews in order to create a possible long-term deterrent to potential persecutors of Israel. The wall of solidarity eventually crumbled before fully achieving its objectives.

What is the moral of this story? With respect to the current Cuban sanctions, I have no doubt that it can legitimately be cited in support of either side of the debate, whether to prove that all attempts at commercial blockade are doomed to failure, or to justify hermetic enforcement of the boycott as the only assurance of its success.

However we choose to interpret the issue, it provides us with an opportunity to retell a fascinating exploit and to make the acquaintance of an outstanding personality from the Jewish past.

SUGGESTIONS FOR FURTHER READING

Roth, Cecil. (1948). *The House of Nasi: Doña Gracia*. Philadelphia: Jewish Publication Society of America.

76

⨯

What are the Origins of Israeli Coalition Bargaining?*

News Item: May 1996—The narrow victory of Benjamin Netanyahu's Likud party requires concessions to the small Orthodox religious parties whose support is necessary for a parliamentary majority.

Yet again we have been privileged to witness the distasteful ritual horse-trading in which the Israeli Orthodox parties extort political favors from a new government in exchange for their coalition support. The process, which is an unfortunate by-product of Israel's proportional representation system, has never reflected favorably on either side in the negotiations and has served to alienate generations of Israelis from their Jewish heritage.

---

*"Coalition Bargaining." *The Jewish Free Press*, Calgary, July 5, 1996, pp. 6–7.

This style of coalition negotiation has quite a long history, antedating the establishment of the state by a full generation. As early as 1918 attempts were made to convene a parliamentary body that would represent all segments of the Jewish populace of Eretz-Israel and serve as a government-in-waiting until the achievement of statehood. Democratic elections were planned for this body, and the entire *Yishuv* (the pre-state Jewish population) made ready to cast their votes.

Well, *almost* the entire *Yishuv*. The Orthodox representatives could not countenance the fact that women would be allowed to participate, whether as voters or as candidates.

Faced with threats that the Orthodox would withdraw and set up an assembly of their own, thereby undermining the raison d'être of the general parliament, the leaders of the secular and religious factions set to work on a solution to the impasse.

Fortunately, both sides were headed by far-sighted and flexible leaders. The socialist David Ben-Gurion and the Mizrachi President, Rabbi Judah Leib Maimon, had been together through imprisonment in Turkey and exile in America and shared similar visions of Zionist priorities. (The fact that Rabbi Maimon's sister, Ada, was one of Labor's most outspoken feminist activists may also have facilitated matters.) An initial compromise was achieved when Ben-Gurion consented to emend the name of the proposed parliament from a Founding Assembly—with its implications of a permanent, constitutional status—to the less explicit Elected Assembly.

Unfortunately, this agreement did not prove sufficient. Five days before the date set for the polling, eighty-five rabbis, among them Rabbi Abraham Isaac Kook, issued a solemn proclamation declaring that all Godfearing Jews should boycott the elections since women's participation would constitute a gross violation of Jewish law and tradition.

Faced with this new obstacle, Rabbi Maimon acted decisively. The Mizrachi Party flatly refused to follow the unsolicited rabbinic decision, insisting that the formulators of that decision merely intended it as advice and not as a halakhic ruling. Mizrachi members were encouraged to take part in the elections.

After many delays, most of the Jewish population finally went to the polls on April 19, 1920. However, Arab riots in Jerusalem caused the elections there to be postponed until May 2. The riots had the additional effect of strengthening support among the Orthodox for this demonstration of national pride and solidarity. Even Rabbi Kook retroactively conceded to the Mizrachi position (which he described as "providential") and planned to cast his own vote.

There remained, however, a slight problem: Rabbi Kook would not agree to participate unless separate booths were provided for the women. The secularists were equally adamant in their refusal to yield to the clerical reactionaries.

A further meeting was convened at which Rabbi Kook discussed his position with representatives from the opposing groups. Initially, the sage proposed that the dispute be resolved through semantics: It would be the men, rather than the women, who would be segregated at the polls. The delegates were not appeased.

The solution that did emerge was so outrageous that to this day no one is entirely certain how it came to be accepted. Apparently, out of desperation to secure Orthodox participation in the process, the democratic majority consented to a procedure whereby the patriarchs of Orthodox Jerusalem families would be granted the right to cast votes on behalf of their wives and daughters!

The prize for this suspension of democratic principles was that Rabbi Kook actively urged his constituency to take part in the balloting, and the Elected Assembly was ultimately elected from all major segments of the Jewish populace for whom it claimed to speak. Once that milestone had been reached, the original disputes faded into the background, and the Elected Assembly—as well as its successor, the Israeli Knesset—conducted all subsequent elections in conformity with fully egalitarian standards.

The dynamics of that episode appear to have set the pattern for all future coalition haggling in the Jewish state. Those earlier pioneers were gifted with a remarkable ability to define priorities and to wisely discern when principles must be compromised in the broader national interest.

In those earlier days, both sides were arguing over values and ideological principles. I doubt that the same can be said about their present-day successors.

SUGGESTIONS FOR FURTHER READING

Teveth, Shabtai. (1987). *Ben Gurion—the Burning Ground: 1886–1948.* Boston: Houghton Mifflin.

77

⤜⤏

Is Relevance Irrelevant?*

News Item: October 1994—The Ministry of Advanced Education of the Province of Alberta issued its "White Paper on Adult Learning." This dealt with, among other things, the roles of the universities and their faculty members.

As I understand them, our present provincial leaders are not favourably disposed towards any form of higher education that is not directed towards the employability of its graduates

From out here in the pedagogic trenches, this strikes me as a frighteningly shortsighted notion of what higher education should be about—and all the more so when viewed from the perspective

---

*"On Education and Employability." *The Jewish Free Press*, Calgary, October 10, 1996, p. 8.

of a Jewish tradition for whom schooling has always been seen as a way of molding the student's intellectual and spiritual character.

To be sure, Jewish tradition is unequivocal about acknowledging the parental obligation to teach one's children a useful trade; to do otherwise, the Talmud states, would be tantamount to actively recruiting them into the criminal underworld. The ancient rabbis offered practical guidance in selecting vocations that allowed their practitioners to work in dignity, if not in affluence.

In fact, by reading the rabbis' career recommendations, historians have been able to learn a great deal about the vicissitudes of economic conditions in talmudic times.

Thus, the severe decline in agricultural profits in the third century, a consequence of political instability in the Roman empire, was exemplified in two contrasting statements by Rabbi Eleazar ben Pedat. Initially, he echoed the traditional Jewish preference for the farming life when he declared that "a man without land is not a man" (No, the saying was not invented by Duddy Kravitz's *zeideh*). In later years, however, the harsh economic and social realities of his day prompted him to observe that "there is no profession more degrading than agriculture," thereby reflecting the experience of the thousands of his contemporaries who were being forced to forsake their fields and flock to the crowded cities.

The fickleness of the economy should, of itself, be sufficient reason for concluding—as our political leaders and administrators apparently have not done—that a real education must be based upon more substantial and lasting foundations.

At any rate, for our sages, education was not a matter of acquiring technical skills, but a means of participating in civilization and of shaping moral and spiritual character.

Even the champions of the European Jewish Enlightenment, who insisted that Jewish schools ought to be teaching their students to become economically productive members of society, did not imagine that the inclusion of practical subjects would come *in place of* the traditional academic and religious curriculum.

Indeed, the time-honored pedagogic agenda of the talmudic yeshivah promotes many of the ideals associated with liberal education. Firmly rooted in ethical values, it is at the same time committed to critical analysis. The teachings of earlier authorities are subjected to the most uncompromising investigation, challenged by logic or by texts such as the Bible. Sloppy reasoning is not tolerated.

Admittedly, one area in which the Talmud can hardly claim to excel is that of practical relevance. For the most part, the rabbis had far more interest in subtle conceptual definitions than in the pragmatic application of Jewish law. We often receive the impression that the more implausible the situations, the greater the likelihood that they would be heatedly debated in the academy.

But, of course, relevance can be a matter of perspective. Just as many of our most useful technological and scientific breakthroughs have resulted accidentally, from disinterested theoretical inquiry, so have several of the farfetched constructions in the Talmud anticipated developments in the real world.

Rabbi Adin Steinsaltz has collected several fascinating examples of bizarre-sounding talmudic speculations that would take on actuality centuries later. He notes, for instance, the recurrent mentions of the "tower floating in the air," a hypothetical construct that would allow a person to traverse an impure place without actually touching the ground or breathing the air.

What was once the farfetched imagining of an unbridled legal imagination has since become a commonplace of aviation; and the halakhic concepts formulated in those ancient discussions can be profitably applied to contemporary questions as diverse as overflight rights and environmental protection.

It is precisely that freedom to indulge in fruitless impracticalities that defines us as civilized human beings. And one cannot help but be dismayed by people who have gone astray after the idolatries of practicality and relevance.

SUGGESTIONS FOR FURTHER READING

Sperber, Daniel. (1978). *Roman Palestine 200–400: The Land.* Bar-Ilan Studies in Near Eastern Languages and Culture, Ramat-Gan: Bar-Ilan University.
Steinsaltz, Adin. (1978). *The Essential Talmud.* Translated by Chaya Galai. New York: Basic Books.

78

Can the Government Run a Road through Your Property?*

***News Item: September 1996—A proposed expansion
of a major Calgary thoroughfare, which will require
expropriation of residential properties, is viewed
by some as a threat to the local Jewish community
and its institutions.***

Any project that involves major road building will inevitably cause inconveniences to those residents whose property lies in the path of the bulldozers. This appears to be the case with regards to Calgary's plans to expand 14th Street SW, as described in recent issues of this newspaper.

Of course this is not a new or unique problem. Most law-based societies have had to cope with these sorts of conflicts,

---

*"Encounter with a Lion." *The Jewish Free Press*, Calgary, October 24, 1996, p. 8.

where benefits to the majority are achieved at the expense of a minority.

Jewish legal literature discusses several scenarios in which a public thoroughfare impinges on the property of individuals. In most cases, the interests of the public are given overriding priority.

A classic case that is discussed in the Talmud involves a public road that passed through a privately owned field, prompting the field's owners to take matters into their own hands by diverting the road to an alternate route through the same field. In such an instance, the rabbis ruled that not only would the public have the right to hold on to their original road, but the owners would be penalized by having to forfeit the replacement road as well!

As representatives of the public interest, the Jewish courts saw themselves as the custodians of far-reaching powers that could be traced back to Biblical times. Indeed they cited the precedent of Joshua and the tribal chiefs of his day, who had exercised similar authority when apportioning the land among the tribes of Israel.

Somewhat more complex were the extensive powers assigned to the Jewish kings with regard to the expropriation of property for personal or national purposes. The biblical precedents appear ambivalent in their attitude towards royal power. Even while seeking to alarm the people with the prospect of rapacious leaders who would "take your fields, and your vineyards, and your oliveyards," (I Samuel 8:14) the prophet Samuel was introducing measures designed to prevent the kings from exercising arbitrary authority over the citizens' property.

Some commentators pointed to the biblical account of how the wicked monarchs Ahab and Jezebel had to arrange for the judicial murder of Naboth in order to confiscate his vineyard. Did this not demonstrate that even tyrants did not have the authority to seize private property at will, even though they were ready to offer compensation!

The Mishnah appears to be more generous about authorizing the king to confiscate property: "The king is permitted to break down fences in order to obtain access, and none may protest. No limits are set to the dimensions of the King's roadway." Commentators add that this prerogative also extends to the demolition of buildings.

Medieval halakhic authorities were of several minds when it came to defining the scope of these royal powers. It would be interesting to speculate on the degree to which their positions on this question might have been influenced by their cultural and political environments.

Thus Rashi, who lived in a feudal society where power was wielded arbitrarily by kings and barons, extends the king's right of expropriation even to matters of personal convenience.

A very different approach was professed by Maimonides, whose depictions of royal conduct are always guided by rationality, echoing the Platonic ideal of the philosopher king. In Maimonides' view, the king is permitted to seize private property only in time of war or other urgent necessity, and the owners must be fairly compensated. Some interpreters subjected these rights to further conditions; insisting that the expropriated lands be returned to their owners if no longer needed.

Thus, the threat of possible expropriation hovers over all property owners.

Under the circumstances, we can better appreciate the interpretation that Rabbi Simeon ben Lakish applied to the prophet Amos' image "As if a man did flee from a lion" (5:19). As understood by Rashi, this picture alludes to the plight of "a man who went out into his field and there encountered the municipal surveyor."

SUGGESTIONS FOR FURTHER READING

Blidstein, Gerald J. (1983). *Political Concepts in Maimonidean Halakha.* Ramat-Gan: Bar-Ilan University Press.

Cohn, H. (1968). "Courts as Expropriators." In *Fourth World Congress of Jewish Studies in Jerusalem*. World Union of Jewish Studies, 267.

Federbush, S. (1978–). *Mishpat ha-melukhah beyisra'el*. Jerusalem: Mossad Harav Kook, 1973.

Zevin, S. J. et al., ed. *Talmudic Encyclopedia*. Jerusalem: Talmudic Encyclopedia Institute.

79

꒥

What Lies under the Temple Mount?*

News Item: September 1996—The opening of an archeological tunnel under the Temple Mount leads to fierce and prolonged rioting by Arabs in Israel.

I trust that most of my readers are more knowledgeable and discerning than the news media and were not taken in by the hysterical Arab fabrications about the Western Wall archeological tunnel somehow penetrating under the Al-Aqsa mosque and threatening the stability of the Temple Mount.

The Israeli Antiquities Authority is well aware of the religious and political sensitivity of that site and has scrupulously excluded it from the scope of their otherwise ubiquitous digging in Jerusalem's old city.

---

*"Excavations and Imaginations." *The Jewish Free Press*, Calgary, November 7, 1996, pp. 10, 11.

No doubt the decision-makers have not forgotten the sad fate of the English Captain Montague Parker who, in 1911, conducted excavations in Jerusalem's Siloam pool and Ophel. Unfortunately, Captain Parker could not resist the temptation to extend his research beneath the Temple Mount. Though he tried to evade detection by doing his work under cover of darkness, word of his clandestine activities eventually got out, and the rumor spread that he had actually succeeded—as had been his undeniable intention—in unearthing and removing the cherished treasures of the Temple.

So great was the ensuing uproar among the irate natives that, in true "Indiana Jones" style, Parker's team had to flee to Jaffo, where their yacht set sail only moments before the arrival of the Turkish police.

The expectation that the Temple's vessels are still concealed beneath the earth has been fueled by the sector's very inaccessibility. As often happens, legend and imagination have ventured into those realms from which empirical investigation has been excluded.

According to a tradition that is recounted in the Palestinian Talmud, a priest in the Second Temple, while at work chopping wood for the altar, became aware of an unevenness in the Temple floor. Before he had a chance to show the spot to a companion, he immediately expired. This was viewed as proof that the holy ark was buried under that location, and that its whereabouts were not ready for public disclosure.

Muslim traditions also speak of treasures from the Jewish Temple being housed in a cave under the Dome of the Rock. Access to this cave is obstructed by a large slab of marble. In Arabic the cave is designated *Bir al-Arwah*—the Well of the Spirits—and legend has it that Abraham, David, and other Biblical saints assemble there for prayer. The sixteenth-century Egyptian Rabbi David ibn Zimra relates that the cave's entrance had been sealed by the kings of an earlier era because none of the emissaries who were sent to investigate it ever emerged alive.

The entrance to the Cave of the Spirits is actually situated in another cave, which, in turn, is carved into the great rock (*al-Sakhra*) from which the mosque gets its name. This rock is well-known from ancient Jewish sources where it is referred to as *Even ha-shetiyyah*. While the Hebrew expression might originally have denoted a fire-stone (a meteorite), it came to be universally understood as the Foundation Stone. Rabbinic lore saw this rock as the kernel from which God began to fashion the world, of which the Temple Mount was the centre.

Jewish legend lovingly elaborated upon the miraculous qualities of the Foundation Stone. The midrash identified it with the stone that served as Jacob's pillow while he dreamed at Beth-el, a belief that was later reiterated by a twelfth-century Christian pilgrim. Several Jewish writers accepted the Arabic claim that the rock actually hovers in the air.

The *Zohar* stated that the rock had been quarried directly from the divine throne of glory, and that it had furnished the tablets that were given at Sinai. Other sources told how the secret name of God was engraved on the rock, so that special defenses had to be devised to prevent unscrupulous individuals from using the mystical name to divulge divine secrets. Some people, including Jesus, were clever enough to bypass the security system and use the name for sorcery.

The Muslims evolved their own beliefs about the wonders of *al-Sakhra*, linking it to the stones in the Garden of Eden or to episodes in the life of Muhammad.

Contrary to the impressions that are created by recent events, the devotion of two communities to a single holy site does not inevitably lead to conflict. A more harmonious scenario is suggested in the following tale, which builds upon the affinity between the Jerusalem Foundation Stone and the black rock that is housed in Islam's holiest site, the Kaaba in Mecca.

Accordingly, a Muslim sage speaks of a great day in the time of the future Resurrection, when the stone of the Kaaba, escorted by all the inhabitants of Mecca, will travel to the Temple Mount in Jerusalem, where it will be united with the Foundation Stone. At that point (the story goes), the Jerusalem rock will greet its Meccan cousin with the hearty blessing of "Peace to the great guest!"

SUGGESTIONS FOR FURTHER READING

Ginzberg, Louis. (1909–39). *The Legends of the Jews*. Translated by H. Szold. 7 vols. Philadelphia: Jewish Publication Society of America.

Mazar, Benjamin. (1975). *The Mountain of the Lord*. Garden City: Doubleday.

Vilnay, Zev. (1973). *Legends of Jerusalem*. Edited by Z. Vilnay. 1st ed., *His The Sacred Land, vol. 1*. Philadelphia: Jewish Publication Society of America.

80

∿

Did Jews Cheer for
the Home Team?*

*News Item: Frequent occurrence—The Calgary Flames
lose another hockey game.*

My beloved Calgary is a city that takes its sports very seriously.

I have had occasion to point out the difference between the Calgarians' unconditional loyalty to their home teams and the sensible attitudes of the pagans of old, who, when vanquished by a mightier army, easily transferred their devotion from their own ineffectual deities to the victorious gods of their conquerors. Not so the good people of Calgary, who will continue supporting their losing athletes in defiance all reasonable hope!

The adulation that is currently heaped upon hockey and football players was once the privilege of chariot racers. In ancient

---

*"Home Team Blues." *The Jewish Free Press*, Calgary, December 19, 1996, p. 8.

Rome their popularity surpassed that of statesmen and generals. Under the Christian Byzantine empire, they rivaled even the monks and saints as heroes of the masses.

The residents of the Holy Land were not immune from the general enthusiasm for chariot racing. King Herod is said to have erected a hippodrome in Jerusalem, and a fourth-century author counts Caesarea among the world-class centres of that sport. So famous was it that a Hebrew mystical text speaks of celestial fire-eating horses whose mouths are so immense that they can be measured as "three times the size of the Caesarea stable doors."

To be sure, there was a cost to this manifestation of civic pride. The local chariot teams were subsidized by tax moneys, and aristocratic citizens were under strong social pressure to contribute to their sponsorship, even if this caused them considerable financial hardship.

Society, in those days, was split between the supporters of the Blues and of the Greens. The devotion of the fans to their teams was so volatile, often leading to violent riots and rebellions, that historians have sought a social, political, or religious background to the rivalries. At any rate, graffiti cheering on the favored team have been unearthed at various sites in Israel, including a Greek inscription from Jerusalem that reads "Good luck, let the Blues win: Long life to them!" A seventh-century monk laments that the Blues and Greens of Jerusalem were evil and unruly men who filled the holy city with bloodshed.

Tales of brutal outbreaks between Blue and the Green supporters are well attested. Sometimes the fans would support rival political leaders, with the conflicts erupting into uprisings and civil wars. Under different circumstances, the two factions were also known to join forces to combat a common enemy.

The Jews were involved in at least one such outbreak in Caesarea in 555, though historians are not in agreement about how to interpret the evidence. A witness to the events reports that the Samaritans and the Jews made common cause "in the manner of the Blues and Greens" in a violent attack on the Christians that led to several deaths and the burning of churches.

The report, with its comparison to the racing clubs, is susceptible to several possible interpretations. Some scholars see it as a mere figure of speach, indicating that though Jews and Samaritans were normally as antagonistic to one another as supporters of the rival blues and greens, on this occasion they joined in common cause against a mutual foe. However, most historians, conscious of Caesarea's reputation for fierce sport loyalties, believe that the attack was actually connected to these team loyalties. Perhaps an altercation that began as a sports riot snowballed into a full-fledged insurrection.

What team did the Jews support? Apparently, it was the Blues. This is explicitly documented with respect to the Jewish community of Antioch and finds indirect corroboration in a medieval midrash about "the throne and circus of King Solomon." The author of that work depicts Solomon and his entourage in accordance with the conventions of the Byzantine imperial court, including the obligatory sponsorship of monthly athletic contests. In that portrayal, they are likened to the Blue team arrayed in the hippodrome: The king, the sages, disciples, priests, and Levites were garbed in the blue *tekhelet* used for the ritual fringes, whereas foreign visitors, who gathered from afar to see the races and bring tribute and gifts to the Israelite king, were clothed in green.

SUGGESTIONS FOR FURTHER READING

Dan, Yaron. (1977). "The Circus and its Factions (Blues and Greens) in Eretz Israel during the Byzantine Period." *Cathedra* 4: 133–47.

Jellinek, Adolph. (1967). "Salomo's Thron und Hippodrome." In *Bet Ha-Midrasch*, ed. Adolph Jellinek. Reprint ed. Vol. 5, pp. xvi–vxii, 34–9. Jerusalem: Wahrmann.

Patlagean, E. Ville, (1962). "Une Image de Salomon en Basileus Byzantin." *Revue des Etudes Juives* 71: 9–33.

81

⚬⟋⟍

Is *Star Wars* a Kabbalistic Myth?

News Item: January 1997—Twenty years after its original release, George Lucas' Star Wars trilogy returns to the cinema screens in an enhanced version.

"They fought from heaven," sang Deborah in the Bible, "The stars in their courses fought."

Well, I have finally gotten around to seeing the movie *Star Wars*, even if it took me twenty-five years to do so, and I thoroughly enjoyed the technological swashbuckler.

I am certainly not the first to comment on the religious dimensions of *Star Wars*. Though some of its motifs are patently un-Jewish ("Obi-Wan died so that others might live," observed a writer

---

*"The Force Is with Us." *The Jewish Free Press*, Calgary, March 6, 1997, pp. 10–11.

318

in another newspaper last week), there are, nonetheless, some tantalizing affinities with traditional Jewish themes.

Most remarkably, its depiction of the epic struggle between the cosmic forces of Good and Evil evokes some well-known themes from Jewish mystical lore.

The notion that the battle against evil should involve the rescuing of a captive princess from the dark forces is a commonplace in Kabbalistic literature. For our mystics, the princess is a personification of the Divine Presence, the *Shekhinah*, who has become separated from her divine bridegroom and now participates in the sufferings and exiles of the people of Israel. In keeping with this perspective, redemption demands that she be freed from the clutches of the Dominion of Evil and restored to her proper place in the celestial hierarchy.

Needless to say, this motif is not uniquely Jewish. It has furnished countless plots for chivalrous romances, Germanic fairy tales, and computer games, even as it has inspired the allegorical parables of the *Zohar* and Rabbi Nahman of Bratslav.

Another interesting twist of the *Star Wars* story is the idea that in order to achieve ultimate liberation from evil, the powers of virtue must actually descend into the realms of darkness. This is an idea that also has a venerable history in the Kabbalah, symbolized for example, in the descent of Abraham, Jacob, and Moses into the metaphysical immorality of Egypt. This theology was stretched to radical extremes when devotees of Shabbetai Zvi interpreted their messiah's conversion to Islam as his own penetration of the Deathstar in order to purify evil itself, in what was anticipated to be the ultimate stage of the redemption.

All in all, I discerned the most remarkable parallels to Jewish mystical concepts in the idea of The Force, that spiritual power that permeates the universe and which can be channeled to moral objectives by the upright Jedi knights. The belief that an understanding of the divine creative process can allow humans to manipulate that power is undoubtedly central to Jewish esotericism. However, the similarities do not stop there.

What I found particularly fascinating about it all was the premise that the Lord of Evil, Darth Vader, was himself an adept of The Force, a former Jedi knight—who had learned to cultivate the dark side of The Force.

Now the perception that Evil constitutes the flip side of Holiness is a distinctively Kabbalistic response to the classical philosophical conundrum of how evil can exist and thrive in a universe controlled by an omnipotent and beneficent deity.

Religious thinkers have wrestled with this question for millennia, offering a plethora of unsatisfying answers. Some traced the sources of evil to a cosmic satanic power that acted in defiance of God; whereas others tried to argue that evil is merely an illusion, an absence of God, or an optical illusion created by our inability to see the larger picture.

The Kabbalah, however, teaches that evil is not so much tolerated by God as it is an essential ingredient of the metaphysical structure of the cosmos.

Although there are different opinions about exactly how evil fits in to the larger scheme of things, most Kabbalistic authorities acknowledge that it is closely related to the divine attribute of Justice, the aspect of God that is responsible for keeping the universe under control and maintaining the limits and borders between the different domains. This necessarily involves the creation of destructive capabilities so that sinners can be deterred or chastised. Once the arsenal of destruction has been set loose in the universe, it can scarcely be restrained. These impure realms are known in Kabbalistic terminology as the "Other Side" (*Sitra Ahra*).

In the theology of Rabbi Isaac Luria, the very existence of the universe would have been impossible were it not for those powers of repulsion and separation, since they issue from the same ultimate principle that separates God from his creation. Were it not for them, God would be indistinguishable from his world, and there could be no creation.

The Kabbalistic imagination populated the invisible world with vast armies of demonic soldiers serving under the satanic command of Samael, a nefarious host far more horrific than *Star War's* Imperial Storm Troopers.

Jewish religious history also knew its share of individuals whose obsession with the occult led them to the "dark side." The Talmud relates that Rabbi Elisha ben Abuya, the notorious "Other," was induced by his mystical pursuits to forsake his faith and his people.

And there was the case of the fifteenth-century Spanish Kabbalist Rabbi Joseph Della Reina who become so caught up in messianic frenzy that he was impelled to conjure up Samael himself with a view to forcing his hand at hastening the Messiah's coming, but was instead tricked by the arch-demon into worshipping the evil powers, with disastrous consequences.

Predictably, the cautionary legends that evolved around Joseph Della Reina came to incorporate motifs from similar stories in other cultures, including the anti-hero's involvement with the "queen of Greece," likely a borrowing from the tale of Dr. Faustus' preoccupation with Helen of Troy.

Indeed, who knows how long it will take before episodes from *Star Wars* begin to be cited as "midrash" from our synagogue pulpits?

SUGGESTIONS FOR FURTHER READING

Dan, Joseph. (1974). *The Hebrew Story in the Middle Ages.* Keter Library, Jerusalem: Keter.

Idel, Moshe. (1988). *Kabbalah: New Perspectives.* New Haven: Yale University Press.

Lachower, Yeruham Fishel and Isaiah Tishby. (1989). *The Wisdom of the Zohar.* Oxford: Oxford University Press.

Scholem, Gershom. (1933). "Le-ma'aseh yosef della reyna." *Zion* 5: 124–31.

———— (1974). *Kabbalah*. Meridian ed., New York: New American Library.

Urbach, E. E. (1967). "The Traditions about Merkaba Mysticism in the Talmudic Period." In *Studies in Mysticism and Religion Presented to Gershom G. Scholem*. Edited by E. E. Urbach, et al. pp. 7–28. Jerusalem: Magnes Press.

82

৵৽

What Does Judaism
Say about Cloning?*

*News Item: Amid much controversy, Dolly, the first
successful clone of an adult mammal, is produced by
Dr. Iam Wilmut and his team of scientists in Edinburgh.
Dolly is the product of a donor cell of one ewe,
combined with a modified donor egg of another ewe,
which was then implanted into the uterus
of a third ewe which gave birth to the clone.*

As I write these words, the moist eyes of Dolly, the cloned
sheep, still adorn the front pages of the newspapers, and learned
philosophers and columnists are busily speculating about the
imminent cloning of human beings. Several have even alluded to
the reputed creation of golems by Jewish mystics and magicians.

---

*"Dolly and the Golem." *The Jewish Free Press*, Calgary, April 7, 1997,
pp. 8–9.

Indeed, if we are to believe the Talmud, the creation of a living mammal in a laboratory was accomplished by two rabbis as early as the third century, though their choice of animal was a calf rather than a sheep: "Rav Hanina and Rav Hosha'ya used to convene every Friday and occupy themselves with the 'laws of creation.' They were able to fashion a calf one-third grown, which they ate." (Sanhedrin 65b) This seems to have been a routine matter for them, and they had no qualms about serving up the delicacy as the entrée at their Sabbath table.

What were those "laws of creation" that served as the instruction manual for the calf-cloners? Scholars are unsure whether to identify them with the treatise called *Book of Creation—Sefer Yetzirah*—that was familiar to Jewish mystics in the Middle Ages.

Sefer Yetzirah is one of the most unusual works in Jewish literature. Attributed to the Patriarch Abraham, it represents a Jewish version of neopythagoreanism, an ancient philosophy that viewed the mystical combinations of number patterns as the key to the mysteries of the universe. The author of *Sefer Yetzirah* takes this theme one step further. In addition to elaborating on the mysterious potencies of the ten decimal numbers, he expands upon an idea, found in the Talmud, of creation accomplished by means of combinations of the letters of the Hebrew alphabet. According to the ancient rabbis, this was how the Torah's supreme artisan Bezalel was able to fashion the sacred implements of the Tabernacle.

The medieval *Book of Creation* is founded upon the principle that the structures of mathematics and language reflect the metaphysical configuration of the universe. From this it follows that one who has mastered those principles will be able to imitate the divine process of creation.

If this was the method employed by Rabbis Hanina and Hosha'ya in the Talmud, then perhaps it would not be inappropriate to draw analogies between their permutations of letters and modern scientists' permutations of genetic codes. An ingenious medieval tradition claimed that the calf was served at the *siyyum*, the festive meal that was held in honour of the rabbis' completing their study of *Sefer Yetzirah*.

The ancient rabbis appear to have been less daunted than their modern counterparts by the prospect of manufacturing artificial human life. The Talmud ascribes such an achievement to the sage Rava. Apparently, the creature was a credible enough imitation to pass itself off as fully human—but for the fact that it could not speak. The faculty of speech, traditionally equated with the uniquely human capacity for reason, continued to elude mortal imitators of the creative process. Later writers disagreed whether or not this limitation was insurmountable.

For all its deficiencies, Rava's creature was the first documented case of a *golem*. The Hebrew word *golem* denotes an unformed substance, especially a lump of clay or earth. The word is sometimes used with reference to the earth from which the first human being was fashioned, before God imbued it with the breath of life. By extension, it was applied to similar beings that were brought to life by human creators.

It was the thirteenth-century German-Jewish mystics and pietists, known as the *Hasidei Ashkenaz*, who were the most fervent in their attempts to produce a golem. Rabbi Eleazar of Worms composed an extensive manual in which he detailed all the incantations and intricate alphabetical combinations that were needed to fashion a viable humanoid. Upon its forehead was inscribed the Hebrew word *Emet*, truth, which was also considered a name of God.

In the Middle Ages, the making of golems was restricted, for the most part, to ecstatic trances; they did not have any existence in the real world. Legends that purport to tell about great rabbis, such as Rabbi Samuel the Pious in Germany and Solomon Ibn Gabirol in Spain, who fashioned golems to serve as their personal attendants, gained circulation only in later eras.

As we come closer to modern times, the methods of golem manufacture become more varied, reflecting some of the current scientific thinking. One writer speaks of combining organic ma-

terial in a vessel, and another of a mechanical contraption assembled from boards and hinges.

The golems were also becoming more dangerous. Their sheer
size, if allowed to develop unchecked, was seen to constitute a
threat. It was related that Poland's most renowned golem-maker,
Rabbi Elijah of Chelm, was killed, or at least injured, when he
was crushed while deactivating his overgrown creation. By the
nineteenth century, even as alarm at the relentless pace of indus-
trial and technological progress was inspiring works like Mary
Shelly's *Frankenstein*, Jewish legends were also imagining golems
who could run wild and wreak destruction. In order to destroy the
golem—as was necessary on occasion, since otherwise they would
continue to grow uncontrollably—one had to reverse the order of
the divine letters from which it had been formed, or erase the first
letter of the word *emet* on its forehead, transforming it into *met*,
dead—at which point it would crumble back to lifeless dust.

Notwithstanding the circulation of such horror stories, it appears that the predominant concern was less with the monster's
going on a rampage or turning on its creator than with the moral
and theological implications of the endeavor.

For all the satisfaction that might result from this ultimate
expression of our divine image, there remained a powerful anxi-
ety that people might thereby obscure the distinction between
the Eternal Creator and his mortal imitators and come to treat
the latter as objects of idolatrous worship. The permissibility of
playing God was in itself questioned; and not all aspiring creators
were convinced that Rava's inability to produce a speaking or reasoning being was a systemic limitation. And, of course, there were
always skeptics who insisted that the real golems were the aspiring sorcerers, not their fictitious creatures!

Truly, the discussion sounds very much like the current one
surrounding Dolly, the sheep.

We might do well to keep in mind that the Talmud introduced
the whole topic in order to illustrate its claim that "if the righteous wished, they could create a world."

It seems to follow from that statement that those who are really righteous will have the discretion to refrain from usurping a function that rightly belongs only to the Creator.

SUGGESTIONS FOR FURTHER READING

Idel, Moshe. (1990). *The Golem: Jewish Magical and Mystical Traditions on the Artificial Anthropoid.* SUNY Studies in Judaica, Albany: State University of New York Press.

Scholem, Gershom. (1965). *On the Kabbalah and Its Symbolsim.* New York: Schocken.

Trachtenberg, Joshua. (1970). *Jewish Magic and Superstition.* 1st Atheneum ed., New York: Temple Books.

83

‰

Can Jewish Workers
Go on Strike?*

*News Item: June 1997—Labor unrest in Calgary.
Workers at the Safeway supermarket chain have been
on a prolonged strike, and the teachers in the local
public school system have also threatened to go to the
picket lines at the beginning of the school year.*

As I write these lines, a prolonged strike of supermarket employees is just concluding, and the teachers union has declared a labor dispute of its own. Developments of this kind are, of course, a natural part of modern economic life.

The right of workers or craftsmen to organize themselves into guilds or unions has roots in a talmudic law that asserts the authority of citizens to determine such matters as measures, exchange rates, and salaries. The medieval commentators extended these prerogatives to professional organizations as well, granting

---

*"Striking Similarities." *The Jewish Free Press*, Calgary, June 26, 1997, p. 8.

them the privilege of enforcing their collective decisions upon individual members.

In modern times, the concept was further applied to trade unions by authorities of the stature of Rabbis Ben-Zion Ouziel and Moshe Feinstein.

Nevertheless, in Jewish law the definition of permissible grounds for a strike has generally been more limited than what is accepted in our society, reflecting the ideal of a community whose constituent segments must subordinate themselves to the common good. Most authorities are clearly more comfortable about allowing strikes in cases where the employer has reneged on an existing contract or violated accepted conventions. Presumably the wage-cuts and reassignment of tasks that occur so frequently in our economy could fall into that category. And at least one authority has explicitly extended it to encompass situations where the objective circumstances, such as inflation or market conditions, have altered so significantly that they effectively undermine the purposes of a existing contract.

More problematic from the perspective of Jewish law is the question of whether a decision by a union or guild has the status of an accepted convention for purposes of enforcing it upon an unwilling employer. In general, talmudic law has looked askance at unilateral strikes under such circumstances where the grievances of the workers were not formulated in consultation with the broader community leadership, preferably its rabbis, whose position in the process bears some resemblance to those of labour courts in our society.

On these grounds, one Eastern European rabbi ruled against the local slaughterers when they walked out unilaterally in support of wage demands. In his responsum, the rabbi declared that those slaughterers had consulted no rabbinic authority about their demands, and hence their employers were within their rights to hire outside workers to keep their businesses in operation.

In a similar spirit, Rabbi Abraham Isaac Kook stated that a strike may be declared only as a means to enforce an existing decision by an authorized Jewish court, and only after the employees had exhausted other means of legal recourse.

Assuming that the sanctions themselves are deemed to lie within the permissible parameters, does Jewish law permit them to keep out scab labor?

This question is subsumed under the more general one of whether a guild or union has the right to prevent outside workers from setting up shop within their domain, an issue that arose frequently in Jewish history.

Although the Talmud appears to deny them such a right, several authorities have understood the extent of that decision somewhat differently. In particular, Rabbi Joseph Colon, writing in fifteenth-century Italy, argued that the Talmud meant only to say that the guild could not rely on the court to enforce their monopoly; however, if they possessed the power or pressure to enforce it by themselves, then the law would not stand in their way.

Rabbi Colon's position was vehemently opposed by Rabbi Joseph Karo, the author of the *Shulhan 'Arukh*, but accepted, nonetheless, in Rabbi Moshe Isserles' Ashkenazic glosses to that law code. In the responsa of subsequent authorities we encounter a continuing controversy on this question.

Responding to an inquiry concerning the legality of a strike by teachers at an American yeshivah, Rabbi Moshe Feinstein was most generous in defining the powers and rights that he conceded to striking unions. Not only did he assert that workers could go on strike to defend their interests without consulting a rabbi or community leader, and that the vote of the majority was binding upon the whole union; but he went on to rule, albeit with considerable hesitation, that the union could impose its will on nonmembers as well. All this, he emphasized, was on the condition that the strike itself was a legal and nonviolent one.

An even stronger advocate of the power of the labor unions was Rabbi Abraham Isaac Kook whose words echo the prevailing socialist ideals of pre-state Israel: "The organization of workers for purposes of protection and defense of working conditions is a legitimate expression of justice and social reform. . . . Unorganized labour causes harm to the workers. Nonunionized labourers work under inferior conditions to unionized ones, and thereby cause losses not only to themselves but also to the proletariat as a whole."

Such talk makes a person want to rush out immediately and rally to the cause of the exploited Jewish newspaper columnists.

SUGGESTIONS FOR FURTHER READING

Warhaftig, Shilem. (1982). *Jewish Labour Law*. 2nd, revised ed., Publications of the Faculty of Law, University of Tel-Aviv, Jerusalem: Ariel United Israel Institutes and the Harry Fischel Institute for Research in Jewish Law.

Yaron, Zvi. (1974). *Mishnato shel ha-Rav Kuk*. Jerusalem: [Jewish Agency].

Jewish Scholarship

84

⨾⨾

How Do They Study Talmud in College?*

𝒫eople who feel little discomfort at the idea of the Bible being studied in secular universities nevertheless display a certain surprise and uneasiness at the notion of extending this academic recognition to the Talmud.

The Bible is, after all, a recognized pillar of all of Western Civilization, while the Talmud has always been the exclusive and esoteric possession of the Jews. Its notorious hairsplitting dialectic and frequently trivial-sounding subject matter also tend to produce some embarrassment and a certain disbelief that anyone on the outside could find the Talmud of interest.

Yet the Christian world has long expressed an interest in the study of rabbinic literature, initially limited to those aspects which

---

*"The Talmud Goes to College." *The Jewish Star*, Calgary/Edmonton, June 1987, pp. 4–5.

would help illuminate their own scriptures (and indeed, the Jewish context of Jesus' biography is so strong that a Jew reading the Christian Bible is likely to doubt the possibility of a non-Jew's ability to understand much of his own scriptures).

When Jews began to apply critical methodology to the study of the Talmud, it was also with various ulterior motives.

Thus, the ideologists of the German Reform movement in the nineteenth century sought talmudic precedents for their claims regarding the flexibility and universalism of Judaism. No less a figure than Rabbi Israel Salanter, the founder of the Lithuanian *Musar* [moralistic] movement, believed that the introduction of talmudic study into the curriculum of the German universities would be of value not only to Jews (as a defence against the misrepresentations of the Talmud with which we Albertans are all too familiar), but also to the gentiles, who would benefit from familiarity with rabbinic logic and reasoning.

The situation has progressed considerably until today, when there is a general realization that the study of Judaism is not only as legitimate as that of any other culture or civilization, but also that it holds a special place of interest because of its centrality to Western culture.

AT THE UNIVERSITY

Rabbinic thought and literature are naturally recognized to be preeminent expressions of Judaism. Gone are the days when Judaism was only regarded as a prelude to Christianity. This recognition depends, of course, on the resources and scope of the particular program.

Talmud may be squeezed into a half-hour lecture in a survey course on world religions or it may merit its own department, as is the case in the major rabbinical seminaries (which function on the whole as full-fledged university-level academic institutions) or the larger Israeli universities.

At the Hebrew University of Jerusalem, for example, in addition to a Department of Talmud, which specializes in close textual and philological examination of rabbinic literature, Talmud can be studied from different perspectives in such departments as Hebrew language or literature, Jewish history, law, Jewish thought, and more. In North American universities, the context for Talmud study could range from a religious studies or Near Eastern studies department to a specialized department or program in Jewish studies.

The logic of academic study is such that a university is not merely a channel through which a given body of learning is presented to the students. In applying the methods of scientific analysis to a given topic, the scholar is making a new contribution to the scholarship. In our case as well, the university Judaica scholar is not merely reporting the results of the study in the traditional yeshiva, but providing a creative new understanding of the Talmud.

VARIETY OF TEXTS

The academic approach to Talmud study has made a number of such contributions. The first of these is in defining the scope of talmudic literature.

The traditional yeshivot have generally limited themselves to the study of the Babylonian Talmud, which has, for various reasons, been accepted as authoritative. The universities have paid equal attention to the vast variety of literature produced by the same rabbis: including a huge library of legal and homiletical biblical exegesis, law-codes, and more; as well as such areas as the *Talmud Yerushalmi*, produced in the Land of Israel and considered by many to be superior in its intellectual vision to its Babylonian sister.

The *Yerushalmi*, as is the case with many other neglected works, had to be virtually rediscovered by means of a painstaking examination of manuscripts scattered through the libraries of the world.

Another contribution has been in the area of text criticism.

Most of the commonly used editions of talmudic texts emanate from a series of early sixteenth-century Italian printings. Many, like the Babylonian Talmud itself, were published by the Christian Jacob Bomberg!

Much scholarly energy has been devoted to tracing alternate textual traditions from manuscripts (the medieval burnings of Hebrew books has resulted in a relatively small number of surviving manuscripts) and citations in medieval writings. The discovery of the thousand of venerable oriental fragments preserved in the Cairo *Genizah* (now scattered through many libraries, mostly in Cambridge, England) has revolutionized our perceptions of the nature of the talmudic text.

UNIVERSITY AND YESHIVA

The academic approach has also brought the application of other disciplines to Talmud study.

The Talmud has benefited from specialized knowledge of such peripheral fields as ancient languages and cultures (the hundreds of Greek, Latin, and Persian words in the talmudic vocabulary are reflections of complex cultural contacts), the study of ancient history and science, and so forth.

A particularly promising field is the study of the Hebrew and Aramaic languages, especially our appreciation of rabbinic Hebrew as a distinct dialect (and not a corruption of Biblical Hebrew). Much has been learned from the living traditions assembled with the ingathering of various Jewish communities, notably the Yemenites, to Israel.

Similarly, the application of methods of general literary criticism to talmudic texts has proven most fruitful. Someone who does not appreciate the standard literary conventions of the rabbinic homily has about as much hope of appreciating a midrash as does a reader of English poetry who has never been told of the sonnet form. Such studies, generally neglected in the yeshiva curriculum, have been carried out with great success in the university setting.

An additional contribution of the academic approach is in source criticism. This basically refers to a methodological distinction between the final product and the sources which were put together to make it up.

Understandably, the traditionalist tends to be somewhat uncomfortable with the widespread academic assumption that, in the process of editing the various traditions, the redactors of talmudic works frequently (whether intentionally or because of misunderstanding) altered their original meanings. Nonetheless, the critical talmudic scholars have shown that traditional commentators often employed such an approach and have, thereby, come to a clearer understanding of the original significance of many statements by the ancient rabbis. The fact that the Talmud is manifestly a composite and human creation has made this approach somewhat more acceptable to the religious community than it would have been if applied to the Bible.

One of the most interesting phenomena associated with the critical study of the Talmud has been the degree to which it has been accepted by the traditionalists. Not only are the manuscript-based editions of talmudic texts to be found on the shelves of many yeshivot (often with the introductions and title pages removed to mask their heretical origins), but bodies of unquestionable orthodoxy have been in the forefront of such projects as a text-critical edition of the Babylonian Talmud (at the Rabbi Herzog Institute in Jerusalem), the publication of academic studies of the Talmud (at Jerusalem's Rav Kook Institute, or New York's Yeshiva University, for example), and more.

Though we are unlikely to see yeshivot establishing compulsory classes in Greek or Pahlavi, their students are certainly likely to make use of dictionaries that demonstrate such expertise. The fact is that most of the important academic scholars of the Talmud have had traditional religious training.

The marriage between the university and the yeshiva is thus a complex one, but one that promises to prove valuable for both sides.

85

Ꮹ

What is the State of Academic Jewish Studies in America?*

The North American Jewish community did not take much notice of a gathering that took place in Boston last month. Nevertheless, the occasion marked a significant milestone in the development of Jewish intellectual life on this continent.

The event in question was the twentieth annual conference of the Association for Jewish Studies (AJS), the academic organization of teachers and researchers of Judaica at postsecondary institutions in the U.S. and Canada.

The gathering had all the trappings of a typical academic conference. The main activities involved exchanges of scholarship, as some two hundred papers were presented on a remarkable assortment of topics relating to Jewish history, literature, ideas, and social studies. In the background, booksellers were exhibit-

---

*"A Landmark in Jewish Scholarship." *The Jewish Star*, Calgary, Jan. 20–Feb. 16, 1989, pp. 4–5.

ing their wares, candidates were being interviewed for positions, organizational meetings were convened and—what many would consider the most important purpose of such conferences—a venue was provided for informal contacts between scholars to exchange opinions and discuss projects.

This characterization could apply equally to any scholarly conference, whether it be devoted to anthropology or zoology. And indeed it was precisely the normalcy of the conference that was singled out as a significant phenomenon. Twenty years ago, when the founding conference of the AJS was convened at Brandeis University, there were many who could not imagine that a viable organization could be established.

EUROPEAN SCHOLARS

At a special session devoted to the commemoration of the AJS's twentieth anniversary, some of the previous presidents of the organization reminisced about the founding meeting in 1969.

The sixty people who had participated in that meeting accounted for virtually all the teachers of Judaica in North American academic institutions at the time (twenty years earlier the number had been twelve). Though an interest in Jewish studies had blossomed on many campuses, inspired largely by the wave of Jewish consciousness sparked by the Six Day War of 1967, there were few serious academic programs in existence.

The previous generation had been dominated by a handful of European-trained scholars concentrated around the larger East Coast universities and seminaries. Much of the actual teaching on campuses elsewhere was relegated to local rabbis or sympathetic Jewish faculty members who might agree to offer a course in a Jewish aspect of their principal field of expertise (such as Jewish–American writers, Middle Eastern politics, and so forth).

As usual, the established Jewish institutions opposed the new organization, at least until they could find a way to control it.

NEW AMERICAN SCHOLARS

Of great concern to the founders of the AJS was the disturbing lack of an American scholarly tradition of Jewish studies. European Jewish scholars could presume a familiarity with classic Jewish texts and languages—an assumption that was obviously not valid in 1969 America. A real fear was felt that it might prove impossible to train a new generation of Judaica teachers who would uphold acceptable scholarly standards.

The 1988 conference was the finest proof of the groundlessness of the fears—though, to be sure, similar trepidations were still being expressed about the coming generation.

About four hundred individuals participated in the conference, representing a cross section of the state of Jewish studies in North America. Most were young scholars, and many of these had already authored important contributions to Jewish learning. Particularly among those dealing with the more traditional textual subjects, it seemed that the great majority had done some of their studies in Israel. In all, they offered impressive testimony that Jewish studies are alive and well on the North American campuses.

The variety of subjects dealt with at the conference can serve as an index to the present concerns of academic Jewish scholarship. Predictably, sessions were devoted to such traditional topics as Bible, Talmud, midrash, Jewish philosophy and Kabbalah. Many of the papers were concerned with applying to Jewish literature of all periods (including Biblical, Yiddish, and everything in between) the methodologies current in general literary studies. Similarly, the approaches of contemporary social–scientific research were being applied to topics in Jewish history, and especially to the study of the North American Jewish community.

FEMINIST PRESENCE

As has been the case for a number of years now, many sessions were devoted to exploring the place of women in Jewish society, literature, and religious tradition. This pre-occupation reflects the power of feminist ideologies throughout the contemporary academic world, but, of course, is of special concern to Jewish tradition, whose official formulations have almost exclusively been composed by and for men.

Female scholars do in fact play a role in the AJS (the outgoing president is the noted Yiddish scholar Ruth Wisse of Montreal). While much of the feminist scholarship tended to be shallow and doctrinaire, it also inspired fascinating sessions on such topics as "The Experience of Medieval and Renaissance Jewish Women," as well as an interest in popular and folkloristic aspects of Judaism that might otherwise have been overlooked.

The feminist presence also created some extracurricular complications—for example, the meals were arranged so as to avoid the recitation of *Birkat Ha-Mazon*, the blessing after the meal, in order to avoid tension between the feminists and traditionalists over the inclusion of women in public prayers.

Clearly, much progress in Jewish scholarship has occurred over twenty years. This landmark in the intellectual history of North American Jewry offers much hope for the quality of Jewish learning in coming years.

86

⤳

Why Should You Study
Talmud Every Day?*

*I*n February, I reached a landmark of sorts in my Jewish life—I completed study of the entire Babylonian Talmud, a project that took me about six years.

Having done so, I have been giving some thought to how this task has affected me personally, and about the strange love affair between the Jewish people and this strangest of literary creations.

I don't recall exactly when I first decided to make the commitment to make it through the *Bavli*. I had, in the past, taken on some similar obligations. One year it involved reading through the whole of Rashi's classic commentary on the Torah, subsequently graduating to the more expansive one of Rabbi Bahya. More recently, I had made it through the Mishnah (using the readable

---

*"Endings and Beginnings." *The Jewish Star*, Calgary/Edmonton, April 19–May 11, 1989, pp. 11–12.

modern Israeli explanation by Pinhas Kahati). The Babylonian Talmud seemed inevitable.

DAF YOMI

About sixty years ago, Rabbi Meir Shapira of Lublin, one of the leading Orthodox communal activists of his generation, originated the idea of having the whole Jewish world simultaneously studying one leaf of the Talmud every day. At that rate, the entire work could be completed in approximately seven years.

For reasons no longer clear to me, I developed my own accelerated schedule, according to which I would add an extra folio on Shabbat, the holidays, and the days preceding them.

Owing to limitations of intellect and time, I restricted myself to the basic level embodied in Rashi's standard commentary. I am utterly dumbfounded at minds that are able, when studying at such a pace, to delve further into the infinitely profound strata of understanding that the Talmud does contain.

I did not follow the official schedule of the Daily Talmud Page (*Daf Yomi*) that has become so popular among ever-broadening circles in the Jewish religious world. I allowed myself to follow my own interests as the spirit moved me, or as appropriately portable versions came to hand.

This last remark may sound strange, but it should be noted that the luxurious folio volumes with gold leaf bindings that we usually associate with Talmuds are not very convenient for the day-to-day use demanded by my lifestyle. I don't know if anyone has yet tried to study the effects of photo-offset miniaturization on the study habits of Jews, but I would venture to estimate that there has been an appreciable increase in the hours devoted to traditional religious study now that versions of the classical texts are available that can be read, albeit with considerable eyestrain, on buses, under one's work desk, or at odd moments of leisure.

For my part, I find myself overwhelmed by the geographical associations that are evoked by totally unrelated debates on abstruse topics in Jewish religious law. One tractate conjures up associations with the Shi'ite village in Lebanon where I studied it during my Israeli army reserve duty; another page I plodded through while waiting in a queue at Disneyland; still another I read just before my first job interview at the University of Calgary. I imagine that these personal associations will be forever attached to their respective *sugyas* (topics).

WHY THE TALMUD?

At some level of consciousness, I was constantly coming back to a basic question: Of all the great classics of Jewish religious literature, how did it happen that the Babylonian Talmud, a technical work of esoteric and often irrelevant legal argumentation, became the most popular text among such broad segments of the Jewish masses (often to the consternation of leading rabbis of the time)?

The conventional answers that point out the religious motivation underlying Talmud study don't seem to hold water. There are any number of Jewish classics, from the Bible to the products of the nineteenth-century *Musar* (moralistic) movement, that offer much more immediate religious inspiration and fulfilment.

Nor is the Talmud a real guide to day-to-day practice. Talmudic reasoning thrives on unlikely theoretical possibilities, and I doubt that more than ten percent of it relates directly to any problems likely to be encountered by normal people.

Contrary to widespread opinion, while the Talmud is a work *about* law, it is not a book *of* laws. If you really want to know what to do, ask your rabbi or look it up in a code of Jewish law like the *Shulhan Aruch*. Frankly, I am repeatedly amazed at how little my talmudic study has equipped me to actually decide practical questions of Jewish law.

Quite the contrary, the Talmud goes out of its way not to offer direct answers. One of its basic premises is that two or more mutually contradictory positions can both be defended. Also, that no proof—even of a view that you know to be correct—is to be accepted unless it does actually prove what it's supposed to.

Someone who has been brought up on this kind of intellectual diet will not easily be taken in by the various simplistic and fundamentalist ideologies that are constantly being thrown at us. This would appear to be a basic value of Jewish education: that it is more important to teach people *how* to think than to give them set and facile answers. That is what Talmud is about.

TALMUD AS SPORT

But there is much more, much more than I can hope to get into within the space limitations of this article. Let me at least raise one point that I do not feel has been emphasized sufficiently. I will illustrate it with an example.

About a dozen years ago, when Israeli television still had a sense of humour, there was a very funny satirical program called *Nikku'i Rosh*—"Head-Cleaning."

The premise (then considered fanciful) of one episode was based on the idea of what would happen if the religious political parties had control of television. Alongside black-coated versions of various detective thrillers and situation comedies, the producers presented their version of what the sport broadcasts would look like. They brought the viewers into a yeshiva where a group of Talmud students were arguing back and forth, metaphorically thrusting forth with textual proof and defending with logical counterargument.

It turned out that the author of that segment, a well-known left-wing activist, was, in fact, a yeshiva graduate. He had really caught the point. Historically speaking, talmudic study has been the national sport of the Jewish people!

The modes of argumentation are exciting and challenging in a way that noninitiates cannot really appreciate. Yes, the secret is out. The reason Jews have been studying Talmud for so many generations is not only because of religious commitment, not out of idealism, but because it's fun!

The Talmud leagues are now accepting rookies. Try a few innings; it can be contagious.

87

⟶

Can a Gentile Do Work for a Jew on Shabbat?*

$\mathcal{A}$ popular perception that is encouraged by modern apologists for traditional Judaism, as well as by its opponents, portrays Jewish religious law, *halakha*, as a static corpus that has remained unchanged through the vicissitudes of history.

For anyone who has a closer familiarity with Jewish sources, it is clear that this has never been the case.

The halakha, as the principal expression of Jewish religiosity throughout our history, has served as a means by which Jews have interacted, as individuals and as a community, with the realities of life. Halakha does indeed have a history, which is integral to any complete understanding of the Jewish past.

No one has succeeded as well in chronicling the story of Jewish law as Professor Jacob Katz of Jerusalem. His life's work, which

---

*"The Shabbes Goy." (Review article) *The Jewish Star*, Calgary/Edmonton, Feb. 23–March 8, 1990, pp. 7–8.

has earned him the prestigious Israel Prize for Jewish History, has taken him through the dry-looking tomes of talmudic commentaries, Jewish law codes, and rabbinic responsa, in order to unearth new insights into the religious and social history of the Jewish people.

What distinguishes Katz's research is the broad variety of perspectives which he brings to bear on the material. He does not confine himself to explaining the legal argumentation. He also interprets it from the context of religious and intellectual history and as an indication of the workings of Jewish society and economics through the ages.

The current study shows Katz at his finest.

NO BENEFIT

The Yiddish phrase chosen for the title of his book is, in itself, a reflection of the problematic nature of its topic.

The rich Hebrew–Aramaic lexicon of Jewish legal discourse does not have a term to designate the phenomenon under discussion: the employment of non-Jews to perform tasks that a Jew himself cannot perform because of the Sabbath or other ritual restrictions. Although modern Hebrew has coined a phrase, *Goy shel Shabbat*, used as the title of the Hebrew original of this book, that expression is simply a translation of the Yiddish term.

The fact is that Jewish law, as reflected in the Talmud, is quite clear on the point that, just as a Jew is forbidden himself to perform acts of labor on the Sabbath, so is he prohibited from benefiting from work that is done for his sake by a gentile.

Though the prohibition was generally regarded as being of a somewhat lower degree of stringency (of rabbinic rather than biblical origin) and it is subject to some exceptions—in emergencies, for the performance of important religious precepts, in certain types of partnership or contract relationships—is was nonetheless a fact of talmudic law.

Popular practice tended to regard the restrictions from a different perspective. The common people tended to view the Sabbath in a narrow, ritualistic sense, as a set of taboos that only affect the behaviour of individuals but do not prevent Jews from benefiting from actions that are performed for them by gentiles.

TO CURB OR TO COPE

The greater part of Katz's study focuses on the medieval and modern communities of central and eastern Europe. More than their Sephardic counterparts, the Ashkenazic rabbis attached considerable weight to the established customs of their communities, even when the prevalent practice seemed to conflict with the Talmud.

The rabbis would often propose bold reinterpretations of the relevant talmudic passages, seeking to expand the options for permissive rulings. For example, Rabbi Jacob Tam, always a halakhic maverick, argued that the very act of earning a living is in itself a religious *mitzvah* that can serve as grounds for bending the restrictions.

Much of the book consists of meticulous descriptions of the ways in which halakhic scholars coped with the popular tendency to employ gentiles to do jobs that they themselves could not do.

In some instances, this involved straightforward prohibitions. More often, the rabbi would suggest an alternative way of making the situation more acceptable, often through the use of legal fictions such as a formal sale of a business along the lines of the practice used for leaven on Passover.

In most of the cases, it seems that the rabbis were looking for ways to grant retroactive sanction to practices that they could not curb. One of the most commonly repeated phrases in the book is the talmudic dictum, "Better that they should sin inadvertently than by intention," a testimony to the resigned frustration felt by halakhic authorities unable to make their communities conform to the real demands of Jewish law.

The important questions debated by the rabbis relate, for the most part, to economic rather than domestic life. Jews would find themselves involved in businesses that had to remain open on Saturday, either because they were contracted to the government or because the employees were Christian and the five-day work week was yet undreamed of.

In addition to the legal questions involved, Katz uses the halakhic materials to paint a fascinating picture of the economic activities pursued by Jews, especially in the modern era. But to this reviewer's mind, the most interesting sections of this book are those that describe the complex considerations that guided the Orthodox leadership in the polarized Jewish communities of nineteenth-century Russia and Hungary.

The Enlightenment and the Reform movement were making strong inroads, and the Orthodox rabbinical authorities realized that their decisions could not be made simply on the merits of the cases. A ruling that was too lenient could be viewed as a concession to the forces of change, while excessive stringency was likely to alienate those who were sympathetic to the tradition but would find it financially onerous to close their businesses for two days a week.

The rabbis who were consulted tried first to ascertain where the questioners stood ideologically. The general tendency was to choose the stricter options, a decision which seems to contribute to the decline of Orthodoxy in these communities.

In general, this readable book can serve as a model for how the study of halakha can open a window to a dazzling variety of issues in the history of Jewish society and religion.

SUGGESTIONS FOR FURTHER READING

Katz, Jacob. (1989). *The 'Shabbes Goy.'* Philadelphia: Jewish Publication Society of America.

88

୬୬

Are the Dead Sea Scrolls
a Dead Sea Dud?*

Coming from someone who makes his living from the study of ancient Jewish texts, it might surprise some readers when I declare my conviction that the Dead Sea Scrolls are not all that important, and that their impact has been inflated out of all proportion by the media and various interested parties.

The intense public fascination with the Qumran scrolls was fueled by the expectation that documents contemporary with the beginnings of Christianity would provide valuable—or even revolutionary—new insights into the origin of that religion. The Christian scholars who controlled much of the research into the scrolls made every effort to uncover allusions to Christian concerns, and tiny fragments were fancifully pieced together so as to produce theological statements about divine or suffering messiahs. The

---

*"The Dead Sea Dud." *The Jewish Free Press*, Calgary, August 25, 1994, 9.

archeological site at Qumran was even described as if it had housed a medieval European monastery.

These dubious conclusions have been utilized both as confirmation of Christian tradition and as refutations of its uniqueness or originality. Either way, they succeeded in transforming the esoteric world of Dead Sea Scroll scholarship into a lucrative industry whose potential market included much of the Christian world.

Not surprisingly, almost none of these alleged Christian links find factual support in the evidence of the scrolls. The simple truth is that the scrolls contain a representative sample of the diverse literature that Jews were producing during the latter part of the Second Temple Era, a time marked by factionalism and ferment in the Jewish community of Eretz Yisrael. As such, they reflect typical Jewish concerns, most notably in the area of halakhah, Jewish religious law, which, then as today, ignited the most virulent controversies between competing sects. These simple and obvious facts rarely get mentioned in the popular representations of the scrolls.

The scrolls do enrich our knowledge of a very complex time in Jewish history, though much of this knowledge is of value only to scholarly specialists, and even their more substantial contributions (in such areas as the development of the Hebrew language and Jewish legal exegesis) are unlikely to sell a lot of newspaper tabloids or TV sponsorships.

The hoopla surrounding the Dead Sea Scrolls appears even more irksome when we contrast it with a far more important manuscript find that has remained largely unknown even among Jews, precisely because it could not attract the interest of large Christian audiences.

I am referring to the Cairo *Genizah*, a vast repository containing hundreds of thousands of discarded Jewish texts and documents that was maintained since the thirteenth century but which contains much earlier material as well—including at least one work that would later be unearthed among the Dead Sea Scrolls!

Individual items from this collection began to circulate during the latter half of the nineteenth century, but their historic value and point of origin were first noted in 1896 by Solomon Schechter, (then teaching at Cambridge University), who promptly had the remnants of the Genizah transported from Egypt to Cambridge, where they remain today.

The Genizah has revolutionized every area of classical Jewish studies. Not only does it preserve the most accurate versions of ancient Jewish works like the Talmud, midrash, and liturgical poetry—including several that had become lost over the generations—and a rich selection of medieval scienctific and theological works, but even its more mundane documents (letters, bills, and private correspondence) have allowed us to piece together a vivid and intimate portrait of Jewish life in the Mediterranean basin (including the Land of Israel) in all its social, economic, and spiritual diversity. What was considered a century ago to be a dark age in our history has now become one of the most familiar.

Compared to this wealth of cultural and historical information, the conjectural and fragmentary evidence of the Qumran library presents a pathetic picture.

This situation should alert us to the fact that in our sensation-obsessed society, what passes for scholarship is coming more and more to be defined by marketablity rather than by intrinsic value. We must be careful not to be taken in by this trend, especially when it involves our own history and tradition.

SUGGESTIONS FOR FURTHER READING

Schiffman, Lawrence H. (1955). *Reclaiming the Dead Sea Scrolls: The History of Judaism, the Background of Christianity, the Lost Library of Qumran*. Anchor Bible Reference Library, New York: Doubleday.

89

⤜

Who is Lilith . . .
and Who Isn't She?*

$\mathcal{T}$he feminist critique of conventional values has not overlooked the Jewish tradition. Whether or not one acknowledges the validity of all the charges that have been leveled against the treatment of women in Jewish law and theology, it is hardly possible to ignore these issues.

As one who is normally sympathetic to feminist aspirations, I have often been disappointed with the scholarly standards of the debate, especially when it has been directed towards the classical texts of Judaism. In the course of polemical ideological exchanges, I find too frequently that sweeping generalizations are being supported by flimsy or questionable evidence, with a disturbing disregard for factual accuracy and historical context.

---

*"Looking for Lilith." *The Jewish Free Press*, Calgary, February 6, 1995, pp. 8–9.

As an example of this sort of scholarly sloppiness, I wish to discuss an intriguing Hebrew legend that has found its way into dozens of recent works about Jewish attitudes towards women.

The legend in question was inspired by the Bible's dual accounts of the creation of the first woman, which led its author to the conclusion that Adam had a *first* wife before his marriage to Eve. Adam's original mate was the demonic Lilith, who had been fashioned, just like her male counterpart, from the dust of the earth. Lilith insisted from the outset on equal treatment, a fact which caused constant friction between the couple. Eventually, the frustrated Lilith used her magical powers to fly away from her spouse. At Adam's urging, God dispatched three angels to negotiate her return. When these angels made threats against Lilith's demonic descendants, she countered that she would prey eternally upon newborn human babies, who could be saved only by invoking the protection of the three angels. In the end Lilith, stood her ground and never returned to her husband.

The story implies that when Eve was afterwards fashioned out of Adam's rib (symbolic of her subjection to him), this was to serve as an antidote to Lilith's short-lived attempt at egalitarianism. Here, declare the feminists matronizingly, we have a clear statement of the "rabbinic attitude towards women!"

There is only one slight problem with this theory: The story of Lilith is not actually found in any authentic rabbinic tradition. Although it is repeatedly cited as a rabbinic legend or a midrash, it is not recorded in any ancient Jewish text!

The tale of Lilith originates in a medieval work called *The Alphabet of Ben-Sira*, a work whose relationship to the conventional streams of Judaism is, to say the least, problematic.

The unknown author of this work has filled it with many elements that seem designed to upset the sensibilities of traditional Jews. In particular, the heroes of the Bible and Talmud are frequently portrayed in the most perverse colors. Thus, the book's protagonist, Ben-Sira, is said to have issued from an incestuous union between the prophet Jeremiah and his daughter. Joshua is described as a buffoon too fat to ride a horse. King David comes across as a heartless and spiteful figure who secretly delights in the death of his son Absalom, while putting on a disingenuous public display of grief. The book is consistently sounding the praises of hypocritical and insincere behavior.

So shocking and abhorrent are some of the contents of *The Alphabet of Ben-Sira* that modern scholars have been at a loss to explain why anyone would have written such a book. Some see it as an impious digest of risqué folktales. Others have suggested that it was a polemical broadside aimed at Christians, Karaites, or some other opposing movement. I personally would not rule out the possibility that it was actually an anti-Jewish satire—though, to be sure, it did come to be accepted by the Jewish mystics of medieval Germany; and amulets to fend off the vengeful Lilith became an essential protection for newborn infants in many Jewish communities.

Eventually the tale of Lilith was included in a popular English-language compendium of rabbinic legend, and some uncritical readers—unable or unwilling to check after the editor's sources—cited it as a representative rabbinic statement on the topic. As tends to happen in such instances, subsequent authors kept copying from one another until the original error turned into an unchallenged historical fact.

Certainly there are volumes of real texts and traditions that could benefit from a searching and critical feminist analysis, and it is a shame to focus so much intellectual energy on a dubious and uncharacteristic legend of this sort.

SUGGESTIONS FOR FURTHER READING

Dan, Joseph. (1974). *The Hebrew Story in the Middle Ages.* Keter Library, Jerusalem: Keter.
Eisenstein, J. D., ed. (1969). *Ozar Midrashim: Bibliotheca Midraschica.* Reprint ed., [Israel].

Index

About the Author

Originally from Montreal, Eliezer Segal has lived and studied in Israel and is currently the head of the religious studies department at the University of Calgary. Although his academic research focuses primarily on the Talmud and traditional Jewish biblical exegesis, Professor Segal is also the author of a newspaper column, a children's book and a site on the World Wide Web.